GCSE

A-Z

BUSINESS STUDIES

handbook

Arthur Jenkins

Hodder & Stoughton

A MEMBER OF THE HODDER HEADLINE GROUP

Order queries: please contact Bookpoint Ltd, 39 Milton Park, Abingdon, Oxon OX14 4TD. Telephone: (44) 01235 400414, Fax: (44) 01235 400454. Lines are open from 9.00 - 6.00, Monday to Saturday, with a 24 hour message answering service. Email address: orders@bookpoint.co.uk

British Library Cataloguing in Publication Data
A catalogue entry for this title is available from the British Library

ISBN 0 340 68366 X

First published 1998
Impression number   10 9 8 7 6 5 4
Year   2002 2001 2000

Typeset by GreenGate Publishing Services, Tonbridge, Kent.
Printed and bound in Great Britain for Hodder and Stoughton Educational, a division of Hodder Headline plc, 338 Euston Road, London NW1 3BH, by Redwood Books, Trowbridge, Wilts

HOW TO USE THIS BOOK

The GCSE A–Z Business Studies Handbook has been developed along lines similar to the very successful A level Complete A–Z Business Studies Handbook.

The entries cover all the GCSE syllabuses in Business Studies, including the option syllabuses, where applicable. The specifications for the GNVQ Intermediate in Business Studies are also covered. In addition, the book will be of value to students preparing for other syllabuses related to Business Studies, such as Commerce and British Industrial Society and Office Applications.

It is an alphabetical textbook designed to be easy to use. Each entry begins with a one sentence definition. This is followed, in most cases, by some extension or qualification of the definition. This will be helpful in preparing for a number of GCSE questions that require a definition and where additional marks are given for development. Entries that are core ideas in GCSE business studies, or that are more difficult at this level, have been developed further. The entries cover, at least the main points necessary to prepare assignments and answer questions. Formulae for all the numerate elements of the subject at GCSE are included and are developed through the use of worked examples.

The integrated nature of business studies is recognised through the use of cross references. A student preparing an assignment will be able to obtain additional material and information on related topics by following the cross references. They are picked out in the text in italics.

If, for example, the reader looks up the term 'balance sheet':

- There is a brief definition of a balance sheet followed by a specimen example.

- The example contains a number of different terms related to the balance sheet.

- To understand the entry fully the reader needs also to look up the cross referenced terms (i.e. *fixed assets*; *current assets*; *current liabilities*; *working capital*; *net assets*; *issued share capital*; *general reserves*; *capital employed*).

The cross referencing will also be helpful to students who may be confused by the different names given to the same topic in text books and by examination boards. Wherever possible alternative names for the same term are cross referenced.

I hope that the book will be a valuable resource. It is intended to provide a quick and easily understood digest of the main topics and terms used in both GCSE and the Intermediate GNVQ in business studies.

Arthur Jenkins

ACKNOWLEDGEMENTS

The book owes its origins to the considerable success of the Complete A–Z Business Studies Handbook which has given rise to an important series of texts in other subjects at GCE A/AS and GNVQ Advanced levels.

I am grateful to Ian Marcousé for the invitation to prepare a text directed at the GCSE and Intermediate GNVQ in Business Studies. I have also benefited from Ian's assistance, guidance and support during the preparation of the book. This was especially helpful in the early stages of development as we worked towards an acceptable format.

A number of organisations have very kindly provided me with information which was valuable in helping to ensure the accuracy of the entries.

The assistance of Barry Heywood, Regan von Schweitzer and Ged Jones in reading the text and offering suggestions and criticisms have proved invaluable. The fact that I did not always act upon the advice is no reflection on the quality of their suggestions and any deficencies are entirely my own responsibility. I am also indebted to Ann, my wife, for her support and encouragement throughout.

Arthur Jenkins

absenteeism is staying away from work for reasons other than ill health. It is a kind of industrial truancy. People stay away for no good reason.

> ***Explanation:*** Some workers 'take a day off' without good reason. This type of unauthorised absence can seriously disrupt production. For the worker it may lead to loss of wages and, in extreme cases, result in *dismissal*.

ACAS: see *Advisory, Conciliation and Arbitration Service*.

accounting: the reporting, analysis and interpretation of financial information about a business or other organisation over a period of time, usually a year. Accounting is not the actual recording of information: this is done through *bookkeeping*.

Accounting is concerned with:

- The performance of a business: is it making a profit or a loss?
- What has happened to the resources used by the business over the time period?
- Have the values of the *assets* and the *liabilities* increased or not?

accounting equation: all *financial accounting* is based on this equation:

Assets = Capital + Liabilities

Assets are the resources of the business. They are what the business owns.

Capital is what the business owes to its owner(s).

Liabilities are what is owed by the business to other people or businesses.

The value of each item may change but the total of the two sides of the equation must always be equal.

> ***Explanation:*** The assets of a business must be owned by someone.
>
> Either the assets are all owned by the owners, in which case assets are equal to capital.
>
> Or, as is more likely, the business will have bought some things on *credit* and will owe the money for those things. This means it has liabilities, in which case assets = capital + liabilities.

> ***Example:*** A business buys a machine for £50 000. It pays a deposit of £10 000 and borrows £40 000 on credit.
>
> The accounting equation reads:
>
> Assets = Capital + Liabilities
> £50 000 = £10 000 + £40 000
>
> When half the debt is repaid the equation will change to read:

Assets = Capital + Liabilities
£50 000 = £30 000 + £20 000

When the debt is fully repaid the equation will read:

Assets = Capital
£50 000 = £50 000

accounts are individual records of the transactions that financially affect a business or organisation. Accounts are entered in the *ledger*. Each separate account will include the date, the name of other accounts affected by a transaction and the amount.

From the accounts can be seen:

- what the business owns

- what is owing to the business

- what the business owes to others

- details of the transactions that lead to the business making a profit or a loss

- what the business owes to the owner(s) (the *capital*).

acid test ratio is a measure of the money a business has readily to hand with which to pay its debts quickly. *Current liabilities* are usually paid out of *current assets*. Cash is the most *liquid asset*; debtors are the next easiest to change into cash while stock is the least liquid current asset. The acid test ratio is similar to the *current ratio* but stock is left out because it may take longer to convert to cash.

> FORMULA *for acid test ratio:*
>
> **Current assets – Stock**
> **Current liabilities**

If the ratio is 1:1 the business will have enough cash to be able to pay its debts quickly. If the ratio were 0.5:1 the business would have only enough cash to pay half its debts.

2

Worked example: Balance sheet of XYX and Company Limited as at 31 December

	£ 000	£ 000
Current Assets:		
Stocks	140	
Debtors	110	
Cash	70	320
Current Liabilities:		
Creditors	120	
Bank overdraft	120	240

$$\text{Acid test ratio} = \frac{\text{Current assets} - \text{Stock}}{\text{Current liabilities}} = \frac{320 - 140}{240} = 0.75$$

This means that XYX and Company Limited has only enough cash to pay 75p for every £1 it owes. Its liquidity is, therefore, poor.

added value is the amount by which the value of a product has risen as a result of a person's or firm's part in the *production* of that good or service. The actual value of the product is increased at each stage in its production.

Explanation: A product changes as it goes through each stage in the process of production. After each stage the product is worth more than it was at the beginning. This is because extra work (value) has been added. The value added will include the cost of wages and overheads. It will also include an allowance for profit.

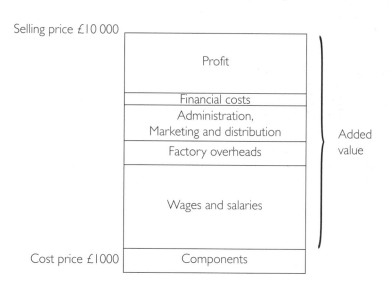

Added value

Example: A car manufacturer buys a large number of components and combines them to make a motor car. Each component by itself may have very little other use. By putting these parts together to make something different the car manufacturer has added value. Similarly, the individual worker on the production line adds value through his/her effort.

Added value is usually measured by the difference between the selling price of the product and the cost of the materials it contains.

advertising is communication with the public through one or more of the range of media available. In business advertising is one aspect of *promotion*.

Functions of advertising:

- To increase consumer awareness by telling the consumer that particular goods exist or where they can be purchased.

- To increase existing demand for a product by trying to increase its *market share*. This may be by creating a new demand for a product by targeting a new group of consumers.

- To create a new or improved image for a product.

Types of advertising:

- **Informative** – lets people know about a product; people cannot buy something they do not know exists or have no information about. (See *informative advertising*.)

- **Persuasive** – designed to persuade the public to buy a particular product.

- **Defensive** – where a company responds to a competitor's advertising claims when it is feared that a rival may win its customers.

Methods of advertising:

- **Direct** – where the advertising is targeted at chosen individuals.

- **Indirect** – general advertising aimed at the public at large or a particular part of the public. For example, specialist magazines, such as PC magazines, are aimed at people with an interest in computers; advertisements for toys are shown during children's television programmes.

Advantages of advertising:

- Different types of markets or customers can be targeted by choosing different places to advertise. Day to day products will be advertised in the popular press and on television. Specialist products will be advertised in the specialist magazines.

- It may result in increased sales and therefore increased employment and profits. If it leads to an increase in sales, costs will be spread over a larger output. Unit costs will be lower. This may lead to a reduction in the price of an article.

- It may result in an increase in demand and *economies of scale*.

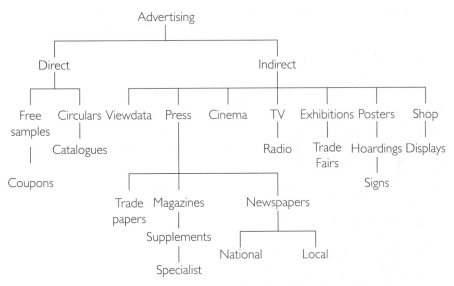

Methods of advertising

Criticisms of advertising:

- It may stimulate socially undesirable habits, e.g. smoking or drinking; it may also stimulate poor attitudes such as greed and envy.

- It may tempt people to buy things they cannot afford or they do not need.

- Higher prices may be caused by increases in advertisers' costs.

advertising agency: a specialist organisation employed to advise on the promotion of a firm's products. An agency will give advice, design and prepare advertisements and place them on television or in the press. It may also carry out market research before and after a promotion. It will be paid a *commission* for its work.

advertising campaign: a planned programme of advertising designed to promote an organisation, its products or services. The campaign must be carried out within a *budget*.

An advertising campaign should:

- be designed for a well defined target audience; this will affect the choice of media and the methods to be used

- cover a specific period of time

- be able to produce results that can be measured.

Advertising Standards Authority (ASA): a body set up for the voluntary *self-regulation* of the advertising industry. It aims to protect the public from irresponsible and dishonest advertising.

Scope: All advertising and *sales promotion* in the United Kingdom, except that on radio and television, come within the ASA's control.

Explanation: The ASA tries to make sure that everyone who orders, prepares and publishes advertisements does so according to the rules set out in the British Codes of Advertising and Sales Promotion. These rules, written by the advertising industry, are enforced by the ASA. Through the codes the ASA tries to make sure that all advertisements are 'legal, decent, honest and truthful'. It is important in *consumer protection*.

Example: The Benetton company used a series of dramatic photographs in its advertisements that included a picture of a newly born baby covered in blood. The advertisement offended many people who complained to the ASA. They upheld the public's complaints and Benetton withdrew the advertisements.

ASA

Features of the Advertising Standards Authority:

- Advertisers can ask for advice about their advertisements before they are published.

- The ASA does spot checks on advertisements to make sure the codes of practice have been followed.

- It investigates complaints from the public and may have advertisements withdrawn.

Main criticisms of the Advertising Standards Authority:

- It has no legal powers to enforce its decisions. It can only persuade advertisers and publishers to accept and observe the codes of practice.

- It is financed by the advertising industry and the public may think it is biased.

- It has been slow to respond to controversial issues such as the use of cartoon characters to advertise alcoholic lemonade (appealing to under-age drinkers?).

Advisory, Conciliation and Arbitration Service (ACAS): an independent body set up by the government in 1975 to promote good industrial relations. It gives information and advice about all things to do with employment law. ACAS cannot impose or even recommend how a dispute is settled. All ACAS services are confidential and free.

Functions of ACAS:

- ACAS helps to settle and prevent disputes before they develop into major confrontations. ACAS staff helps employers and employees to work together to solve problems before they get out of hand. The unions and the employers can jointly, or separately, ask for help.

- ACAS offers conciliation when disputes arise. An ACAS officer will get the two sides in a dispute to talk through their problems until they find 'common ground' as a basis for negotiation. They try to prevent the cases going to tribunal.

- If the two sides have failed to agree through conciliation, they can ask ACAS to provide *arbitration*. ACAS will then help to find either one person or a small group to examine the case and suggest an answer.

affinity card: a *credit card* that is tied in with a particular product, firm or charity.

> ***Explanation:*** These are ordinary Visa or Mastercard credit cards. Although they are issued through a *bank* the name of the bank is replaced by that of a company or charity. There will be some benefit to the company or charity from putting their name to the card.

The GM Card
from Vauxhall

Example: The GM Card is issued by General Motors, the makers of Vauxhall cars in the UK. It is an ordinary Visa or Mastercard credit card. If a person has one of these cards they gain 'points'. The more the card is used the greater the number of points gained. The points can be used to get a reduction on the price of a new Vauxhall.

after sales service: the supply of services to customers after a sale is completed.

After sales service is an important part of many companies' *marketing mix*.

Examples: After sales service can mean providing a repair and maintenance service, as in the case of cars or televisions or other *durable goods*. It may also be the supply of services, such as an up-dating service for *trade directories* or help lines such as software houses offer to users.

agenda: a list of the items of business and the order in which they are to be discussed at a meeting.

agent: someone who has been given the power to act on behalf of another person or company.

Explanation: An agent's job is to bring buyers and sellers together. Agents can make legally binding contracts on behalf of those they are acting for. They are used by sellers to find buyers (e.g. estate and travel agents). They can also be used by buyers to find sellers (for example, a manufacturer may use an agent to find a supplier of components). They are often used when a firm enters a new market. It saves having to open expensive offices in places where the firm is unknown.

Features of the agent's role:

- Agents often specialise in certain products or services. They know their local market well and have good contacts. They will know the best prices that can be obtained.

- Agents are especially useful overseas because they know the local market, local laws and regulations. Overseas customers may be more willing to do business and to trust someone who is from their own country.

- Agents never buy or own the goods and services in which they deal. They sell and distribute goods for others.

- They are paid a *commission* for their work.

AGM: see *annual general meeting.*

amalgamation: where two or more divisions of a company are combined into one new division. This usually happens as part of a *rationalisation* programme.

annual general meeting (AGM): the official meeting of ordinary *shareholders* held by a *public limited company.* The meeting must be held by law. At the meeting the shareholders have the right to:

Propose and vote on resolutions

Ordinary shareholders can put forward resolutions for discussion at the AGM. Ordinary shareholders have the right to vote on anything that affects their rights, e.g. a rights issue. They cannot vote on such things as directors' pay.

Approve the accounts

The *Annual Report* and *Accounts* must be approved by the shareholders.

Approve the dividend

The *final dividend* is proposed by the directors but cannot be paid until it is agreed by the AGM.

Appoint and dismiss directors

The directors are the shareholders' representatives and can only be elected or be re-elected by them.

The AGM is held after the end of the *financial year.* Only *ordinary share*holders can vote at the meeting. It is their only chance to question the directors about the running of the company.

annualised percentage rate (APR): the true annual percentage *rate of interest* paid on a *loan.* Lenders of money must by law state the APR in all advertisements and agreements. This enables borrowers to work out what interest they have to pay. The lower the APR the cheaper it is to borrow. APR can be used to compare the rates being offered by different lenders.

Explanation: The interest on a loan is calculated at a flat rate. This interest is charged on the full amount of the loan for the full period of the loan. However, as repayments are made the amount borrowed becomes less and one would expect the interest to fall. In fact it does not. The APR takes into account that interest is being paid on a smaller amount as repayments are made.

Worked example: A washing machine is bought for £600 on hire purchase, over two years. The flat rate of interest is 15%. The total cost of the machine will be

$$£600 + \left(\frac{15 \times 2}{100}\right) = £600 + £180 = £780$$

By the end of the first year £300 will have been repaid (plus interest) so that only £300 is borrowed in the second year. The interest will still be £90, which gives an interest rate of 30%. The interest is therefore 15% + 30% = 45%, divided by two (the number of years), giving an APR of 22.5%.

Annual Report and Accounts: a report that must be produced by limited companies at the end of the financial year. By law it must include:

- a *directors' report*
- a *profit and loss account*
- a *balance sheet*
- an *auditor's report*.

It must be approved by the *annual general meeting* and a copy sent to every shareholder and the *Registrar of Companies*. Anyone who wishes to know about the company can look at the report at Companies House. Examples of interested people would be those wishing to invest in the company, buy it or do business with it.

APR: see *annualised percentage rate*.

appraisal is a system for evaluating the performance of workers against agreed targets. It is used mainly in very large organisations.

Explanation: Many businesses try to involve their workers in the development of their careers; one way of doing this is through appraisal. An appraisal is usually done, once a year, through an interview, by an employee's boss. Appraisals usually follow the same pattern. The interviewer uses a standard company form which lists the questions to be asked. An appraisal has three main parts:

- a review of the previous year's performance
- agreeing the future needs of the person, their department and the general needs of the organisation

- an agreed action plan that sets out targets for the person; the training and support he or she needs and how it will be provided.

Advantages of appraisal to employees:

- Employees get a chance to talk about all aspects of the job in depth with their manager.

- Their training needs can be identified.

- Job satisfaction may be increased.

Advantages of appraisal to managers:

- Managers get to know the people working for them better. Ways of solving problems can be discussed in a helpful atmosphere.

- Managers have to think about their plans for the next year and how each person fits into them.

- Managers can make it clear to workers what is expected of them and set clear, agreed targets that may be linked to training for their workers.

Appraisal has been criticised because it is often linked to pay. A person who 'fails' the appraisal interview may not get a pay rise while colleagues on the same grade do so.

arbitration: where an independent person is used to help to settle a dispute.

> **Explanation:** When the parties to a dispute cannot agree they may ask an independent person, called an arbitrator, to help them. The arbitrator will listen to the two sides of the dispute and try to find an answer that both sides can accept. Arbitration is a cheaper way of settling a dispute than going to court.

> **Example:** A contractor building a new office block is asked by a client to make changes which add to the cost of the building. The client thinks the contractor saved on other parts of the job and the changes cost much less than claimed. The client refuses to pay more than the contract price. They cannot agree, so an arbitrator is asked to decide whether the client is liable to pay all or part of what the contractor is claiming.

(See also *Advisory, Conciliation and Arbitration Service*.)

articles of association are the internal rules for running a *limited company*. They include such things as: the number of *directors*, how long they serve for and their duties; the date of the end of the *financial year*, and of the AGM; the way the Articles can be changed.

The articles are one of the essential documents that a limited company must have by law. They must be approved by the *Registrar of Companies* before the company can begin to operate.

ASA: see *Advertising Standards Authority.*

assets are all the things owned by a business, organisation or a person, that can be given a money value. For a business to exist it must have assets. Those assets, or resources, must be supplied by someone. In the simplest form of business the only assets may be the owner's skill.

There are two main types of asset:

- **Fixed assets** – such things as premises, machinery, office equipment, vehicles. They have a long life, are used in the business and are only disposed of when they reach the end of their useful life.

- **Current assets** – are stocks, debtors and money in the bank or in cash. They are short-term and change in value from day to day.

audit: an independent check on the truth and accuracy of a business's financial records. It is usually carried out by a firm of professional accountants. An annual audit is a legal requirement for limited companies. The audit is mainly for the benefit of the shareholders. The audit report looks at two main areas:

- the company's accounts and other financial records

- what the company has told its members about those accounts.

authorised capital: the maximum number of each type of share that a *public limited company* is allowed to issue to its shareholders. The authorised capital is stated in the *memorandum of association.* The actual number of shares that are issued may be less than the authorised capital.

automation: the replacing of human labour by machines. The growth of computer-controlled machines has, in recent years, speeded up the move to automation.

Automation happens in offices as well as factories. Banks, for instance, have shed thousands of jobs as computers have replaced people.

Advantages of automation to employers:

- Machines can be employed 24 hours a day without breaks. More can be produced in the same time because there is no break in production due to meals and shift changes. Computer-controlled machines can be reprogrammed very quickly and easily to do other jobs.

- Less labour may be needed. One person may be able to look after several machines, so the costs of production are reduced. Costs can be spread across a larger output, therefore *average cost* is reduced.

Disadvantages of automation to employers:

- Not all companies have enough *capital* to buy the very expensive machinery needed.

- Workers may have to be made *redundant*. This may damage morale and be expensive because of the redundancy payments.

Advantages of automation to employees:

- It may lead to a cleaner and better working environment. Less physical labour may be needed.

- Those that program and maintain the machines will need a high level of skill and constant up-dating. There may, therefore, be greater *training* opportunities and job security.

- Although fewer people may be employed, those that remain may be better paid.

Disadvantages of automation to employees:

- Fewer people are needed and there is a greater chance of being made unemployed.

- Some jobs are de-skilled and skilled workers become just machine minders. For example, robots can spray car bodies more quickly and evenly than humans.

- As more firms automate their production, job opportunities become fewer.

average costs: sometimes called the *unit cost* of making a product. It is calculated by dividing the sum of the *fixed costs* and the *variable costs* by the total output.

> **FORMULA *for calculating average costs:***
>
> $$\text{Average Costs} = \frac{\text{Total costs}}{\text{Output}}$$

Average costs change all the time with output. They do so because the fixed costs are spread across a larger or smaller output.

13

Worked example: A firm buys raw materials for 70p per unit, has fixed costs of £5000 and output that varies as follows:

Output	Variable cost per unit (£)	Variable cost (total) (£)	Fixed cost	Total cost (£)	Average cost (£)
4000	0.70	2800	5000	7800	1.95
5000	0.70	3500	5000	8500	1.70
6000	0.70	4200	5000	9200	1.53
7000	0.70	4900	5000	9900	1.41
7500	0.70	5250	5000	10250	1.37

Average costs explain why the prices of certain goods fall when output increases. Many electronic goods are expensive when they are first introduced. As output increases, the average cost falls and so does the price in the shops.

average stock is the average amount of stock that is held by a firm over a period of time, usually a year.

FORMULA *to calculate average stock:*

$$\text{Average costs} = \frac{\textbf{Total of stock valuations}}{\textbf{Number of stocktaking occasions}}$$

Thus if a firm counts its stock four times a year when it is valued at £25 000, £60 000, £15 000 and £40 000, the average stock is

$$\frac{£140\ 000}{4} = £35\ 000$$

Explanation: The average level of stocks held is important to a business.

- If the stocks are too high a firm might stop buying supplies or cut the amount of goods made. The firm may also find it hard to pay its debts.

- If stocks are too low some customers may be kept waiting for their orders to be met.

- It is best if stocks are kept at a fairly constant level. They should be big enough for a company to be able to deliver orders on time, but not so big that they tie up capital unnecessarily.

BACS: see *banking automated clearing services.*

bad debts occur when someone who owes money fails to pay the amount owed.

> **Explanation:** Most businesses sell goods on *credit.* The people who then owe the money are called *debtors.* Sometimes debtors fail to pay part or all of their debts. When this happens they are called bad debts. A business will try many times to get the money and wait quite a long time before deciding a debt is bad. *Credit control* helps to reduce bad debts.

balance: the difference between the amounts entered on each side of an *account.*

> **Example:**

	Dr		RAY GUNN & CO		Cr
May 1	Balance b/d	120 00	May 12	Bank	110 00
May 20	Sales	700 00	May 12	Discount received	10 00
			May 31	Balance c/d	700 00
		820 00			820 00
Jun 1	Balance b/d	700 00			

Accounts are balanced when they are totalled and the difference between the two sides is calculated. The balance shown at the beginning of the month is called the opening balance. The balance at the end of the month is called the closing or carried down balance (c/d).

See also d*ebit entry, credit entry.*

balance of payments: the difference between the total amount earned from buying and selling goods and services overseas.

> **FORMULA to calculate balance of payments:**
>
> **Total exports – Total imports**

The balance of payments is divided into two parts:

1 The *current account* is the difference between the total value of a country's *exports* of goods and services and the total value of its *imports* of goods and services during a year. This is made up of:

> • the import and export of *goods,* which is called *visible trade*

> • the import and export of *services,* which is called *invisible trade.*

Example

Total exports – Total imports = Balance of payments

£800 billion – £650 billion = *plus* £150 billion

2 The capital account records the movement of large sums of money in and out of a country. Included in the capital account is money invested by foreign firms in Britain or money invested by British companies abroad.

balance of trade: the part of the *balance of payments* that is the difference between the total value of a country's *imports* of goods and the total value of its *exports* of goods. In this case services are not taken into account. It measures only the balance of *visible trade*.

balance sheet: a statement of the value of the *assets* and *liabilities* of a business at a fixed moment in time. It is only accurate on a certain date, so the heading should always be 'as at' the date concerned.

Example: a typical balance sheet

Balance Sheet of XYX and Company Limited as at 31 December

	At cost £ 000		Net value £ 000
FIXED ASSETS:			
Premises	150		150
Fixtures and fittings	70		56
Machinery	170		125
	390		331
CURRENT ASSETS:			
Stock	86		
Debtors	67		
Bank	52		
Cash	18		
		223	
Less CURRENT LIABILITIES			
Creditors		130	
Working capital			93
NET ASSETS			424
FINANCED BY:			
Issued share capital			
400 000 ordinary shares of £1 each, fully paid			400
General reserves			24
CAPITAL EMPLOYED			424

The balance sheet is not an account but a list of the balances in the accounts of the business set out in a particular way. When drawing up a balance sheet certain rules of format should be followed:

- *Fixed assets* should be shown first; followed by *current assets*.
- It is usual to deduct *current liabilities* from the total assets, to show *working capital*.
- *Net assets* must always be equal to *capital employed*.

bank: an organisation that receives deposits from the public which it uses to finance business activity. Banks have three main functions:

- **receiving deposits –** which also provides safe keeping for money
- **transferring of money –** mainly through cheques and credit transfers
- **lending –** to both business and private people.

See also *commercial bank, central bank.*

bank charges are the sums charged by a *bank* for extra services on current accounts. If a customer's current account is accidentally overdrawn the bank will make a charge. This charge will be extra to any interest charged. The bank will also charge if it has to write letters telling customers they are overdrawn. Other charges are for extra work such as preparing a *bank draft* or providing a *bank reference* for a customer. Bank charges are shown on the *bank statement.*

bank draft: a *cheque* that is drawn on the account of a *bank* instead of on the account of a company or a person. The bank must be paid the value of the cheque before they issue the bank draft.

> ***Explanation:*** If a firm is dealing with a customer for the first time it may know nothing about that customer. Or, perhaps a customer's cheque has 'bounced' in the past. To be certain of being paid the firm could ask for a banker's draft. Because the cheque is drawn on the bank's account, the bank guarantees payment and the firm is certain that it will be paid.

Bank drafts are often used in overseas trade because the *credit status* of a foreign company may be unknown. In foreign trade a bank draft can be made out in any currency to suit the company to which it is to be paid.

bank giro credit: see *credit transfer.*

bank loan: a fixed sum of money borrowed from a *bank* for a definite period of time. It can be repaid by instalments or in a lump sum.

- The bank will charge *interest* on the whole sum for the full period of the loan.
- The bank will open a special loan account where interest will be added and repayments shown.
- A bank loan is different from a *bank overdraft*.

Bank of England: the *central bank* for the UK. It is publicly owned but is technically independent of the government. It works closely with the *Treasury*. It is responsible for fixing the bank rate and for the management of the country's money supply.

Functions of the Bank of England:

- the bankers' bank – all the other banks have accounts at the Bank of England
- the government's bank
- the sole issuer of banknotes in England and Wales
- the lender in the last resort – which means that if all the other banks stopped lending money the Bank of England would lend money to enable business to carry on.

bank overdraft: see *overdraft*.

bank rate is the *rate of interest* that the *Bank of England* would charge if it did lend money. The bank rate is important because it sets a pattern which is followed by all other interest rates. The bank rate is fixed by a committee of experts chaired by the Governor of the Bank of England.

bank statement: a list produced by a *bank* of all the money paid into a bank account and all payments out of that account (withdrawals). The bank will provide a statement as often as it is required. A business may have one daily but a private person will probably have one once a month. The bank statement should be checked regularly to make sure that the bank's records agree with the business's accounts.

banking automated clearing services (BACS): a company owned by the banks and building societies, it provides an electronic system for the transfer of money from one bank account to another.

Common uses of BACS:

- paying salaries directly into personal bank accounts

- paying *standing orders* and *direct debits*
- by businesses to pay their *creditors* and to transfer money between branches of a business.

bankrupt: when an individual or a business that is not *incorporated* has more liabilities than assets. That is, if everything owned was sold they would not raise enough money to pay their debts. Once a person has been made bankrupt there are restrictions on what they can do in business; they cannot for example, become a company director. A limited liability company cannot be declared bankrupt. (See also *liquidation*.)

bar chart: a way of showing information in which the length of a bar is used to compare data. The length of the bars is in proportion to the size of what is being considered. The longer the bar, the greater the relative importance of that data. The bars can be drawn either vertically or horizontally.

Example: A survey asked 150 local shoppers where they preferred to do their shopping. The results were:

Corner shop	5
Local shopping centre	14
Out of town shopping centres	58
Supermarkets	42
Town centre shops	31

It is fairly easy to see from these figures which is the most popular form of shopping. It takes a bit of sorting to decide which is the second most popular. It is quite hard to see by how much they vary in popularity. If the same information is put into a bar chart we can see the order of popularity straight away. We can also get a fairly good idea by how much they vary in popularity.

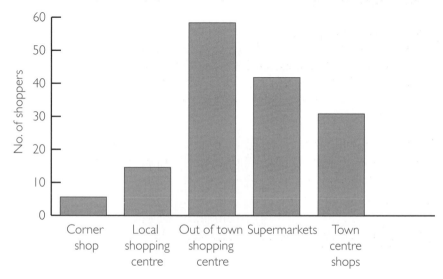

The same information can be shown in a horizontal bar chart.

No. of shoppers

bar coding is a system for identifying goods. The code is made up of a pattern of lines and spaces. It can be used for anything where repeated identification is needed. Most products bought in shops have a bar code. Each country, each manufacturer and each product has its own unique identification number. The individual bar code is made up of a combination of these numbers plus a control digit. The code does not contain the price because different sellers may charge different prices.

FORMULA:

Country + Manufacturer + Item + Control

Country → 5 000127 051096

Manufacturer Product

Uses of the bar code:

- The tills at supermarket check-outs are linked to a central computer which automatically displays the price and prints it on the till roll. It will also enter the sales in the accounting system and updates stock records.

- Bar codes are used by all kinds of organisations for *stock control*. They can be used wherever a unique number can be allocated and records of a transaction are needed.

barter is the simplest form of *trade* when people *exchange* goods instead of using money. It is very difficult to make it work well in a modern society because of the huge choice of goods. You have to find someone who wants what you have to exchange. It is also very hard to find a basis on which to agree a price. For example, if you are a farmer growing potatoes and you want a tractor how do you decide how many potatoes a tractor is worth?

basic pay: the amount a worker is paid for working for a certain time. It is *wages* or *salaries* before *deductions* or the addition of *overtime, bonuses* or *commission*. Basic pay is usually stated as a sum per hour, week or year.

batch production: where identical goods are made in lots or batches. One batch is finished before moving on to the next one. Batch production is used:

- to make goods against a specific order. Just the goods for that order are worked upon until it is finished. Work then moves on to the next order. This system is used, for example, by printing companies

- where the same machine can be used to produce different things by changing the settings. For example, a lathe may be used to turn a certain kind of wooden chair leg on one day; the next day it could be reset to produce a different design

- where goods have the same design but are made to different sizes or colours. For example, a batch of brown, 80 cm waist trousers might be made one day while the next batch could be size 84 cm in a different colour.

block release: when an employer allows an employee to be released for a 'block' (period) of time to attend a training course. The block may be as little as week or as much as a year. While on block release the employee will still be paid but will attend college rather than go to work.

Board of Customs and Excise: see *Customs and Excise.*

board of directors: a committee elected by the shareholders of a *limited company.* It decides policy and makes important decisions about running the company.

Explanation: All the owners (shareholders) of a firm cannot take part in running the company. They therefore choose some shareholders to be their representatives. These are called the directors. A company must have at least one director, but the number of directors on the board will vary from company to company. Directors must report to the other shareholders at the *annual general meeting*. Directors must, by law, always act in the best interests of the company and its shareholders.

Types of director:

- In a large company there will be executive and non-executive directors.

- The *executive directors* are responsible for the day-to-day management of certain aspects of a company's work. They will be full-time employees of the company. The managing director will manage the company as a whole. Other executive directors might manage, for example, sales or personnel aspects of the company.

- *Non-executive directors* do not take part in the day-to-day management of a company. They are usually part-time. They try to make sure that all aspects of the company are run according to the law. They have a duty to see that the company is run in the best interests of all the shareholders.

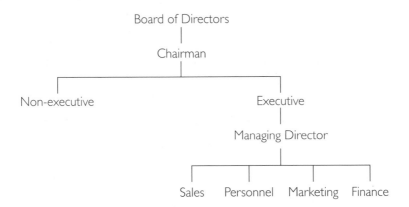

bond: a guarantee backed up by a sum of money paid into a special account; it is a kind of guarantee for customers. If the person giving the bond cannot keep to the guarantee, the money is lost or used to compensate customers.

Examples: two kinds of bond:

1. Travel agents who are members of ABTA (the Association of British Travel Agents) pay a bond which is used if a member company goes out of business. The bond is used to get customers home from abroad and sometimes to pay compensation to people whose holidays have been cancelled.

bonded warehouse: a warehouse, the owner of which has entered into a bond with *Customs and Excise*. The owner guarantees that duty will be paid on the goods stored there. While in the warehouse the goods can be weighed, graded, packed or bottled. They can be sold but they cannot be released from the warehouse until the duty has been paid. Bonded warehouses are often used for tobacco, wines and spirits.

bonds are promises to repay a loan, usually on a fixed date. They are securities issued either by governments or by companies. Companies issue bonds as a less risky alternative to shares. The bondholders are *creditors* of the company and are paid a fixed *rate of interest* before the *net profit* is finalised. Government bonds are called *gilt-edged securities*, or gilts. Bonds can be bought and sold on the *stock exchange*.

bonus: an extra payment over and above the normal rate of earnings. It is most often paid as an addition to wages and salaries. It is often used as an incentive. It may be a payment for good timekeeping, meeting targets or just for long service. A bonus should be easily understood, seen to be fair and easy to calculate.

book value (or net value) refers to the value of a company's assets in its *balance sheet*. *Fixed assets*, other than land, are depreciated, usually annually. They are shown in the balance sheet at their original purchase price (cost) minus *depreciation*, which equals their net or book value.

Example: Balance sheet of XYX and Company as at 31 December

	At cost £	Depreciation £	Net £
Fixed assets			
Premises	150 000		150 000
Furniture and equipment	70 000	14 000	56 000
Machinery	170 000	45 000	125 000
	390 000	59 000	331 000

The book value of XYX and Company's fixed assets is £331 000. This may not be the real value of the assets but it is the value recorded in the company's accounting system.

bookkeeping is the methodical recording, in money terms, of the financial transactions of a business.

Explanation: A record is kept of all financial activities to find out whether a business is making a profit or a loss. This is done through a system of recording money transactions known as the *double entry* system. Under this system every transaction involves two entries, one *debit (Dr)* and one *credit (Cr)* entry. Transactions that do not involve money are not recorded.

boom: a period in the *business cycle* when business activity is at a very high level. During a boom, business confidence, investment and employment will be high. Wages, interest rates and prices will probably be rising.

Boston matrix: a way of showing the position of a firm's products in terms of their share of the market and in relation to the growth of its industry. It is also known as the 'Boston Box' and was developed by the Boston Consulting Group in America.

The Boston matrix

Market growth

- **Stars** have a high market share in a high growth industry. They may require financial support, for promotion, but give a high return. They are at the growth phase of the product life cycle.

- **Problem children** have a low market share in a high growth industry. They may be new products or in a highly competitive trade. They have good potential but are not doing as well as they should and need a great deal of financial support. Some products never get beyond this stage.

- **Cash cows** have a high market share in a low growth or non-expanding industry. They need little financial support and produce more cash than is necessary to sustain their market share. This surplus can be milked to support the 'problem children'. They are at the mature phase of the product life cycle.

- **Dogs** have a low market share in a low growth industry. They are in the decline phase of the product life cycle with no hope of reviving their fortunes. They will probably be dropped when they start to make a loss.

branding: the identification of a product by giving it a unique name under which it is marketed. Goods are branded to make them special in the eyes of consumers.

> ***Explanation:*** A company may make two products that are identical in every way. If they are given different brand names and *packaging* they will be seen by the public as very different goods. This allows producers to market them as separate products.

- A branded product will probably have packaging which people recognise easily and always link with the brand name e.g. Coca Cola.

- The brand name will probably be registered as a *trade mark*. This gives the producers a *monopoly* for their brand.

- Some brand names have become so well known that the product is always known by the brand name, thus Thermos (vacuum flasks), Hoover (vacuum cleaners), Biro (ball point pens).

Advantages to the consumers:

- Branding may widen choice.

- Branding may simplify shopping because products can be easily identified.

- Consumers can be reasonably sure about the quality of branded goods.

breakeven: the output at which a firm's total revenue is equal to its total costs (*fixed costs* plus *variable cost*). This is called the break-even point. At this point the business is making neither a profit nor a loss.

The breakeven point can be worked out either by using a table, a graph or by calculation.

Worked example: A firm has fixed costs of £5000 and variable costs of £2 for every unit it produces; its selling price is £4 per unit. We will assume that all the production is sold. We can show this in a table:

No. of units	Fixed costs £	Variable costs £	Total costs £	Sales £	Profit/ loss £
0	5000	0	5000		(5000)
1000	5000	2000	7000	4000	(3000)
2000	5000	4000	9000	8000	(1000)
2500	5000	5000	10000	10000	
3000	5000	6000	11000	12000	1000
4000	5000	8000	13000	16000	3000
5000	5000	10000	15000	20000	5000

We can see from the table that the breakeven point is 2500 units. If the firm produces less than 2500 units it will make a loss. All output beyond the breakeven point results in a profit. This information can also be shown as a graph:

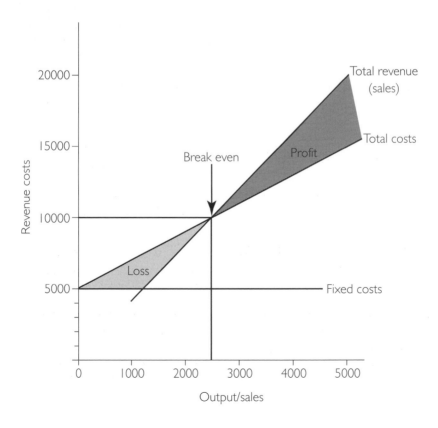

Points to note:

- The vertical axis is always revenue/costs and is measured in money.

- The horizontal axis is always output/sales measured in units.

- The 'total costs' line always starts on the vertical axis at the fixed costs line. This is because the cost of producing zero units is the fixed costs. There are no variable costs at zero output.

- The firm is making a profit to the right of the breakeven point. To the left of the breakeven point the firm is making a loss.

Alternatively we can calculate the breakeven point without having to draw up a table or a graph.

We have said that the variable cost of one unit is £2 and the selling price of one unit is £4. Every unit sold therefore makes a *contribution* of £2 towards the fixed costs.

$$\text{Breakeven point} = \frac{\text{Fixed costs}}{\text{Selling price per unit} - \text{variable costs per unit}}$$

$$= \frac{5000}{4 - 2} = \frac{5000}{2} = 2500 \text{ units}$$

A firm can use breakeven to predict the effect on its profits of a change in its costs, price, sales or output.

breaking bulk: the splitting of large quantities of goods into smaller amounts to suit the needs of buyers.

> **Explanation:** Manufacturers prefer to sell goods in very large quantities. Consumers, however, usually only want small amounts of goods at any one time. Each stage in the *chain of distribution* breaks bulk for the next stage. Manufacturers sell in large amounts to *wholesalers* or the central depots of supermarkets. They break bulk by supplying individual shops with smaller amounts. The shops break bulk when they sell goods in ones and twos to the consumer.

British Standards Institution (BSI): an independent body, responsible for the preparation of British Standards for all industries. BSI is funded by the sale of its standards, certification fees, subscriptions and by government grant.

> **Explanation:** The Institution draws up detailed specifications for a wide range of products. These are called standards. The standards may also lay down details of the materials to be used and the way the product has to be made and tested. Standard sizes are also laid down. All goods made to a standard have the same basic specification. The standards are prepared by committees of experts. They are reviewed at least every five years.

Benefits of standards to industry:

- Having standard sizes makes stock keeping simpler and therefore cheaper, especially for small items like screws.

- Goods produced to a British Standard and independently tested may be able to carry the famous *Kitemark*. This may make them easier to sell.

- Products made to a British Standard are accepted in all EU countries. It is part of the harmonisation of the *single market*.

Benefits of standards to the consumer:

- The BSI contributes to consumer protection:

  - by setting minimum safety standards

  - by encouraging the production of quality goods

  - goods carrying the *Kitemark* are of at least a minimum quality.

- Any fall in costs to manufacturers may be passed on to consumers in lower prices.

BSI represents UK interests, in harmonising European standards and formulating international standards. Examples of goods produced to international standards include those for the size of ship containers, audio and video cassettes and credit cards.

brokers buy or sell goods or services on behalf of other people.

Features of brokers:

- they are found in a number of different industries, e.g. sugar, tea, wool, cotton

- they never directly handle the goods themselves

- they are paid a *commission* for their work.

Examples:

1   Brokers buy and sell shares on behalf of clients on the Stock Exchange.

> **2** Consumers are most likely to deal with insurance or mortgage brokers. For example, a broker will arrange motor or household insurance for a customer (the client). Because they are working for their clients they will try to get the best cover, as cheaply as possible. Insurance brokers do not charge their clients because they are paid a commission by the insurance company for selling the insurance on their behalf.

BSI: see *British Standards Institution.*

Budget (the): the annual forecast of the money the government expects to collect in taxes and so has to spend on services during the *financial year.* It is delivered by the Chancellor of the Exchequer, traditionally in March. It does not come fully into effect until the next financial year, starting in April. Some tax changes may come into effect straight away. If an increase in the tax on wine, for example, was delayed for several weeks people would buy large quantities to avoid the tax increase.

The Budget is usually in three main parts:

- a review of the current financial year

- estimated government income and expenditure targets for the following financial year

- the tax changes necessary to achieve next year's financial targets.

budget: a detailed estimate of the future income and financial needs of a business. Budgets show what resources will be needed and how they will be used over a period of time.

- Budgets are the future financial plans for a business; each part of a business is set targets for income and expenditure.

- Budgets are usually for no more than a year ahead. They can be for short periods like a month or for longer periods of up to five years. They are brought up to date regularly, so that they are as accurate as possible.

The word 'budget' is also used where a sum of money is allocated to a particular purpose such as a building project or for the purchase of a new machine.

The preparation of the plan is known as *budgeting.* The use of the plan in the management of the business is *budgetary control.*

budgetary control is the use of budgets to control the finances of an organisation.

> **Explanation:** Performance is measured against a budget. A department, for example, will be expected to have sold what it said it was going to sell and to keep

its costs within the budget. Checks are carried out to see if all parts of the business are meeting their targets and not overspending. Managers are asked to give reasons for differences between the budget and what is really happening.

Advantages of budgetary control:

- Forecasting and planning are encouraged.
- Agreed targets are set that everyone knows about; this helps to keep expenditure under control.
- Problems can be spotted quickly.

Disadvantages of budgetary control:

- Rising costs are often outside a firm's control (e.g. when the price of materials has risen).
- Budgets can be rigid and reduce flexibility.
- Departments may be tempted to spend up to budget, instead of saving money.

budgeting is the process of financial planning by which budgets are agreed.

Explanation: Each part of an organisation has its own budget. If a business is divided into departments each one will have a budget. Managers of departments are asked to draw up estimates for the coming year against set targets. Once they are approved the budgets for each department are brought together to form a main or 'master budget' for the whole business. Once the budget is agreed it becomes the financial plan for the business. It is then used as the basis for *budgetary control*.

building societies are financial institutions that take deposits from investors. They pay interest on the deposits and lend those deposits to people to buy property, usually their home.

Features of building societies:

- Loans are secured by *mortgages* on properties. The loan and the interest charges are repaid over a fixed number of years.
- Borrowers pay a higher rate of interest than the rate paid to investors. The difference between the two rates of interest is used by the society to pay for premises and other running costs.
- Strictly speaking building societies do not make a profit. They are 'mutual' organisations which means they are owned by their customers (depositors and borrowers) who can vote at the *annual general meeting*.

> • They now offer a wide range of financial services such as cheques, credit cards, insurance and estate agencies.

Several societies, including the Halifax and Abbey National, have become banks that are no longer mutual societies but *public limited companies*.

bulk buying is the purchase of goods in large quantities. Suppliers of goods may give a *trade discount* to buyers, which varies with the size of the order. The more bought, the cheaper the goods. This is an *economy of scale*. Buying in large amounts may mean stocks have to be held for a long time. The cost of holding such stocks has to be set against the advantage of bulk buying. One reason why supermarkets can sell goods cheaper than a small shop is that they buy in very large quantities and receive large discounts. They also sell the goods quickly.

business cycle: every five years or so business goes through a cycle. The cycle seems to have four phases:

> • **boom**

> • **recession**

> • **slump**

> • **recovery** and then back to boom again.

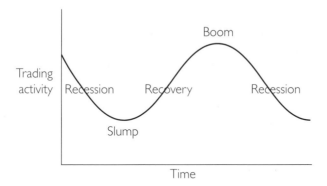

business ethics are the moral principles applied to the running of a business.

These standards:

> • are sometimes set by a code of conduct or a code of practice agreed by the industry as a whole (e.g. banking, the Stock Exchange, doctors)

> • may be a set of principles used by an individual company (e.g. Body Shop do not sell cosmetics that have been tested on animals).

A company's business ethics will often be included in their *business objectives*. Because of the public worries about the environment some companies publicise their business ethics and use them as part of their *marketing*.

business letters are letters that have a business, rather than a personal purpose. They are used in *formal communication*. The style of a business letter will depend on the 'house style' of the organisation. There are some general conventions that should be observed.

Example of the layout of a business letter

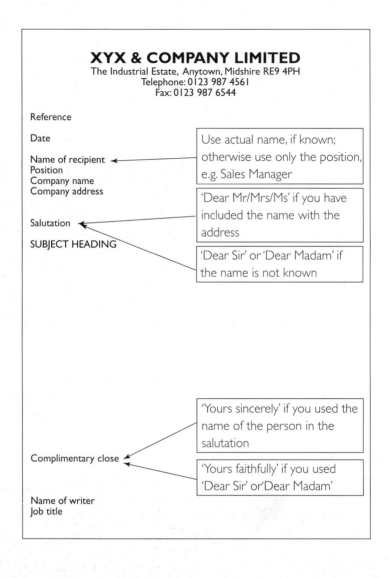

(See also *communications*.)

business objectives are the targets, other than financial, that a business sets for itself. They will vary a great deal depending on the nature of the business and the principles on which it is based. Here are some common objectives which most businesses will have:

- **Survival –** important to everyone connected with the business, including workers, managers, shareholders, suppliers, creditors, banks and other providers of finance. If a business does not survive, money and jobs will be lost.

- **Profit –** making a *profit* is probably the most common and the most important objective. No business can survive for long unless it covers all of its costs. It can only do so if it sells its products or services for more than the price it has to pay for the goods and services it uses in the business. The size of the profit will vary. Some businesses will try to make as much profit as they can (maximise profit). Others will be content to make only enough profit to survive comfortably, (e.g. one man in business, wishing to make a comfortable living for himself and his family, but with no wish to expand).

- **Growth –** some firms want to become larger, or increase their *market share*, or be the biggest firm in their type of business. They may want to drive out their competitors or simply to make a bigger profit. (See also *growth*.)

- **Prestige –** some firms wish to have the prestige of becoming the market leader in their field of business, or they may want to have a reputation for very high quality, (e.g. Rolls Royce). Other firms will think there is prestige in having a reputation for being responsible in protecting the environment; many furniture manufacturers, for example, say their products are made from 'renewable resources'.

business organisations: see *organisations*.

business plan: a detailed outline of a business's intentions over a period of time. Business plans usually cover a relatively short period of between one and three years. This is because it is difficult to look further ahead, with any real accuracy.

Main reasons for a business plan:

- Potential investors can use the plan:
  - to see the return they will get on their investment
  - to gain some confidence in the manager's ability to manage
  - to see that there is a good market for the company's products.

- Banks and other lenders usually insist on a business plan before they will lend money.

- It can be used within the business. Managers can compare what is really happening with the plan. If the business is not meeting the plan's targets they can see where things are going wrong.

Not all business plans look the same but all should contain the following headings:

1. **The business** – the aims and objectives of the business; if it is a new business, what is the business idea? Why start up? If an existing business, how old is it? What is its past performance?

2. **The management** – kind of company, sole trader, partnership, etc; ownership and management of the company.

3. **The market** – who are the customers? Where are they located? Estimated size – what is the competition and where is it located? In what way is the product different? Is there a potential for growth? How can it be achieved?

4. **Marketing plan** – how the product will be sold.

5. **Resources** – premises, number of employees, their skills, estimated future needs.

6. **Financial report** – start up costs (if a new business); capital and who owns it; details of existing loans and how they are being repaid; estimated future capital needs including new loans and how they are to be repaid; must include a *cashflow forecast, profit and loss account* and *balance sheet*.

7. Prospects for the business over the next three to five years.

business rates: a tax paid to local authorities on all premises used for business purposes. The amount of the tax is based on the value and size of the premises. The rate of tax is set by central government.

buyout: this occurs when a group of managers, and often employees too, purchase the company for which they work. They are usually supported by *venture capital* from the banks or specialist financial providers. The buyers will also put some of their own money into the business. All the people who join in the buyout will become *shareholders*. The number of shares they own depends on the level of their personal investment. (See also *management buyout.*)

Circumstances under which buyouts may happen:

- When the original owner decides to sell part of a business (e.g. Cadburys decided to sell part of the business to its managers, who called it Premier Foods).

- When a firm goes into *liquidation* or receivership (e.g. Leyland Daf Vans went into receivership when its Dutch parent company failed; since the buyout it is known as LDV).

- When a company is privatised (e.g. West Midlands Travel, National Freight Corporation).

CAD: see *computer aided design*.

CAM: see *computer aided manufacture*.

capacity: the resources used by an organisation to carry on its business. Its capacity provides a business with the ability to carry out its *objectives*.

> **Explanation:** The capacity of a company includes:

- the size of its premises
- how much machinery and equipment it has
- the number and the skills of its workers.

> If a firm is short of any of the resources needed for a job, it does not have that capacity to do the job. Once a business has reached its capacity it cannot take on extra work. It will then have to decide whether to turn down orders, or increase its capacity. It can do this by buying new machinery, taking on more workers or by expanding its premises.

Capacity is also used in the sense of the total amount that an organisation can produce with the resources it has at present.

capital: the funds invested in a business to enable it to buy the physical *assets* it needs to carry on business. It is everything used by the owners for the purpose of running the business. It is one of the *factors of production*.

> **Explanation:** In everyday speech we think of capital as just money. When someone starts a business they use their money to buy things to use in the business, for example, premises, equipment and stocks of goods for sale or raw materials. These are the *assets* and equal the capital of the business. If, for some reason, a business closes down, all the assets will be sold and debts paid. What is left is the capital. It belongs to the owners. The owners may be *shareholders*, *partners* or a *sole proprietor*.

capital account: see *balance of payments*.

capital employed: the long-term funds used in a business. It consists of the owner(s) funds, *reserves* built up by the business, plus money borrowed for more than a year. The capital employed will be equal to the *net assets* of the business.

capital equipment: the *fixed assets* of a business that are directly used for making other goods and services. It is assets that have a fairly long life, such as machinery and equipment.

capital expenditure is spending on the purchase of new or replacement *fixed assets* for a business. It also includes spending that increases the value of a fixed asset.

Capital expenditure results in an increase in the value of the assets in the *balance sheet*. It has no direct effect on either the *trading account* or the *profit and loss account*.

Examples:

- the purchase of machinery or a new building
- buying a new aeroplane by an airline
- building a new extension to a building or modernising a machine to extend its life.

Compare capital expenditure with *revenue expenditure*.

capital goods are the same as *capital equipment*. They are not goods that are wanted for their own sake. They are goods used in the production of other goods.

capital intensive: where production depends very heavily on the use of *capital equipment*. Other *factors of production*, such as labour, are less important.

Examples:

- car factories using many robots and automatic machinery
- industries that have a continuous process such as chemical factories, power stations and oil refineries.

capitalism is an economic and social system where the allocation of the *factors of production* is left to the market mechanism. The government interferes as little as possible in controlling the way the economy works.

> **Explanation:** Under capitalism *market forces* decide how the *factors of production* are allocated. Efficient businesses will be rewarded with big profits. They will be able to buy up-to-date equipment and attract the best workers, because they can afford to pay them well. Weaker firms will make smaller profits, and will not be able to afford the best equipment or workers. The good firms will get better and the weaker firms may close.

cash: the notes and coins used in a country to settle debts. Other methods of paying off debts have replaced cash to some extent, for example *cheques, credit cards* and *debit cards*. Cash is the most liquid of all assets. The order of *liquidity* of other assets is measured by how easy they are to turn into cash. The main use for cash is in making small payments to other people or in shops.

Disadvantages of cash:

- Cash is bulky and heavy to carry in large amounts and takes a great deal of time to count and check.

- There is a security risk both in carrying and storing cash. It cannot be safely sent through the post.

cash budget: an alternative term for a *cash flow forecast*.

cash discount: a *discount* given by a seller for prompt payment for goods bought on *credit*. Often, the sooner the bill is settled the bigger will be the discount.

Example: An *invoice* may say 'Terms: 3% 7 days; 1% 14 days'. This means the trader will reduce the bill by 3% if it is paid within seven days but by only 1% if it is paid in 14 days. After 14 days no discount will be given.

cash flow forecast: a specialised *budget* which shows the cash flowing in and flowing out of a business over a given period. For these purposes cash includes money in the bank.

Explanation: A business may have to wait several weeks or months after it has produced and sold goods before it is paid for them. Money does not come into a business evenly through the year. Firms need cash to pay their suppliers and to pay workers on time.

A cash flow forecast shows the main sources of money and the main spending headings. It also shows the months where there may be a surplus or a shortage of cash. If the business knows well in advance when it is going to be short of cash it can arrange an *overdraft* with the bank.

Example: a typical cash flow forecast for four months

	January £000	February £000	March £000	April £000
CASH IN				
Capital	50			
Cash sales Dept A	15	10	30	36
Dept B	10	15	28	28
Debtors		12	19	27
Total cash receipts	75	37	77	91
CASH OUT				
Set-up costs	21	3		
Wages and salaries	1	1	1	1
Rent	5			5
Rates	1.5	1.5	1.5	1.5
Other overheads	3	3.5	2.5	6.5

(continued)	January £000	February £000	March £000	April £000
Cash purchases	30	30	35	40
Creditors	1.5	15	30	35
Total cash payments	63	54	70	89
NET CASH FLOW	12	(17)	7	2
add opening balance brought down	0	12	(5)	2
Cash balance carried forward	12	(5)	2	4

cash on delivery: a method of payment where customers pay for goods when they are delivered. A delivery driver will not hand over the goods until the customer has paid. It is a method of payment used by mail order firms who have a problem in making sure they are paid for goods. Sales by *credit card* have largely replaced this method of payment.

caveat emptor: Latin words meaning 'let the buyer beware'.

> **Explanation:** *Consumer protection* law has made illegal many of the most common ways of cheating the buyer. However, buyers cannot rely entirely on the law for protection. The consumer must still be very careful because 'good offers' are not always what they seem to be.

CBI: See *Confederation of British Industry*.

cell production: where the workers on a production line do several operations instead of just one. They do blocks, or cells, of work.

> **Explanation:** Usually the workers on a *mass production* line only have to do one very small operation before the job moves on to the next person. This is very boring for the workers. Under cell production, workers, usually working in small teams, carry out a number of operations and produce a complete part of the product. The workers have more control over their work and are less bored. They can see what they have produced and can take pride in their work. They have to solve their own problems as a team. Examples can be found at Rover, Honda and Nissan.

central bank: is the national bank of a country, responsible for the issue of notes and coins on behalf of the government. All countries have a central bank. It is usually the government's bank and the bank at which other banks have their accounts. It will be responsible for controlling and regulating the banks in its country. The central bank of the UK is the *Bank of England*.

central government: the national government, responsible for the running of a country as a whole. The central government is responsible for things like defence and managing the economy. It makes policy for the country as a whole on, for example, education, health, transport and relations with other countries (foreign policy).

It is very difficult for the government to know every detail about every part of a country. Therefore, most countries have different levels of government. As well as the central government they will have some kind of *local government.*

centralisation: where the control of an organisation is concentrated in a relatively small number of managers at a head office. They will usually give instructions to the various departments or branches. In a centralised organisation there is very little *delegation* and decisions can be made quickly. Centralisation is the opposite of *decentralisation.*

> **Example:** Banks and most retail *chain stores* are centralised.

- Branch managers are given very detailed instructions on how to run their branches. They have no control over finance. All supplies will be bought centrally.
- Managers send regular sales reports to head office. They are used for ordering new stock and to measure the branch's success.
- The branch managers' main job is to see that the branch is run according to company policy. They can only make decisions and hire staff within limits set by head office and only with their permission.

Advantages of centralisation:

- Everything is done in exactly the same way in all parts of the organisation. Staff can be moved easily from one branch to another.
- It provides *economies of scale* because there is less repetition of jobs and bulk buying is possible.

Disadvantages of centralisation:

- The people 'on the spot' may be unable to take decisions without asking head office. Decision making becomes slow. Local managers may lose motivation and good business opportunities may be lost.
- The people who make the decisions are remote.

Certificate of Incorporation: a certificate issued by the *Registrar of Companies* once he/she is satisfied that all the legal requirements for setting up a new limited company have been followed.

The effect of the Certificate of Incorporation is to give the company a legal existence of its own, separate from the people who own it. It also means that the company can begin to use its name, including the word 'limited' if it is a *private limited company* or 'plc' if it is a *public limited company.*

chain of command: the route through which instructions are issued by managers. It also shows how matters are passed upwards for a decision. The chain of command is the communications route in an organisation. The length of the chain of command will depend on the number of levels there are within a firm. It may vary from one department to another within the same organisation. The chain of command for a finance department may be quite short while that for production may be quite long, with several different layers of management.

Example: a typical chain of command

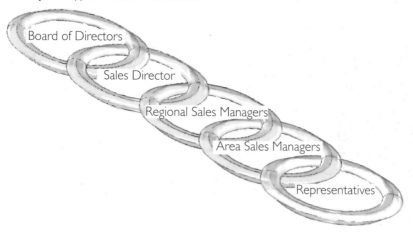

chain of distribution: the stage in the *chain of production* that takes goods from manufacturers to the final consumer. The chain of distribution will vary depending on the product.

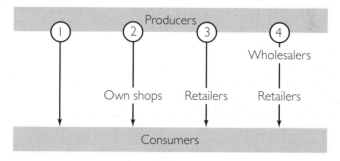

Examples: different chains of distribution

1	Goods sold directly by producers to the consumer; e.g. farmers sell directly to consumers through farm shops.
2	Goods sold to the consumer through shops owned by the manufacturer; e.g. Multiyork and Wesley Barrell both make furniture which they sell to the public through their own shops. It is an example of forward vertical *integration*.

41

3 Goods sold directly by the manufacturer to the retailer. Most of the large supermarket chains buy goods in bulk, directly from the manufacturer.

4 Goods sold by the manufacturer to a wholesaler, who sells to the retailer, who then sells to the consumer. Shops selling specialised goods and the corner shops buy their goods from a *wholesaler*.

chain of production: the stages through which a product passes during *production*. The chain of production will be different for different products. There will be *added value* at each stage in the chain of production.

Example: a typical chain of production

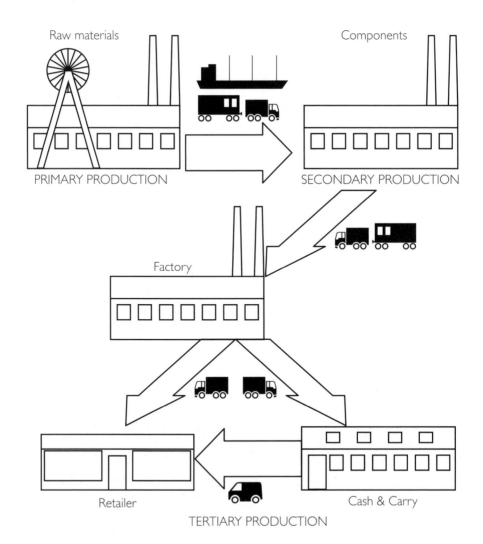

PRIMARY PRODUCTION

Raw materials

Components

SECONDARY PRODUCTION

Factory

Retailer

Cash & Carry

TERTIARY PRODUCTION

chairperson (chair or chairman): a person elected by the members of an organisation to be in charge of meetings. The chairperson may also represent the organisation and speak on its behalf. Between meetings the chair often makes urgent decisions on behalf of the organisation.

A company chairperson will be the leader of the company and will chair meetings of the *board of directors*. The chair may be responsible for the long-term aims, policy and strategy of the company. The managing director will be responsible for carrying out policies, once they have been agreed by the board of directors.

chamber of commerce: an association of business people who represent and promote business interests in their area. It acts as a *pressure group*. Large chambers of commerce have full time staff and offer a wide range of business services to their members.

Services provided include:

- information about sources of funding and finance, overseas law and trading regulations, importing and exporting procedures and documents, business opportunities at home and abroad

- informing local and central government about the area's business

- help for businesses at home and abroad to find *agents* or suppliers, either in this country or overseas. Chambers of commerce also organise trade missions abroad to promote the area's business.

channels of distribution are the same as the *chain of distribution.*

charge card: a method of paying for goods instead of using cash or cheques. Charge cards are similar to *credit cards*, but the balance owing has to be paid in full each month. They are aimed mainly at business people.

A statement is sent every month showing how much has been spent, when and where and includes records of all receipts. The total amount due must be paid within a certain number of days. None of the balance can be carried forward to the next month.

Features of a charge card:

- The cardholder pays an annual fee to the card company.

- No interest is charged.

- There is no pre-set lending limit. As long as the account is paid on time each month cardholders can spend as much as they like.

The best known charge cards are American Express and Diners Card.

charge card

cheque: an order in writing to a *bank* to pay a named person an exactly named sum of money. Cheques are usually printed forms supplied by the banks free of charge to their customers.

Parties to a cheque:

- **the drawee** – the party ordered by the drawer to make the payment (always a bank)

- **the drawer** – the account on which a cheque is drawn

- **the payee** – the person or organisation to whom a bank is ordered to pay the money.

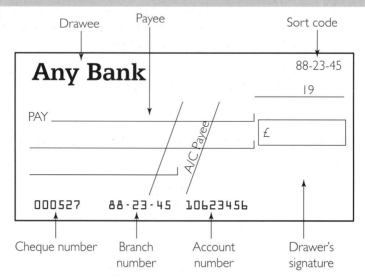

A cheque is a way of transferring money from one bank account to another.

cheque clearing: the system for settling the amounts owed between banks as a result of the cheques drawn by customers on their accounts. (See also *banking automated clearing services*.)

cheque guarantee card: a card issued by a *bank* to a customer. The bank guarantees that any *cheque* drawn by the customer will be met up to a certain value. For the guarantee to work the person receiving the cheque must write the details, from the card, on the back of the cheque.

> *Explanation:* When a customer writes a cheque the trader receiving it does not know whether there is enough money in the customer's bank account to cover the amount of the cheque. To encourage the use of cheques, banks introduced cheque guarantee cards. The bank guarantees the cheque as long as the trader has written the card number and expiry date on the back of the cheque. Most cards guarantee cheques up to £50 but they can be had for larger amounts, up to £250.

chief executive: the person who has overall charge of the day-to-day running of a business. In the UK the job has usually been known as the 'managing director'.

> *Explanation:* Chief executive is an American term that has become more popular, especially in big companies. He or she will be responsible to the *chairman* of the *board of directors.*

choice is a very important economic idea. It could be said that all business is based on choice.

> *Explanation:* Everyone has a very large number of wants. Wants are, therefore, said to be unlimited. No one has enough *resources* (money) to be able to satisfy all their wants. Resources are, therefore, limited. Because wants are unlimited and resources are limited, people must choose which wants to satisfy. Some wants, like food and shelter, have to be met in order to live. For other wants there is a greater choice. It is not only individuals that have to make choices because resources are limited, governments and businesses also make choices.

When a choice is made there is an *opportunity cost,* that is, once the choice is made another want remains that has not been satisfied.

CIM: see *computer integrated manufacture.*

circulating capital is a term sometimes used to describe the *current assets* of a business.

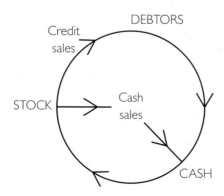

Explanation: The term circulating capital is used because cash, debtors and stock circulate all the time. Cash (including money in the bank) is used to buy stock which is sold either on credit or for cash. Debtors pay their debts in cash which is used to buy more stock and so it keeps going round and round.

The value of each item of circulating capital is changing all the time.

Citizens' Advice Bureau: a chain of independent advice centres staffed by some professional counsellors and by volunteers.

clearing: see *cheque clearing.*

closed questions (in a questionnaire): where the person answering has to choose from a number of pre-set answers. Usually they are answered by ticking a box. There are no other possible answers allowed.

Examples: typical closed questions

Do you eat chocolate?

Yes	
No	

How often do you eat chocolate?

Every day	
Twice a week	
Once a week	
Once a month	
Once a year	
Never	

Advantages of closed questions:

- People may be more willing to answer them because the tick boxes are easy to complete.
- They are easy to check; some are checked using a scanner.
- They are easy to summarise and analyse because only a limited choice of answers is possible.

Disadvantages of closed questions:

- It is impossible to write answers that will cover all possible responses.
- There is no scope for people to express an opinion.
- People may refuse to fill in some questions because the answers they are offered do not fit in with what they think.

closing stock is the stock of unsold goods held by a business at the end of its financial year. The amount of the closing stock will be shown in the *Trading Account.*

code of practice: a set of rules followed by members of an organisation when they are doing business. It is a form of *self-regulation* and is usually voluntary. A code of practice may be drawn up by an *employers' association* or by a *trade association*. For example, the advertising industry has a code of practice prepared by the *Advertising Standards Authority*; the financial services industry is covered by a code of practice prepared by the industry *regulator*.

collateral is the security demanded by a *bank*, or other lender, when making a loan.

> **Explanation:** When a bank lends money, the borrower will promise to repay the loan within a certain time. The bank will, however, want more than a promise to repay. They will ask for collateral *security*. This is something valuable that the bank can sell if the borrower fails to pay off the loan. Usually the banks will want property but they will accept things like insurance policies or shares.

collective bargaining is where *trades unions* negotiate with an *employer*, or a group of employers, on behalf of all their members. They may negotiate on wages, holidays, hours of work or other working conditions and practices.

> **Explanation:** It would be very difficult for each worker to negotiate with their employer. They would not have the skill to do so and the employer would be in a much stronger position. It would take too long and cost too much for employers to negotiate separately with every employee. They might also end up with many different rates of pay and conditions which would be complicated and costly. It suits both employers and employees to have collective bargaining, where unions negotiate on behalf of all the employees.

Negotiations can be at several levels:

- **National –** for all branches of a large company, or for a whole industry (e.g. teachers' and nurses' pay).

- **Local –** at the individual branch level; often called *plant bargaining*. Sometimes these are local agreements in addition to a national agreement (e.g. part of nurses' pay is agreed nationally and part locally).

In recent years there has been a move away from national pay bargaining to local plant agreements.

command economy: see *planned economy*.

commerce is the part of *production* concerned with all aspects of getting goods to the final *consumer*.

> **Explanation:** Commerce is about the *distribution* of goods and services. To get goods from the manufacturer to the final consumer they have to pass along a *chain of distribution*. Goods may be sold and bought at each stage of the chain of distribution before they finally reach the consumer. This buying and selling is *trade*.

Goods have to be distributed to the consumer at the right place in the right quantities at the right time. There are a number of practical problems that have to be overcome in getting the goods to the consumer. The solution to these problems is provided by commerce.

Distribution problem:	Solution
• **Distance –** most producers will be some distance from their market.	Transport
• **Risk –** possibilities of theft, fire or damage to the goods, premises, transport.	Insurance
• **Time/storage –** goods have to be stored ready for distribution to consumers.	Warehousing
• **Finance –** producing and buying stock before it is sold may need finance.	Banking
• **Information –** people need to be told what goods are available.	Advertising

Commercial business can be summarised in a diagram.

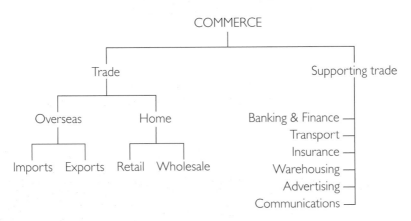

commercial banks are banks that deal directly with the public. They are *public limited companies* that make a profit. They receive *deposits* from the public on which they pay *interest*. Because it is very unlikely that all depositors will want their money back at the same time a bank is able to lend a large part of its deposits. It charges interest on the loans. The difference between the interest charged on loans and the interest paid to depositors is a bank's profit. Examples of commercial banks are Lloyds, Midland and Abbey National.

commission: a payment for services based on the value of the service provided. It is usually paid as a percentage of sales.

Examples: situations where commission may be paid:

- A salesman may be paid a basic salary and also receive a commission if he sells more than his target.

- A travel *agent* will be paid a commission by the tour operator for every holiday sold.

- Estate agents are paid a commission by the seller when they sell a house.

Commission for Racial Equality (the): this body was established under the *Race Relations Act 1976*. Its job is to enforce the Act and to promote equal opportunities in matters of race and colour. The commission gives help and advice to people who feel they have been discriminated against. It also encourages organisations to develop *equal opportunities* policies and to carry them out.

COMMISSION FOR RACIAL EQUALITY

communications is the passing of information between one person or organisation and another. Good communications are essential for a business.

Good communications are:

- clear and simple

- appropriate

- accurate

- complete.

Types of communication:

Internal communications occur within an organisation. Communications may take place at many levels. They may be between branches nationally or internationally or they may be local, within a branch or an office.

External communications are with people or other organisations outside the business. These may include customers, suppliers, trades unions, local and central government departments.

Methods of communication:

Written

Written communications are less open to interpretation than other methods. Copies of all written communications can be kept so there is a record (and proof) of what has been written and when it was sent.

- **Letters** – used mainly for external communication but may also be used internally for communication between branches of an organisation. There are some internal situations when a letter is the best method of communication, for example giving an employee a *written warning* or informing an employee of a promotion within the firm. (See also *business letters*.)

- **Memorandum** – used for internal written communication to give instructions or for correspondence between departments. They are unlikely to be used for external purposes. (See *memorandum*.)

- **Reports** – internal reports may be about policy or for information, for example, to give the *board of directors* the results of a marketing campaign or to suggest an answer to a problem. Most reports are internal but there may be external reports from consultants giving advice on, for example, a company re-organisation. Limited companies must produce their *Annual Report* and *Accounts* for their *shareholders*. Organisations will also consider reports issued by external bodies (e.g. the CBI). (See also *reports*.)

- **Business forms** – used mainly for internal purposes, they will include job application forms and forms for taking supplies out of stock.

- **Notices** – some notices, like Health and Safety Regulations may be required by law. Other notices will be to keep workers informed, perhaps about holiday dates or social club events. Notice boards are a cheap way of informing all employees.

  Notices can be used for special external purposes. For example, there may be a public notice when *planning permission* for a large project is applied for.

- **News letters** – used by many large organisations to inform their employees. They help to develop a *corporate identity*.

Face-to-face

These may be informal chats at which quite important business takes place. There will be no record of such meetings and each person present may remember different things about it.

Meetings may also be formal, with an *agenda*. In this case all the important decisions will be recorded in the minutes. Those present will have a chance of challenging the minutes if they disagree with the record.

Visual

Information may be presented in a visual form. Many people can understand and remember information much better if it is presented visually. Information may be presented at meetings using an overhead projector. Complicated statistics can be communicated in the form of charts and diagrams.

Videos are an important part of visual communication. They may be used by sales people to make presentations about their product, in which case they can be professionally produced and are often more effective than the individual sales person.

Electronic

Electronic methods of communication are becoming increasingly important for both internal and external communications. The main methods available are:

- **Telephone** – it is quick and the person wanted can be directly spoken to. It can be used to speak to someone in any country in the world and is fairly cheap.

  The main disadvantage is that there is no record of the conversation and the persons in the conversation may not agree on what was said.

- **Pagers** – widely used by people who travel or move around large sites. To some extent they have been overtaken by the growth in mobile telephones.

- **Facsimile (fax)** – see *facsimile*.

- **Video conferencing** – it may be very expensive for a business to gather a group of executives from all over the country for a meeting. They can instead be connected for sound and vision using telephone links. This saves on cost and on time wasted in travel and hiring expensive conference rooms. International video conferences are also possible.

- **Electronic mail (e-mail)** – see *electronic mail*.

- **Internet** – see *Internet*.

competition: firms in the same market that vie with one another to gain customers for their product or service. The more sellers there are in a market the greater the competition. Firms will try to increase their *market share* so that they become the largest in their market. The bigger they are, compared to their competitors, the more they can influence prices.

There can also be competition between buyers, for example, at an auction.

competitive pricing is where companies base their prices according to the prices charged by their competitors. Companies want to make a profit, so they will not fix their prices so low that they make a loss.

Explanation: A company will look carefully at the prices charged by its competitors. It will not always fix its prices at the same level as the other companies in the market.

- It may market its product as being of better quality or different to other products. In this case it may fix its prices higher than its competitors.

- A new company in a market will try to gain *market share* by fixing prices below its competitors. It will still want to make a profit but accepts a low *profit margin* in the short term.

competitive tendering is where local councils must, by law, invite *private sector* firms to supply services provided only by local councils in the past.

Explanation: This is a form of *privatisation*. Some believe that local government is inefficient and expensive in the way it provides some services. *Private sector* firms have, therefore, been invited to tender to supply those services. The tendering firm makes an offer to do the work at a set price. As a result of this policy some jobs that used to be done by council departments are now done by private contractors. Often the contractors employ the very people who used to do the same work for the council.

Examples of competitive tendering include school cleaning services, refuse collection, parks' maintenance.

computer aided design (CAD) is when a product can be designed or its design modified using a computer program. The main advantage of CAD is that it speeds up designing. Designers no longer have to make complicated drawings by hand. A design can be looked at from all angles on screen. The effects of changes to a design can be tested. CAD is especially useful in industries where the design of products has to be changed regularly, for example, with fashion goods.

computer aided manufacture (CAM): CAD-produced designs can be transferred directly to program some of the machines used in manufacture. CAM may have a wider meaning to include any use of computers in production planning and control.

computer integrated manufacture (CIM) is where computers are used to control large parts of the manufacturing process. A central computer may co-ordinate the flow of parts to the production line. It may also directly control robots and other automated equipment.

conciliation: an attempt by both sides in a dispute to understand, and come to terms with, one another's point of view. The *Advisory, Conciliation and Arbitration Service* (ACAS) may help by finding an independent person to act as a conciliator. The conciliator will listen to both sides and try to find common ground. He/she will try to get the two sides to take the other's views into account and to reach a compromise that both can accept.

conditions of employment are the terms on which someone is employed. They will be set out in a *contract of employment* that will state whether the job is full-time or part-time, permanent or temporary. Details of pay, working hours, holidays and any *fringe benefits* will also be included.

Confederation of British Industry (CBI) is the main employers' organisation in Britain. It is funded entirely by its members. Most of its 250 000 member companies are quite small firms, employing fewer than 200 people.

What does the CBI do?

- Because of its wide membership the CBI can speak on behalf of business nationally and locally. By lobbying government and Parliament on the needs of industry and putting forward the business point of view it acts as a *pressure group*. It represents the views of UK industry within the *European Union* and internationally.

- It carries out regular surveys of its members which provide valuable *indicators* of the state of business confidence and performance. It undertakes research on behalf of its members.

conglomerate: a company that operates in a number of different, unconnected industries. It will probably be made up of a number of *subsidiary* companies. The main strength of conglomerates is *diversification*. If one industry is doing badly, any losses can be offset by another industry that is doing well.

constructive dismissal may have occurred where an employee resigns from a job because of some action of the employer. If the employers' action makes it impossible for the employee to stay in the job it may be a constructive dismissal. Constructive dismissal is grounds for taking an employer to an *industrial tribunal*.

Examples: grounds for constructive dismissal:

- sexual or racial harassment and discrimination
- changes in conditions of service without consultation
- changes in job descriptions or location without negotiation.

consultation is asking people for their views about a matter that is likely to affect them, before a decision is taken. Sometimes consultation takes the form of a public enquiry (e.g. when a new motorway is proposed). Views received should be seen to be taken into account when the final decision is made, otherwise people see the process as a waste of time.

Forms of consultation:

- an informal chat if the matter is fairly simple
- the bigger the decision the more formal will be the consultation; it might mean getting views in writing and having several meetings
- in the workplace consultation may take place regularly through the *trades unions*.

consumable: any product that can be used or consumed only once. The term 'consumables' may be used in manufacturing for things like raw materials. In an office, consumables will include things like paper, pens and pencils.

consumer: the final user of a product. Consumers are the last link in the *chain of distribution*. It is not only individuals that are consumers. Businesses may be consumers, for example, when they buy supplies of stationery.

Consumer Credit Act 1974: this sets out the rules that must be followed when selling goods on credit. It is designed to protect consumers by making sure they know the true cost of buying goods on credit.

Under the Act:

- Only firms licensed by the *Office of Fair Trading* can offer credit. These include banks, building societies and credit card companies.
- Customers must be told the cost of credit. They have to be shown the cash price, the total credit price and the *annualised percentage rate* being charged. All advertisements and displays must include the APR where credit terms are being offered.
- The customer must be given copies of the credit sale agreement. Customers that sign a credit agreement at home, have a 'cooling off period' of 15 days. This gives them time to change their mind.

consumer durables are long-lasting goods owned by households. They are consumed over a period of time, rather than at once. Examples include furniture, televisions, washing machines.

consumer goods are goods and services produced for use by *consumers*. They satisfy consumers' wants. Some satisfy a want at once, for example, food. Other consumer goods satisfy needs over a period of time (e.g. *consumer durables*). (Compare with *capital goods*.)

consumer protection: a group of laws and organisations set up to protect consumers from unfair trading methods.

> ***Explanation:*** The suppliers of goods and services are well organised and well funded. They can afford to employ expensive experts to protect their interests. Consumers usually have to look after their own interests. They are rarely organised and have little financial support. For these reasons a number of laws have been passed, especially in the last 25 years. These laws give consumers certain basic rights and force suppliers to obey some rules. If these rules are broken, sellers can be prosecuted and may have to pay heavy fines.

A number of organisations have been established to help defend consumers' interests. Some of them have been set up by law (*statutory bodies*). Other private organisations exist to keep consumers informed. They may also act as *pressure groups*.

> ***Examples:*** consumer protection laws
>
> The list below shows the main Acts, but is not a complete list of the legislation.

Consumer Credit Act 1974	Sale of Goods Act 1979
Consumer Protection Act 1987	Sale of Goods and Services Act 1982
Fair Trading Act 1973	Trade Descriptions Act 1968 and 1972
Financial Services Act 1986	Unsolicited Goods and Services Act 1971
Food and Drugs Act 1955	Weights and Measures Acts 1963 and 1979

> ***Examples:*** consumer protection organisations

Independent	*Statutory or government funded*
Advertising Standards Authority (ASA)	Office of Fair Trading
British Standards Institution (BSI)	National Consumer Council
Citizens' Advice Bureau (CAB)	The industry regulators for the
Consumers' Association	privatised industries e.g., OFGAS,
Good Housekeeping Institute	OFTEL, OFWAT
	Independent Television Commission (ITC)
	The trading standards offices of local
	authorities

Consumers' Association: an independent organisation, entirely funded by its members' subscriptions. The association publishes the magazine 'Which?'. Each month it publishes the results of tests on various makes of a product and lists the 'best buys'. There are very few other sources of independent advice about the quality of goods. There are specialist 'Which?' magazines for motoring, gardening and holidays. The association also acts as a *pressure group*.

contract: an agreement between two or more parties which the law will enforce.

> **Explanation:** Each of the parties to a contract promises to do something. Usually, one agrees to provide goods or services while the other party agrees to pay for them. As a result of the contract each side has some rights and also some responsibilities. If either party fails to meet their duties the law will make them do what they promised. Contracts do not have to be in writing. A verbal agreement can also be enforced in law.

contract of employment: a legal document that sets out the rights and duties of both the *employer* and an *employee* with regard to a job. The employer must let an employee have a written statement of the terms and conditions of employment. This has to be issued within 13 weeks of starting work.

Among the things included in a contract of employment should be:

- the names and addresses of the employer and the employee
- the job title and a brief statement of the nature of the job
- the date on which employment begins
- details of pay, rate of pay, the pay scale that applies; how and when wages or salaries, bonuses and overtime payments are to be paid; details of fringe benefits
- hours of work, holidays and holiday pay, details of pension schemes and arrangements for sickness and maternity
- arrangements for ending the contract and length of notice.

contracting out is where a firm sends out some parts of its work to be done by another business. This may happen for several reasons:

- The firm is very busy and cannot handle the work itself but does not want to lose the order.
- There may be some aspects of the job that are too complicated for the firm to handle itself, or special equipment may be needed that the firm does not have.
- Some services may be cheaper for a firm than doing the job itself; cleaning services, for instance, are often contracted out for this reason.

Competitive tendering by local councils is a form of contracting out.

contribution: is the selling price of a product *minus* the variable costs for that product.

Explanation: Suppose an article sells for £10.

Variable costs are   £4

the remainder is   £6

The *fixed costs* and the *profit* have to come out of that £6. The £6 is the 'Contribution' to the fixed costs and the profit. If the fixed costs are less than £6 per unit then there will be a profit.

Therefore:

Contribution — Fixed costs = Profit

Worked example: If a company produces 10 000 items sold at £10 each, then:

	£
Total sales revenue	100 000
less variable costs	40 000
Contribution	60 000
less fixed costs	40 000
Profit	20 000

Contribution is a very useful tool. Firms can use it to calculate the *breakeven point* or to see the effects of changes in sales, fixed costs or variable costs.

Worked example: Suppose that fixed costs in the above example increase to £50 000. Assume variable costs remain the same but the directors decide that they wish to make the same profit of £20 000. They hope sales will stay the same at 10 000. What would be the new price?

Contribution = Fixed costs + Profits

£50 000 + £20 000 = £70 000
Variable costs = £40 000
£110 000

New price = £110 000 ÷ 10 000 = £11

---

controlled economy: the same thing as a *planned economy*.

convenor: the most senior trade union official at plant level in a large company. The convenor will be a shop steward elected by the other shop stewards. The convenor acts as the chairperson at shop stewards' meetings, and will be the main negotiator for the trades union's side in *plant bargaining*.

co-operative: a form of business organisation where a business is owned by its members. The members may be either the customers or the people working in the business.

Features of co-operatives:

- Co-operative members provide the capital through *shares*. They receive dividends on the profits. The shares cannot be sold on the *stock exchange*. They have to be sold back to the organisation.

- Members have a say in how the business is run by voting at the *annual general meeting*. Voting is through one vote per member. This stops any one shareholder becoming dominant A management committee will be elected to run the organisation on the members' behalf.

- Co-operatives are an important form of ownership. There are co-operatives in all parts of the world.

Types of co-operatives:

- **Retail co-operative societies (CRS) –** such as the 'Co-op' shops found in all parts of the country. The shops are owned by a local or regional CRS. Each society is separate from the others. The retail societies buy many of their goods from the Co-operative Wholesale Society (CWS) which is entirely owned by the retail societies. They share any profits that it makes.

- **Workers' co-operatives –** these are often formed by a workers' *buyout* when a company is in danger of closing. They may also be formed by groups of workers to share facilities, for example a group of artists sharing a building divided into workshops. Workers may buy supplies as a group and share some equipment. Members will try to benefit from *economies of scale.*

- **Agricultural –** farmers may form a co-operative to sell and distribute their products. They will also buy seed and equipment through the co-operative. Such co-operatives are especially important in developing countries.

- **Others –** in Britain there is a Co-operative Bank while the Co-operative Insurance Society (CIS) is one of the larger *insurance* companies.

corporation: an organisation that has been *incorporated*. Corporations are artificial 'persons' created by the law. They can be set up in one of three ways; by:

1	Royal Charter (e.g. the British Standards Institution)
2	statute; that is they have been created by an Act of Parliament (e.g. the Post Office)
3	incorporation under the Companies Acts; most *limited companies* will be set up in this way.

corporation tax is a *direct tax* paid by companies on their net profits. Corporation tax is a sort of company *income tax*.

cost centre: departments of a business to which costs are allocated.

> **Explanation:** All businesses try to keep their costs under control. If all the costs are paid centrally it is hard to see which part of the business is responsible if costs increase. To overcome this difficulty departments are made responsible for their costs and become cost centres. Each cost centre is given a *budget*. A department that overspends can be quickly spotted.

cost effective: a judgement about whether a project or activity has been worthwhile. If it is thought that the result was worth the money spent, then it can be said to be cost effective. A *cost benefit analysis* might be used to make such a judgement.

cost of goods sold is the actual cost of making or buying the goods sold by a business. The cost of goods sold will be shown in the *Trading Account*. It is calculated by:

> **FORMULA** *for calculating cost of goods sold:*
>
> $$\text{Cost of goods sold} = \text{Opening stock} + \text{Purchases} - \text{Closing stock}$$

Opening stock is the stock of goods, held for sale at the beginning of a *financial year*.

Purchases are goods bought for re-sale during the financial year.

Closing stock is the stock of goods left unsold at the end of the financial year.

These three items are calculated at their *cost price,* not the price at which they are sold.

Example of a firm's Trading Account

Trading Account of XYX & Co for the year ended 31 December

	£	£
Sales		1 000
Opening stock	300	
add Purchases	2 000	
	2 300	
Less Closing stock	1 500	
	800	
Cost of goods sold		800
Gross profit		200

cost of living index: see *retail price index*.

cost of sales: another way of saying *cost of goods sold*.

cost price is the price that a trader pays for goods which are then resold at a profit.

> **FORMULA to calculate cost price:**
>
> **Cost price = Selling price – Gross profit**

cost-based pricing is where the price of an article is based on its cost of production. The price will include a percentage for profit, added to the cost. This method of fixing prices does not take into account the prices being charged by competitors, or what customers are willing to pay.

cost-benefit analysis: the weighing up of the advantages and disadvantages of a project, in money terms. It takes into account the whole community. The financial and *social costs* of a project can be compared with the financial and social gains. This makes it possible to compare the benefits of a project with those of other possible uses of resources.

> **Explanation:** Decisions on whether to go ahead with projects are not usually made purely on the basis of their financial cost. Social costs may be involved as well as money. For example, building a new factory may cause noise and pollution. Cost-benefit analysis can be used to help to decide the best use of an organisation's resources.

- The social and financial benefits should be greater than the social and money costs.

- The people receiving the benefits will not always be the same as those paying the costs. For example, in government projects the government pays but society should get the benefits.

Example: A new dual carriageway by-pass is proposed around a large town that regularly has long traffic queues in the town centre.

Costs	Benefits
Financial:	Financial:
planning, designing cost, buying land for the by-pass, compensation to land owners, cost of public enquiry, cost of construction of by-pass, loss of income from passing trade in the town.	reduced travelling time, therefore less cost (commercial transport companies will benefit most), lower maintenance cost for town roads, town buildings will need less maintenance.
Social:	Social:
damage to green belt, environmental damage.	less traffic in town therefore safer, less noise and traffic pollution in town, increased employment during construction.

costing: the process used to calculate the cost of producing or supplying goods.

cost-plus pricing is fixing the price of a product by adding a percentage allowance for profit (the *mark-up*) to its *cost price*.

Examples:

- A shop buys goods at £15 each and decides that it wants a gross profit of 33.3%. The selling price will be £15 + (£15 × 33.3%) = £15 + £5 = £20

- A manufacturer's costs of production average £8 per unit. It expects a profit of 25% of costs. The selling price will be £8 + (£8 × 25%) = £8 + £2 = £10.

Explanation:

- One advantage of cost-plus pricing is that any increase in cost can be calculated and may be easily passed on to the customer.

- This method of pricing does not take into account what the customer is prepared to pay, or the prices competitors are charging.

cost-push inflation: see *inflation*.

craft union: a *trade union* set up to look after the interests of workers who have a particular set of skills. 'The Knitwear, Footwear and Allied Trades Union' is an example. Originally the members would usually have served an apprenticeship. Many of the craft unions have now been *amalgamated* with other unions.

credit is where goods or services are bought without paying for them at once. The buyer is given a period of time in which to pay. Payment may be made in instalments or in a lump sum.

Features:

- Goods bought on credit are owned by the buyer straight away. (This is not true of goods bought on *hire purchase*.) A buyer can use the goods or sell them.

- Trade buyers hope to sell the goods before they have to pay for them. A buyer needs less *cash* or *working capital* when goods are bought on credit. The seller is helping to finance the buyer.

credit card: a method of obtaining credit using a small plastic card, issued by banks and building societies. They are part of either the Visa or the Mastercard world wide networks. Cards can only be used in places that show the logo for their card (Visa or Mastercard). Some major *chain stores* also issue credit cards for use in their shops only.

> ***Explanation:*** A credit card is not always accepted straight away. Beyond a certain amount the trader will ask for 'authorisation'. This means checking with the card company that the card holder has not gone beyond his/her credit limit. This check may be by telephone but many tills are now linked to a terminal that automatically checks with the credit card company.

Card holders:

- are given a credit limit. This is the maximum amount of money they can owe on the card at any time

- are sent statements every month which show when and where their cards were used and the amounts spent. Each statement shows a minimum amount that has to be repaid, by a given date

- can pay the full amount shown before the payment date. *Interest* is not then charged. If less than the full amount is paid, interest will be charged on the *balance* due.

credit control is used by companies to try to reduce the risk of *customers* failing to pay their debts. Checks are usually made on customers' credit records before letting them have credit. To keep *bad debts* to a minimum many large companies have a credit control department to check on customers' creditworthiness.

Explanation: When a company does business with someone for the first time they often know nothing about them. It would therefore be foolish to let them have credit. However, they will not want to lose the business. A company needs to be as sure as possible that customers will pay their debts. It can do this in the following ways:

- by asking the customer for references from their bank; the bank will confirm that they have reasonable balances

- by asking the customer for *trade references;* these will be at least two traders with whom the customer has done business on credit in the past

- by checking through a credit agency; these are firms that specialise in finding details about individuals' and companies' payment records

- by looking at a copy of the customer's *Annual Report and Accounts* at Companies House.

Companies will often only sell for cash at first. If after two or three orders there have been no problems they may allow the customer to have credit.

credit entry (Cr): an entry on the credit side of a *ledger* account. In *double entry* accounting a credit entry is always on the right-hand side of the *ledger.*

credit note: a note issued by a supplier to a buyer to change the amount due on an *invoice.* A credit note will reduce the amount the buyer owes to the seller. It is usually printed in red.

Explanation: When goods are sold on credit the seller will send the buyer an *invoice.* If the amount due on the invoice needs to be changed, the seller may send the buyer a credit note. Reasons for sending a credit note include the following:

- There may be an error on the invoice. This might be because the wrong price has been quoted or because although the price per item is right the quantity shown is wrong.

- The customer has been overcharged.

- Goods have been returned by the buyer because they are faulty, damaged or unsuitable.

Example: a typical credit note

XYX & COMPANY LIMITED
The Industrial Estate, Anytown, Midshire RE9 4PH
Telephone: 0123 987 4561
Fax: 0123 987 6544
VAT Registration No.

Credit Note No

Date

To: The Village Stores
Alderminster
Warwickshire
CV37 9QJ

Reference:

Invoice No.

Invoice Date:

Quantity	Description	Unit Price	Total Price	VAT		

---

credit rating: a system used by banks and financial organisations to decide a customer's creditworthiness. It is a kind of scoring system, to decide whether or not credit should be given. It is also used to decide the maximum amount of credit that may be given. Many organisations use credit reference agencies to provide a credit rating that is based on credit records. Firms given a high rating by the agencies will find it fairly easy to get credit.

credit sale: where goods are sold on credit. The buyer receives the goods at once and pays later. (See also *credit.*)

credit status means the same as *credit rating.*

credit terms are the conditions on which credit may be given. They will be shown on a *quotation* and an *invoice.*

Among the terms will be:

- the maximum amount of credit allowed and the length of time before the debt must be paid (e.g. a month, three months)

- whether interest will be charged; and if so, how long before interest starts to be added

- whether a *cash discount* will be given for prompt repayment.

Businesses may not treat all their customers in the same way. The credit terms will partly depend on a customer's *credit rating*.

credit transfer: a system for transferring money from one bank account to another. It is also known as *bank giro credit*.

> **Explanation:** To use this system the debtor must complete a form. The form gives details of the bank and the account to which payment has to be made. Often the forms appear as a tear-off slip at the bottom of *invoices* and *credit card* statements, with all the details already printed. When several payments have to be made at the same time one *cheque* can be used to cover them all.

Two advantages of credit transfer:

- Payments can be made in cash at a bank. For people without bank accounts it is safer than sending money through the post.

- It is cheaper and quicker than making payments by post.

Two disadvantages of credit transfer:

- The name of the *payee's* bank, the branch and the account number must be known before this method of payment can be used.

- Banks often make a charge if the payer does not have an account with that bank. But the gas, electricity and telephone companies, for example, have special arrangements with the banks not to charge people paying their bills by credit transfer.

creditors are those to whom a firm owes money. They will mainly be *trade creditors*, that is, other firms it has bought goods from on credit, but has not yet paid. Creditors will be shown as *liabilities* in the *balance sheet*.

cumulative preference shares: see *preference shares*.

currency is the unit of money in use in a country. It is the money people in that country are willing to use and accept to settle debts. Every country has its own currency. In the UK the currency is the pound sterling, in the USA it is the US dollar. A country's currency is controlled by its *central bank*.

> **Explanation:** The currency in which it trades is important to a business. Currencies are bought and sold on world markets. The price a currency will fetch against another currency is the *exchange rate*. Firms trading overseas may choose

to be paid in either the foreign currency or in their own country's currency. The choice may be difficult because exchange rates vary daily. Some goods are always traded in the same currency all over the world. Oil, for example, is always traded in US dollars.

current account (balance of payments): the balance between total *exports* and total *imports* of goods and services. This is in contrast to the *capital account*.

current account (in banking): an account held at a bank where the money held on deposit must be repaid on demand. It is the account on which, for example, *cheques, standing orders* and *direct debits* are drawn.

current assets are *assets* that will change in value during the next twelve months. They consist of cash (including money in the *bank*), debtors and stock.

current liabilities are the part of an organisation's liabilities that will have to be paid within twelve months of the date of the *balance sheet*. They usually consist of *trade creditors*, bank *overdrafts*, *corporation tax* due and proposed *dividends*.

current ratio is the ratio of current assets to current liabilities. It is also called the *working capital ratio* or liquidity ratio.

FORMULA *for calculating current ratio:*

$$\text{Current ratio} = \frac{\text{Current assets}}{\text{Current liabilities}}$$

Explanation: This ratio measures the relationship between current assets and current liabilities. A business needs to have enough current assets to be able to pay its creditors when payment becomes due. A company considering giving another firm credit would look at the balance sheet to calculate the ratio as part of its *credit control*. There is no ideal current ratio. It is generally thought that a ratio of about 2:1 is satisfactory.

Worked example: A company has the following current assets:

	£
Stocks	52 000
Debtors	8 000
Bank	15 000
Gas	6 000
	81 000

Its current liabilities are £45 000

$$\text{The } current\ ratio \text{ is: } \frac{\text{Current assets}}{\text{Current liabilities}} = \frac{£81\ 000}{£45\ 000} = 1.8$$

curriculum vitae (CV): a summary of an individual's personal details, education, qualifications and experience. It is used when applying for a job. It is sometimes used instead of an application form.

The CV should always be typed and well presented. It is often the first contact a potential employer has with someone. It should also be kept up to date.

customers are the buyers of goods and services from suppliers. A customer may be a firm buying from another firm. For instance, manufacturers are the customers of the firms that supply them with raw materials or components. When customers buy goods from a shop for their own use then they are the *consumers* of those goods.

Customs and Excise: the government department responsible for collecting *indirect taxes.* Among the taxes it collects are *VAT, customs duties* and *excise duties.*

customs duties are taxes on *imports* into a country. They are also called *tariffs.* Not all goods imported into the country have to pay customs duties. The duty on goods imported into *European Union* countries from other EU countries has been phased out over a number of years.

CV: see *curriculum vitae.*

cyclical unemployment: see *unemployment.*

data are all kinds of facts in both verbal and numerical form. Both kinds can be classified as either primary or secondary data.

- **Primary data** – facts collected first hand. For example, market research through a questionnaire is primary data because the facts have been obtained by asking people directly. It is found by *primary research*.

- **Secondary data** – data collected from existing sources. It may be found in books or published reports. It is obtained by *desk research* or *secondary research*.

Data Protection Act: an Act that protects the rights of individuals when information about them is held by someone else. All organisations holding information about people must register with the Data Protection Registrar.

Under the Act:

- Everyone is entitled to have access to the information stored about them.

- They also have a right to question any information they consider inaccurate.

database: the collecting of data into files in a systematic way, usually on a computer. Databases can be assembled to suit the needs of the user. The users decide what information they need to collect. A typical database would have details of a company's *customers*. It might also include customers' ages or jobs. A database can be 'interrogated' for particular information.

day release is where a person is given paid leave from a job to attend training for a day each week, on a regular basis. Usually the release is for *off-the-job training* on a college course.

debentures: certificates issued by a company acknowledging a type of long-term loan.

Explanation: A business may need to raise extra capital for some long-term purpose. Instead of issuing more *shares* it may decide to borrow the money. One way of borrowing is to issue debentures. The debenture is simply a document stating that the money has been borrowed. It states the terms of the loan and the conditions on which it will be repaid. Debentures can be bought and sold like any other stock. Debentures may be given security against the company's *assets*. In some cases they may be able to sell the assets if the company fails to pay the interest or repay the loan.

Features of debentures:

- The holders are paid a fixed *rate of interest.* The interest is payable whether the company makes a profit or not. The interest is an expense shown in the company's *profit and loss account.*

- Debentures may be issued for a fixed period; 20 years is common. Sometimes a definite date for repayment is given e.g. 1 January 2020.

- Debenture holders are *creditors* of a company and have no say in running the business.

debit card: a card issued by a bank that can be used instead of a *cheque.* The card is the same size and looks very like a *credit card.* When goods are bought the card is presented, and the buyer's *current account* at the *bank* is debited (the money is withdrawn). Examples of debit cards include Switch, Visa Delta and Connect.

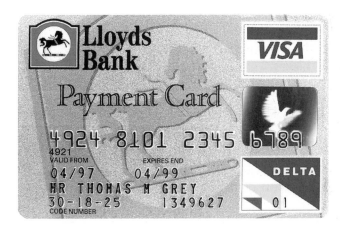

Explanation: Instead of writing out a cheque a buyer can present a debit card. The seller deals with it in exactly the same way as a credit card. Like a credit card, large payments have to be authorised. The transaction is shown on the buyer's *bank statement* in the same way as a cheque would be. There is no separate statement for the card. Many banks now issue one card that acts as a cheque guarantee card and a cashpoint card, as well as a debit card.

Advantages to the buyer:

- It is quick. No time is wasted writing a cheque and waiting for the seller to enter the cheque guarantee card details.

- It can be used up to any amount as long as there is enough money in the cardholder's current account.

Advantages to the seller:

- Sellers are guaranteed the full amount of the payment, once the card is authorised.

- Payment is quicker than with a cheque. It is usually cleared in three working days.

debit entry (Dr): an entry on the debit side of a *ledger* account. In *double entry* accounting debit entries are always on the left-hand side of a ledger account.

debit note: a note sent by a seller to a buyer to correct a mistake on an *invoice* when a buyer has been undercharged. The effect of the debit note is to increase the amount the buyer owes. The debit note contains the same details as a *credit note*.

debt factoring: see *factoring.*

debtor: someone who owes money to an organisation. Debtors are mainly trade debtors, that is, people and organisations they have sold goods or services to on *credit*. The debtors will be shown in the *balance sheet* as *current assets*.

decentralisation is where important decisions in an organisation are delegated to managers of divisions. The organisation may be divided into a number of *profit centres,* each of which will have a manager. Managers are given the freedom to make the decisions they think best for their profit centre. Decentralisation is the opposite of *centralisation*.

Advantages of decentralisation:

- Decisions are made by managers on the spot, who understand their local situations.

- Decisions are made more quickly because fewer people have to be consulted.

- There are more opportunities for managers to show initiative. Managers are better motivated because they have more responsibility.

Disadvantages of decentralisation:

- The organisation is harder to control.

- Local decisions may not always be in tune with company policy and strategy. They may not always take the interests of the organisation as a whole into account.

decline is the stage in the *product life cycle* when the sales of a product begin to fall. Profit will also be falling and consumers will be switching to alternatives.

decreasing balance: see *reducing balance.*

deductions: money that is deducted from *gross pay* to arrive at *net pay.* *Income tax* and *National Insurance* contributions are compulsory deductions. Other deductions might include superannuation or some other pension scheme. Some deductions such as *trades union* membership fees are voluntary.

deed of partnership: a written document that sets out the relationship between the partners in a *partnership.* There does not have to be a written agreement. If there is no formal agreement between the partners, the law assumes all profits and losses will be shared equally.

Key points in a deed of partnership:

- The amount of capital that each partner contributes and whether they will be paid interest on their capital.

- The voting rights of partners and the way profit and losses are to be shared.

- Whether any of the partners will have a *salary* as well as a share of the profits. Junior partners often cannot afford to provide much capital. Their share of the profits will therefore be small. They may need a salary to give them a reasonable income.

- The rules for admitting new partners and ending the partnership.

deficit is where spending is greater than income. The term is not usually used for companies. It refers mainly to *non profit making organisations*, such as charities or clubs. The term is also used about government accounts. A deficit is the opposite of a *surplus.*

deflation: a government policy designed to reduce *inflation* in an economy. The government aims to reduce demand by making less money available for spending. Deflation differs from inflation in that it does not just happen of its own accord. The government has to take definite action.

de-layering: means cutting down the number of levels of management in an organisation.

> ***Explanation:*** Many companies try to cut costs and improve the speed at which decisions are made. One way of doing this is to remove one or more layers of management. After de-layering perhaps only two levels of managers have to be consulted before a decision is made, instead of three or four.

The effects of de-layering include the following:

- The *chain of command* is shortened and costs reduced.

- It may increase the *motivation* of the managers that are left as they will have more responsibility.

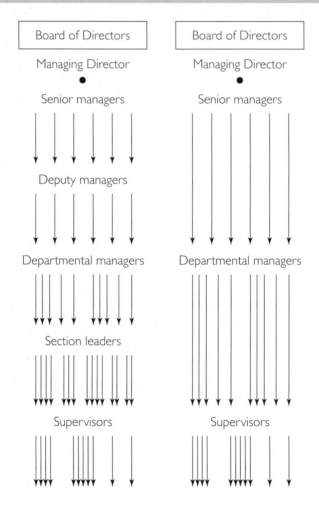

delegation simply means to 'pass on'. It happens in business when authority is passed on to someone else lower down the organisation. He or she is given authority to make decisions on behalf of a more senior person.

Explanation: The bosses in an organisation cannot do everything themselves. As a business grows there is a greater need for delegation. The *board of directors* will concentrate on policy. It delegates the day-to-day running of the business to managers who may, in turn, delegate to other managers within their *span of control*.

If delegation is to work properly:

- Those given the job must be given the authority to carry out the duties.

- Everyone must be clear what authority and decision-making powers have been delegated.

- Those given the responsibility must have the confidence of their boss.

delivery note: a document that lists the goods being delivered to a buyer. It contains all the details shown on the *invoice* except the price and the total amount owing. The buyer should check the goods against the delivery note. If satisfied, the buyer signs the note and gives a copy to the delivery person. If the buyer cannot check the goods on delivery the buyer signs the delivery note 'goods received but not checked'.

demand: is the amount of a product or service that will be bought at a stated price during a given time.

Explanation: Demand is not the same thing as wanting something. Wants only become demand when goods are actually bought.

- Demand is always at a certain price. If the price of one article is too high something else might be bought instead (a substitute).

- For the term demand to mean anything we must know how often the goods are demanded. To say that a family demands six loaves at 60p per loaf does not mean very much. Is it six loaves per day, or per week?

- A demand curve shows the relationship between the demand for a product and its price. It will usually slope down from left to right. Thus the lower the price the more people will buy of that article. The graph below shows that as price falls so demand will increase.

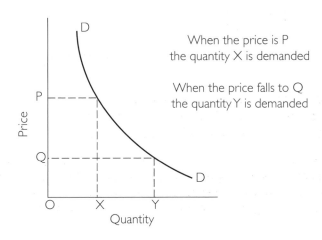

When the price is P the quantity X is demanded

When the price falls to Q the quantity Y is demanded

demarcation is the creation of dividing lines between one job and another. Traditionally these divisions have been between trades, for example, between a carpenter and a plumber. There have also been divisions between skilled workers and unskilled workers. Modern methods of production, using teams, have made the divisions less clear cut. Workers now are often *multi-skilled*. For example, instead of using two people, one maintenance engineer may be able to do mechanical and electrical repairs.

demarcation dispute: a dispute about who should do what work. Such disputes may arise because someone has tried to change the demarcation lines between jobs. Demarcation disputes are often between two *trades unions*.

Department of Trade and Industry (DTI): the department responsible for the government's regional policy, competition policy and overseas trade.

The DTI:

- offers support and advisory services to industry and commerce

- acts as a *regulator* for trade and industry; it sets rules to ensure that companies act lawfully and do not defraud the public. It investigates companies suspected of not acting properly

- is responsible for the *Monopolies and Mergers Commission* and for carrying out rulings by the *Office of Fair Trading.*

deposit: the part of the purchase price for goods or services paid in advance of the goods/services being delivered. When ordering goods it is common to be asked for a deposit as a token of good faith. It shows that the person making the deposit intends to pay for them, when the goods are actually delivered.

deposit account: a type of *bank* or *building society* account that receives long-term deposits from the public. They are usually called 'savings accounts' or 'investment accounts'. Some accounts allow 'instant access'; others need notice of withdrawals. The accounts earn *interest*. The *rate of interest* varies according to the amount deposited.

depreciation is the reduction in the value of a *fixed asset* arising from wear and tear and the passage of time.

> **Explanation:** Assume a business buys a van for £10 000. After three years it is sold for £5000. The difference between the original price of the van and its resale value, £5000, is depreciation. Instead of having to bear all the loss in value at once, businesses make an allowance for the loss, each year in their accounts. This allowance is called depreciation.

The £5000 loss in value can be looked at as an expense. It is the cost to the business of having the use of the van for three years. Like all other *expenses*, depreciation is shown in the *profit and loss account*. The effect of depreciation is to reduce profit. It is better to reduce the profit by a certain amount each year than in one lump sum at the end of the asset's life.

There are two ways of calculating depreciation:

- the *straight line* method
- the *reducing balance* method.

Depreciation applies only to *fixed assets* other than land. This is because land tends to increase in value, very rarely losing in value. The value of the *fixed asset* shown in the *balance sheet* is its value after depreciation has been deducted. This is called its *book value* or net value.

depression: a time when business activity is at a very low level. It is an extreme form of *recession*. It can be said that it is a recession that goes on for a long time. During a depression there is negative *growth,* that is, the total wealth of the country falls. Many businesses fail, unemployment is high and there is little investment by business.

deregulation happens when the government removes some of the rules and regulations that apply to business. This is done to increase *competition* by making it easier for firms to compete and for new firms to enter markets. Examples of deregulation include the increase in the number of radio stations and bus companies in the 1980s. Deregulation should result in:

- lower prices for *consumers* because firms will want to sell cheaply to attract customers
- higher quality goods and services because companies will compete not only on price but also on quality

desk research is where *data* are collected from existing, published information. The term is often used in *market research*. Instead of collecting information directly (e.g. by using a *questionnaire)* such *secondary data* are obtained from books or reports.

Possible sources of secondary data:

- official reports and statistics from, for example, the *European Union*, government and local government
- Chamber of Commerce

- trade magazines and trade associations

- other reports and statistics.

Example: Suppose someone needs to find how many people live in their local town, their ages and the number of men and women. Rather than count them all it would be easier to do some desk research at the local library, looking up the last census report.

desk top publishing: a type of computer software used to organise text and illustrations. Different fonts and font sizes can be used. The material is displayed on a VDU and moved around to get the best effect before outputting. The finished documents can look as though they have been professionally laid out.

devaluation occurs when a government decides to reduce the value of a country's *currency* against other currencies.

Explanation: Assume that £1 will buy FF10 (10 French francs). If the government devalues the pound against the franc by, say, 20%, £1 will then only buy FF8. This will have two effects:

1   British goods sold in France become cheaper.

    For example, an article that cost £2 in Britain sold in France for FF20 (£2 × FF10). After devaluation the price in France will be £2 × FF8 = FF16.

2   French goods sold in Britain will cost more.

    For example, an article that sold in France for FF20 sold in Britain for £2 (FF20 ÷ 10 = £2). After devaluation the price in Britain would be FF20 ÷ 8 = £2.50.

British consumers will either have to pay more for the French goods or buy similar goods manufactured in Britain.

When a government devalues its currency it hopes:

- that *exports* will increase because the country's goods will be cheaper abroad

- that *imports* from other countries will fall. Foreign goods become more expensive so people buy home-produced goods instead. This will lead to more business for the country's firms and may increase employment

- if exports increase and imports fall the *balance of payments* will improve.

development areas are geographical areas chosen by the government to receive special help. They are usually areas of high unemployment. They tend to be areas where the traditional heavy industries of coal, steel and shipbuilding have closed. The special help is in the form of grants and other financial incentives to companies to locate to these areas. Factories may be built in advance or let rent free for periods of up to five years. Many of the grants are paid for out of *European Union* Regional Development Funds.

differentials are the differences in rates of pay between different grades of workers. These differences are usually measured in percentage terms. They are affected by differences in the length of training or the level of qualifications and experience needed to do a job. Differentials are often taken as a measure of the differences in skill and responsibility between workers.

In general:

- managers expect to be paid more than the people working for them

- skilled workers expect to be paid more than trainees or unskilled workers.

direct costs are those costs that are a direct result of producing a particular product. Direct costs include the *wages* of the workers used to make a product, the costs of running the machines and the cost of the raw materials used. Direct costs do not include the general costs of running the business which are classed as *overheads*.

> *FORMULA* **to calculate direct costs:**
>
> **Direct costs = Direct labour costs + Cost of raw materials**

direct debit is a method of transferring money between two bank accounts. It is used to pay regular bills, where the amount to be paid may vary.

Explanation: There are some bills that have to be paid regularly, such as annual subscriptions and quarterly bills for gas, electricity or the telephone. However, the size of the bill may vary from quarter to quarter, or year to year. Direct debits can be used to pay such bills. The *customer* signs a form that tells the bank to make a payment when it is asked to do so by the company to be paid. The customer can cancel this 'authority' at any time. The *utilities* companies prefer their customers to use direct debits because it cuts the cost of collecting money. People using this method do not forget to pay and reminders do not have to be sent. The money is paid automatically and promptly into the company's bank account.

Compare direct debits with *standing orders*.

direct labour: this term may be used in two ways:

> **1** The labour directly used to produce a particular product. If a company is producing a number of different products, the direct labour has to be identified for each product separately. Direct labour gives rise to a *direct cost*.

> **2** When a local council uses its own labour force instead of using outside contractors to do certain jobs this can be referred to as direct labour. The amount of direct labour has been reduced since the introduction of *contracting out*.

direct mail: advertising or promotional material sent directly to selected addresses drawn from a mailing list. The receivers are chosen because they fall within some classification being targeted by the senders. It is often called 'junk mail'.

direct marketing is where goods and services are marketed directly to the *consumer*. It may consist of *direct mail* 'shots', or *telesales* or advertisements in which people are given a telephone number to call if they are interested in a product. It also includes door-to-door and catalogue selling.

direct sales: where a producer sells goods directly to consumers. There are no *middlemen*.

> **Explanation:** Some producers wish to keep control over the selling of their products. They try to make the *chain of distribution* for their product simple and quick. Trade selling is usually direct: suppliers of components for example, will sell directly to their customers.

> **Examples** of direct sales:

> • Farm shops or factory shops; many shops are directly owned by manufacturers e.g. Clarks Shoes, Body Shop.

> • Sales through 'mail shots', leaflets in magazines or telephone numbers included in advertisements e.g. by insurance companies, Readers Digest.

direct tax: a tax charged against the income or wealth of a person or company. *Income tax* and *corporation tax* are both direct taxes.

> **Explanation:** They are called direct taxes because they are charged directly on those who have to actually pay them. The tax cannot be passed on to anyone else. (Compare with *indirect taxes*.)

director: someone elected by the *shareholders* to the *board of directors* of a *limited company*. The directors are given the responsibility and power to run the company on behalf of the shareholders. Directors must, by law, act in the best interests of the organisation. The number of directors will vary with the size of the firm. In a *private limited company* the minimum number is one, in a *public limited company* the minimum is two.

disciplinary procedures: a set of procedures used by an organisation when employees break its internal rules.

> ***Explanation:*** Most organisations have a formal set of procedures to be used when employees break the rules. Serious 'offences' such as stealing or fighting may be gross misconduct and lead to instant *dismissal*. Usually, breaks in the rules are less serious. For example, someone may often be late or fail to wear proper safety clothing.
>
> The procedures set out the steps that must be followed. At each stage in the procedure the employee is interviewed and if the employee has broken the rules they will be given three warnings. On a first offence a *verbal warning* is given followed the next time by a *written warning*. On a third offence a final written warning is given and if the rules are broken again within twelve months the employee may be dismissed. Disciplinary procedures may contain other sanctions such as loss of a grade or reduced pay.

discount: an amount of money deducted from the selling price of a product. There are two main types of discount:

> 1 **Trade discount** – a discount given for buying in bulk. The more goods that are bought the greater the discount given. Where companies sell to both the general public and to people in the trade, the trade buyer will get a discount. For example, builders merchants charge one price to the general public, a builder would get the goods more cheaply.
>
> 2 **Cash discount** – a discount given for paying a bill promptly. The sooner the bill is paid the bigger the discount.

discounting is where an amount of money is deducted from the price of goods in order to increase sales. 'Sales' and special promotions are an example of discounting. Shops may cut their prices because they have stock left over at the end of a season. They need to sell the goods to make way for new stock.

discrimination occurs where people are treated differently because of their colour, race, sex, religion or disabilities. It is an offence to treat people differently when advertising jobs, employing, or promoting staff or in any other way at work. Someone who thinks they have suffered from discrimination can appeal to an *industrial tribunal*.

diseconomies of scale occur when costs rise because of the size of an organisation. They are the things that add to the costs of running a very large business rather than a smaller one.

> ***Explanation:*** Here the word 'scale' means size. There are many advantages to being a large company; however, size also causes some disadvantages. As an

organisation gets bigger it becomes harder to manage. It is these difficulties that are called diseconomies of scale.

Examples: diseconomies of scale:

- To cope with the size more layers of management have to be added. Decisions take longer because more people have to be consulted. The longer decisions take the more expensive they are.

- *Communications* become more difficult and the amount of paperwork increases; this adds to the costs of administration.

- Quality may suffer because workers may feel more remote and care less about their work.

- Large firms cannot take up new opportunities quickly; they are less flexible. They will not be able to change production quickly due to a sudden change in *demand*.

dismissal is the proper word for 'sacking', which is when an *employer* ends a *contract of employment*. Employees may be dismissed because, for example, they cannot do the job, or for bad behaviour. An employer normally has to give notice of dismissal. Dismissal is not the same as *redundancy*. (See also *disciplinary procedures*.)

disposable income is the money a person has left to spend after *deductions*, that is, tax and National Insurance, have been paid. It is a person's *'net pay'* which they can use as they wish.

disputes procedure: the formal procedures that a company has for settling disputes with their employees. The procedures are usually in writing and agreed with the *trades unions*. Such procedures are intended to avoid industrial action.

distribution is the process of getting goods and services to the final consumer; it is more than just selling goods in the shops. It also includes the storing and transporting of goods at various stages on their way to the shops. It is the job of distribution to get goods to the consumer in the right amounts at the right place at the right time. (See also *chain of distribution*.)

diversification is when a business expands by moving into new markets. The new markets will be in goods that are different from those dealt in before. It often means moving into a completely new industry.

Explanation: There is some risk in most businesses. Some firms try to spread these risks by working in several industries or markets. The chances are that when one industry is doing badly others will be doing well or less badly. When a company produces different products aimed at different markets it is said to diversify.

dividend: the share of the profits paid by a company to its *shareholders*.

Explanation: Once a company's *net profit* has been calculated the directors decide how much money will be placed in *reserves*. They then recommend to the *annual general meeting* how much dividend should be paid to the shareholders.

The holders of *ordinary shares* are paid a dividend only if there is enough money left after the holders of *preference shares* have been paid their fixed dividend. The ordinary dividend varies. The dividend is usually stated as a percentage of the total number of shares issued. (See also *issued capital.*)

Worked example: A firm has issued 100 000 10% preference shares at £1 each and 200 000 ordinary shares of £1 each. In year one the firm made a profit of £17 000 and put £6000 to reserves. In year two, profits were £50 000 and £10 000 was put to reserves. What dividend will it pay its shareholders?

	Year 1 £	Year 2 £
Net profit	17 000	50 000
Less reserves	6 000	10 000
Available for dividend	11 000	40 000
Less preference shares dividend = 100 000 × 10%	10 000	10 000
Available for ordinary share dividend	1 000	30 000

In year 1 it is unlikely that the ordinary shareholders would get a dividend because there is not enough money left to pay them. In year 2 the firm could afford to pay the ordinary shareholders a 15% dividend:

$$\frac{£30\ 000 \times 100}{£200\ 000}$$

---

dividend yield: this measures the real amount earned by investing in *shares*. The dividend is calculated as a percentage of the price at which the shares are sold on the market (the *Stock Exchange*).

FORMULA to calculate dividend yield:

$$\text{Dividend yield} = \frac{\textbf{Dividend per share}}{\textbf{Market price per share}} \times 100$$

Worked example: Using the information in the second example above and assuming the market value of the shares is £4 each, then

$$\text{Dividend yield} = \frac{\text{Dividend per share}}{\text{Market price per share}}$$

$$= \frac{£1 \times 15\%}{£4} = \frac{£0.15}{£4} \times 100 = 3.75\%$$

> **Explanation:** The dividend yield is important to investors. They can compare it with the return they get from, for example, a *building society* account. If they get more interest at the building society than the dividend yield it may be worthwhile for them to sell the shares.

division of labour is the splitting of a job or process into a number of smaller parts. Each part is performed by a different person who will become a specialist in that part.

> **Explanation:** Most tasks can be broken down into a number of small parts with one worker specialising in each part. In this way the task will be finished much more quickly than if each worker had to do the whole job. For example, it would probably take one person well over a year to build a house on his or her own. By using specialist bricklayers, carpenters, plumbers and so on the house can be built in a few weeks.

Modern *mass production* methods are based on this idea. A job is broken down into a number of smaller operations. Each operation is performed by one person, possibly on a *flow production* line. They only do that one operation all day, every day. They therefore become very expert at that one very small task.

Advantages of the division of labour:

- Production is quicker and total output is therefore increased.
- Workers' skills are increased through repetition. They concentrate on what they do best.
- Machinery and tools are used more efficiently because they are being used all the time.
- Time is not wasted in moving from one job to another. Less time is needed to learn the job.

Disadvantages of the division of labour:

- Jobs can be very boring because they are repetitive.
- Because they are not interested in their work, workers may have no sense of responsibility for the job.
- Workers may be so narrowly specialised that they cannot use their skills anywhere else. There may be a loss of craftsmanship and workers may find it hard to change jobs.

double entry bookkeeping is an accounting system that records the double effect of all money transactions.

Explanation: Every time we buy something there is a giving and a receiving. When we buy a loaf of bread we receive an article that increases our stock of goods. At the same time we give money in exchange so our store of cash goes down. Double entry recognises these two effects. There is always a *debit entry* and a *credit entry* for every money transaction. The same thing happens when goods are bought on *credit*. Goods are received, but instead of handing over cash, there is a promise to pay later. Because that promise has a cash value it is recorded in the accounts.

doubtful debts: money owed to a business for some time, which is unlikely ever to be paid. A business will have tried most ways of recovering the debt. Doubtful debts are written off in the *profit and loss account* before becoming *bad debts*.

drawings are money taken out of a *sole trader* or *partnership* business by the owners for their personal use. It is the owners' income.

Explanation: Owners, in partnerships or as sole traders, depend on the business for their income. They will not know how much profit the business has made until the end of the financial year. Most people cannot afford to wait until the end of the year for their income. So most owners therefore take drawings out of the business for their personal income at regular intervals during the year.

durable goods: the *fixed assets* of an individual or household. (See also *consumer durables*.)

earnings: the earnings of a business are its net profit after tax has been paid. Individuals' earnings are the total of their incomes from all sources.

EC: see *European Community.*

ECGD: see *Export Credits Guarantees Department.*

economic growth is the increase in the wealth of a country over a period of time. Economic growth is shown by the growth in the *real income* per head of the population. It is measured by the increase in a country's *gross domestic product (GDP)* from one year to another.

economic indicators: these are the official statistics which provide pointers as to how well a country's economy is performing. They also provide pointers to future prospects and may be used as a basis for decision. Among the important indicators will be employment statistics, the *retail price index*, balance of payments figures, average earnings and government borrowing.

The CBI and other organisations carry out surveys among their members and publish the results. They all help to give a detailed picture of the economy.

economies of scale occur when the *average costs* of running a business fall as a firm increases its *output* and size.

> **Explanation:** When a firm grows in size its costs do not grow at the same rate. It can use its resources more efficiently. Although they will eventually increase, *fixed costs* stay more or less the same over quite a large range of output. If the firm doubles in size its costs may not double. The cost of producing each unit of output will probably therefore fall. This happens because there are some advantages in being larger. These advantages are called economies of scale. They are of two kinds, internal and external.

Internal economies of scale:

They are economies that benefit only a particular business.

- It is possible to increase the *division of labour.* Jobs can be broken down more and the workers become more specialised and efficient.

- Bigger machines can be used which may replace a number of smaller ones. The bigger machines can be used up to their *capacity*. Newer machines will be more efficient and probably faster. One worker may be able to supervise several machines instead of one worker per machine.

- Larger firms find it easier to raise *capital*. They can offer more and better *security* and may have to pay less to borrow money.

- There may be marketing economies because they can advertise nationally. Sales may, for example, increase by 200 000 as a result of spending £50 000 on an advertisement. A small firm may spend £5000 in a regional newspaper but only increase sales by 1000.

- The bigger the firm the more stocks it needs. Because of *bulk buying* it will be able to buy its stocks much more cheaply than a firm buying smaller quantities of the same goods.

- There will probably be some management savings. If a firm doubles in size it does not need to double the number of managers. Large firms will be able to employ specialist managers.

- Large firms can undertake *research and development*, enabling them to keep their products up to date. They can also plan new products several years in advance.

External economies of scale:

These are economies that benefit all the firms in an industry or an area.

- Some industries have become concentrated within a particular area. For example, carpet making around Kidderminster and the production of fine china in the Potteries, around Stoke on Trent. Suppliers tend to be drawn to the area. They benefit from the growth of the industry. They may themselves gain internal economies of scale as the industry expands.

- When an industry becomes concentrated in an area there will be a pool of labour with the specialist skills needed by the industry.

- Specialist training and other facilities may be available in the area to support the industry.

- Firms can co-operate to promote a particular industry. They may set up joint research and development facilities. For example the motor industry have set up a research association at Nuneaton in Warwickshire, close to the West Midlands motor industry.

efficiency means using resources as well as possible. It means using labour and machinery and the other resources of a business in such a way that the firm gets the most benefit from them.

EFTPOS: see *electronic funds transfer at point of sale.*

electronic funds transfer at point of sale (EFTPOS) is a way of paying for goods that involves the transfer of money electronically from customers' bank accounts to a retailer.

Explanation: When goods are bought a *debit card* may be presented to the retailer. The retailer is able to 'swipe' the card through a slot on the till or through a special machine connected to the till. The machine makes electronic contact with the appropriate bank. If there is enough money in the customer's account the sale will be cleared. The money will be automatically transferred to the retailers account. If there is not enough money in the customer's bank account to meet the payment the sale will not be authorised and no transfer of money takes place.

'Switch', 'Delta' and 'Connect' are examples of cards that can be used.

electronic mail (e-mail) is a method of communication that conducts messages between computers linked through a network or a modem to the telephone system. Every user has a unique mailbox that can be protected by a password. Messages are sent to a mailbox where they are stored until it is 'opened'. Messages can be printed, deleted or redirected. E-mail can be used for all types of data.

Advantages of e-mail:

- It provides more or less instant communications between firms and between different branches within a firm. Branches can, for example send daily returns to head office.

- Communication can continue 24 hours a day, anywhere in the world, as long as the machines are switched on.

- A 'hard copy' can be kept at both the sending and receiving ends, if necessary.

embargo: a situation where trade with a country is forbidden. It may be as a sanction against that country's policies. After the Gulf War for example, the United Nations put an embargo on trade with Iraq, other than for food and medical supplies. An embargo can also mean a ban on a particular product. The European Union imposed a worldwide embargo on the sale of British beef in 1996.

employee: someone who works for an organisation in return for a wage or salary. There is a contract of employment between the employee and the employer. Employees may be temporary or permanent, full-time or part-time.

employer: a person or organisation that engages someone to undertake work in return for an agreed payment. An employer and its employees are parties to the contract of employment.

employers' associations are where employers join together to promote their common interests. In many ways they are a kind of employers' 'trades union'. They are usually based on a particular industry, such as the Federation of Engineering Employers and act as a pressure group promoting the interests of their industry from the employers' point of view.

Employment Acts 1980, 1982, 1988, 1989, 1990: a series of Acts that reduced the powers of *trades unions*. Controls were introduced so that unofficial strikes and secondary *picketing* became illegal. There must now be a ballot of members before strike action. Union officials must be elected by postal ballot every five years.

employment agency: a private organisation that helps clients to recruit staff. The agencies try to match people to the kind of job being offered by an employer.

> ***Explanation:*** Some employers prefer to use an agency to help them find staff rather than do the whole thing themselves. For full-time staff the agency obtains a detailed job specification from the employer. The agency will carry out the advertising and preliminary interviews. It gives the employer a *shortlist* of two or three names from which to make the final choice. The agency is paid a fee for its work.
>
> Organisations also use agencies to recruit part-time, seasonal and temporary staff. Agencies hold lists of people suitable for various jobs. If a regular employee is ill an employer can ring an agency and ask for a 'temp'. The temp is usually paid by the agency. Agencies are paid fees for their services.

employment contract: see *contract of employment.*

Employment Protection Acts 1975, 1978: these were intended to increase the security of employment for workers. The Acts cover the main parts of the *contract of employment*. They also protect employees from *constructive dismissal* and *unfair dismissal. Industrial tribunals* were also established under these Acts.

EMU: see *European monetary union.*

entrepreneur: someone who spots a business opportunity and carries it through. The entrepreneur organises, manages and takes the risks of running that business.

> ***Explanation:*** If a business is going to make a profit someone has to organise and manage the *assets* and the workers. There are also risks in all business; the 'goods' produced may not sell. The business risks making a loss, or so small a profit that it would be better to invest the capital in some other way.

There are, therefore, always two aspects to the entrepreneur:

- the organisation and management of the resources of the business so as to make a profit

- accepting the risks of being in business. Economists say that profit is the entrepreneur's reward for taking the risks. The greater the risks the greater should be the profit.

environmental policy: a written statement of how an organisation intends to control and prevent damage to the environment by its activities. The policy may also set targets on the kinds of processes and materials used which can mean expensive changes.

Environmental policy may include a number of different things:

- the way waste is to be handled and disposed of; for example, the recycling of all waste paper, or the fitting of expensive smoke cleaning equipment on a factory chimney

- the way energy is used and the establishment of a programme for energy saving

- the use of materials that are 'environmentally friendly' (for example, to use only packaging materials that can be recycled or furniture manufacturers who use only wood that comes from renewable sources).

A company's environmental policy may be the result of government regulations or *European Union* directives. There are also international treaties that set targets for countries. All of these initiatives are meant to make business accept its social and environmental responsibilities.

equal opportunities: the rights people have not to be discriminated against because of their sex, colour, race, religion or disability. This applies to people already in work and to those who are looking for work. Organisations should make sure that their recruitment and promotion methods do not discriminate. In the UK, people have some protection by law through the *Sex Discrimination Act* and the *Race Relations Act*. People who feel they have been discriminated against can ask the *Equal Opportunities Commission* or the *Commission for Racial Equality* for advice. If either of the commissions thinks someone has suffered discrimination it will help to take his/her case to an *industrial tribunal*.

Equal Opportunities Commission: a body set up to promote equal opportunities between the sexes at work, in advertising and in education. It also helps to enforce the *Sex Discrimination Act* and the *Equal Pay Act*. The Commission can help people who have been discriminated against to take their cases to either an *industrial tribunal* or a court. It can carry out investigations and force organisations that discriminate to stop doing so.

Challenging inequalities ⊜ *between women and men*

EQUAL
OPPORTUNITIES
COMMISSION

Equal Pay Act: this Act established in law the right to equal pay for equal work. The Act, which came into force in 1975, covers overtime pay, bonuses, piecework rates as well as basic rates of pay. Also covered are holiday and sick leave entitlements and conditions of service. It applies to full-time, part-time and temporary workers of either sex.

equilibrium is the point at which the supply and the demand for a product are equal. In economic theory the *free-market* price of a product or service is fixed at this point. At the equilibrium point the price will ensure that there is just enough of the product offered for sale to meet the demand.

equity capital is that part of the *capital* of a *limited company* that is held in *ordinary shares.*

> **Explanation:** Equity consists of the ordinary shares actually issued by a company. Each ordinary shareholder has equal rights. He or she will each get the same dividend per share and have one vote for every share owned. There is equality (*equity*) between the shareholders. Most of a company's capital comes from the sale of shares.

ERM: see *European exchange rate mechanism.*

estimate: an indication of the probable cost of a task. The estimate will be based on a fairly quick review of the work to be done. However, an estimate must be realistic because the decision to proceed may be based on the estimate. (See also *quotation.*)

EU: see *European Union.*

European Central Bank: the proposed central bank that will manage the single European currency. It will be independent of the governments of the member countries and the Community and will be the *central bank* for the *European Union.*

The European Central Bank:

- will authorise the use of the Euro
- will fix interest rates and carry out international negotiations on monetary issues
- will eventually define the general economic and monetary policy for the Union. It will be left to the central bank of each country to carry out the policies.

European Commission: the civil service of the European community. It manages the day-to-day running of Community policies. There are 17 members (commissioners), at least one person from each member country. Each commissioner is in overall charge of some area of policy.

The Commission has three main functions:

- to carry out decisions taken by the Council of Ministers

- to make proposals for new policies and new European laws

- to make sure that Community rules and decisions are carried out properly, as the 'guardian of the treaties'. It can take decisions in some policy areas, such as competition policy.

European Community (EC): called the European Economic Community (EEC) until 1991, the dropping of the word 'economic' from its title was important. It showed that it was being seen as more than a group of countries working together on trading matters. The EC still exists as the basis for the *European Union* (EU). The EC and its institutions form the organisation around which the European Union is to be built.

On 1 January 1993 the EC became a single market with no internal frontiers. From that date people, goods, services and money have been able to move around as freely as they can within a country. This has had important results:

- European firms now have a huge 'home market' of over 340 million people. This is bigger than the home market of the USA. Firms based in the EC can sell their goods and services in any EC country as if they were selling them in their own country.

- *Capital* can move freely within the Community. *Banks*, individuals and companies can invest their money in any EC country they choose.

- People can move freely and look for work in any EC country. In practice language difficulties and different working practices may make it difficult.

Advantages of the European Community:

- The large home market may result in *economies of scale*:

  - lower *unit costs* because of longer production runs

  - fewer different types of the same product because they all have to meet similar standards and regulations

  - more competition for services such as insurance should make them cheaper.

- The increase in competition may result in more efficient firms, leading to cheaper goods. This may mean that firms can compete better in world markets.

- Risks are cut because firms depend less on the market in their own country. A fall in one market can be covered by selling more in another part of the EC.

- There is access to more capital because banks and the *financial institutions* are able to invest freely in any part of the EC. *Investment* from outside the Community is attracted by the size of the market.

Disadvantages of the European Community:

- The budget is very large and is not always well controlled. There are worries about fraud and corruption.

- The Common Agriculture Policy has resulted in food prices being kept high. *Subsidies* to farmers have stopped prices from falling. It protects the small inefficient farms, especially in France.

- Language difficulties make trade very difficult. It is hard to find staff that can work in several languages. Costs are increased because instructions, information and publicity have to be produced in several languages.

- There are political worries, especially in Britain, about the EC taking over too many powers that should be left to national governments. Some people also think the bureaucracy is too big and that there are too many rules which often seem to be about trivial things.

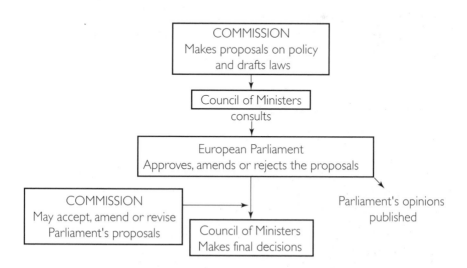

COMMISSION
Makes proposals on policy
and drafts laws

Council of Ministers
consults

European Parliament
Approves, amends or rejects the proposals

COMMISSION
May accept, amend or revise
Parliament's proposals

Council of Ministers
Makes final decisions

Parliament's opinions
published

(Based on EC/EU Factbook by Alex Roney 4th edition. Published by London Chamber of Commerce and Industry, 1995.)

European Council of Ministers: the main decision-making body for the Community. It is made up of the heads of government and their foreign ministers. They meet every six months with the President of the *Commission*. The council agrees the main decisions on Community policies. These policies are decided on the basis of proposals put forward by the Commission. No major new laws can be passed unless the Council agrees.

The term 'council' also refers to meetings of other ministers. There will, for example, be meetings of the ministers of finance, agriculture, transport, industry and consumer affairs. These meetings are also able to make decisions. Most subjects are decided on a majority vote.

European Court of Justice: this is made up of judges appointed by agreement between the member countries. It sits in Luxembourg.

- The court interprets and applies the various European treaties and Community law.

- It rules on complaints concerning Community legislation. It also rules on decisions taken by the Commission and other community institutions.

- It is the final court of appeal. The court's judgements overrule those of national courts, in matters over which it has authority.

European exchange rate mechanism (ERM): this links the *exchange rates* of the currencies of those countries that have joined the ERM. The countries in the ERM must not let their currencies vary by more than a certain percentage from a central rate. The range within which a currency value can move is known as a band. If a currency goes outside the band the member countries must help to support the currency.

European monetary union (EMU) is the process that will lead to a single *currency* for the *European Union*. The single currency is to be called the Euro.

- It is expected that the Euro will replace the existing currencies of at least some EMU members from 1 January 1999.

- Before countries can start to use the single currency they have to meet certain conditions. These are called the 'convergence' terms or criteria.

- The criteria lay down strict rules about the rate of *inflation*, the size of a country's *budget* deficit, *interest rates* and *national debt*.

Advantages of a single currency:

1 The risks arising from changes in exchange rates will disappear for all trade within the EU. At present, the exchange rate, and therefore the prices of goods, can change between the time goods are bought and the time when they are delivered and paid for.

2 Prices can be quoted in one currency and there will be no need to work out the exchange rates. Firms will be able to see the real costs of the goods straight away. Catalogues and price lists will be simpler and there will be savings in printing costs.

3 The single currency is likely to be stronger in international markets than the separate currencies and the costs of exchanging currencies will be saved.

4 People travelling to several countries will not need to carry several different currencies. Travellers' cheques issued for Euros can be used anywhere in the EU. There will be big savings on the commission paid when exchanging money.

Disadvantages of a single currency:

The main disadvantages are political.

- Countries would lose the currency they have had for a long time.
- The *central banks* of member countries will have to give up control over the issue of money to a new European Central Bank.
- *Interest rates* will be controlled by the new European Central Bank, the governments of each country losing their total control over *monetary policy*.

European Parliament: this body has 567 members (MEPs) who are directly elected every five years. The UK has 87 members of the European Parliament. It meets for one week in every month, except August. Proposals from the *European Commission* are looked at by specialist committees.

The powers of the parliament are limited:

- It has a say in appointing members of the Commission.
- It is consulted about new European legislation. Only the Commission can propose new laws. Laws are approved by the Council after consulting the Parliament.
- It must approve the Community budget. It has the final say on 'non-compulsory' spending but the Council has the last word on all compulsory spending (mainly money spent on the Common Agricultural Policy).

European Union (EU): created by the Maastricht Treaty, it is the *European Community* (EC) plus the moves to develop political union. It is said to have three pillars.

FIRST PILLAR	SECOND PILLAR	THIRD PILLAR
European Community	Co-operation on a common foreign and social policy	Justice and home affairs
	Any action under these two pillars has to be by co-operation between the national governments. Although the EU can make laws about these matters the national governments have a veto.	

exchange is the buying and selling of goods and services for money. Exchange is the basis of all business activity.

> ***Explanation:*** In a modern society people have very many *wants*. They are unable to satisfy most of those wants themselves. Everyone has some skills. They sell (exchange) those skills to an *employer* in return for money in the form of a *wage* or *salary*. They exchange that money to buy food, pay for their housing and buy the other things they need. Thus exchange is the basis of modern business.

exchange controls are limits, imposed by law, on the movement of a country's *currency*.

> ***Explanation:*** Many poor countries are short of money. They find it hard to earn overseas currencies with which to buy foreign goods. They can only buy foreign goods if they have earned enough foreign currency to pay for them. The governments of such countries may keep very strict control over the buying of foreign goods. Their citizens are only allowed to buy goods from abroad with government approval. In this way the government controls the exchange rate of their currency.

exchange rate: the price at which one *currency* can be bought or sold in terms of another currency. It is the rate at which one currency can be exchanged for another.

> ***Explanation:*** Like any other commodity, currencies are bought and sold on world markets. The price is stated in a country's own currency. In Britain we look at the price in terms of the pound sterling. British people want to know how many dollars or marks (or any other currency) they can get for £1. In other words they want to know the price of the foreign currency they want to buy. A fairly small change in the exchange rate can be important for a business. It can make the difference between selling goods at a profit or a loss.

Worked example: A British firm sells goods into France for 8000 French francs.

> If the exchange rate is eight French francs to one pound sterling, then the firm will receive:

FF8000 ÷ 8 = £1000
If the exchange rate goes down to FF7.5 to £1, the firm will receive:
FF8000 ÷ 7.5 = £1066
If the exchange rate goes up to FF8.5 to £1, the firm will receive:
FF8000 ÷ 8.5 = £941.18

excise duty is a tax imposed on certain goods produced within a country. In Britain, among the goods on which excise duty is charged are beer, spirits, tobacco and petrol. The tax is collected for the government by the Board of Customs and Excise.

executive director: a member of the *board of directors* of a company with overall responsibility for one of the company's main functions (departments). An executive director will be a full time employee of the firm, e.g. sales director, finance director. Such directors will have executive responsibility for their department. That means they can make decisions on behalf of the board.

expenditure is the money spent by an organisation. It can mean either the total spending, or it can be spending on a particular part of the firm's activities. It is either *capital expenditure* or *revenue expenditure*.

expenses are the costs of running the business. They are often called *overheads* and include *fixed* and *variable costs*. They are listed in the *profit and loss account* for a business and are deducted from the *gross profit* to arrive at the *net profit* for a business.

Export Credits Guarantee Department (ECGD): a government department that insures exporters against the *risks* of overseas buyers failing to pay for goods. By reducing the risks it helps to promote and encourage exports. Although it is a government department it is run like a business. It charges a *premium* for its services in the same way as any other *insurance* business.

exports are goods and services sold overseas.

> **Explanation:** Selling goods overseas is harder than selling in the home market. Exporters face a number of difficulties:

- It may be hard to communicate with overseas buyers because of language problems. It may be hard to prepare marketing literature in the foreign language. The right documents have to be completed correctly.

- Understanding local laws and regulations may be a problem. Exporters have to be careful not to offend local customs and religions.

- There may be differences in units of measurement and in matters such as electrical voltages.

- There are risks in providing credit to overseas customers whose *credit rating* is hard to assess. There will be currency risks because the exchange rate may change. Costs such as insurance and transport costs will be greater.

external costs are costs to a business that result from other organisations' activities.

> *Explanation:* Firms that cause harm to the environment are often not affected by the pollution they cause. If such pollution does not affect them it may not cost them anything, so they have no reason to change their behaviour. Their actions may, however, result in costs to other firms. For example, a firm might have such a noisy factory that people working in the offices of a firm next door cannot work properly. The firm affected has to fit expensive sound insulation so that its staff can get on with their work. The cost of the insulation is an external cost. It is a cost caused by someone else's actions.

external economies of scale are benefits that a firm gains from being in an area where all the main producers in its industry are located. (See also *economies of scale*.)

externalities are costs and benefits over which a business has little or no control. They have no direct effect on a firm's profits.

> *Examples:*

- an external *benefit* – easy access to a good local transport system

- an external *cost* – heavy local traffic congestion.

extractive industry: industry that takes the gifts of nature from the ground. It is the same as *primary* industry. Extractive industries include mining, forestry, farming and fishing.

ex-works price is the price at which the manufacturer sells a product. Sometimes called the ex-factory price, it is the *cost price* charged to bulk buyers like *wholesalers* and large *retailers*. It does not include the cost of transporting the goods to the wholesaler's or retailer's warehouse.

facsimile machine (fax): a method of rapidly sending and receiving written material between two machines, using the telephone system. The fax (or telephone) number of the machine to be contacted is keyed in and the documents fed into a fax machine. The message is then printed out on the receiver's machine within a few seconds.

Advantages of fax transmission:

- Machines can be left on all the time so that messages can be received even when a machine is not attended.

- For international companies the time differences between countries can be ignored.

- Unlike telephone conversations the fax provides a written record of the message transmitted.

factor: a bank or specialised agency that provides a *factoring* service. Banks usually provide the service through specialised subsidiaries.

factoring: a service that allows firms to be able to get a cash advance against their debts instead of having to wait for their debtors to pay.

Explanation: Instead of waiting for money owed to it by its *customers* a business can *factor* the debt. The factor will pay 80% of the amount due straight away. The factor collects the debt in due course and pays the remaining 20%, minus the factor's *commission*.

Advantages of using a factoring service:

- The certainty of 80% now is better than the promise of 100% in the future.

- Factoring helps to avoid *cash flow* problems. The 80% received as cash can be used in the business straight away. The commission may be cheaper than interest on an *overdraft.*

- Factoring saves time and the cost of having to chase the debt. The factor takes the risk of *bad debts.*

A variation on factoring is where a specialist debt collecting agency buys the whole of a debt. This is more expensive than factoring.

factors of production are the resources used in production. These factors fall into four groups.

- **Land –** this includes not only the land itself but all the 'gifts of nature' such as all the minerals in the ground, fish in the sea, forests and the fertility of the soil; land earns *rent.*

- **Labour** – all human resources including both physical and mental ability; anyone capable of doing work for which payment may be received is part of labour; labour earns *wages* or *salaries*.

- **Capital** – goods and equipment of all kinds used in production, not just money; capital earns *interest* for its use.

- **Enterprise** – the factor that organises the other factors of production to make them economically effective; enterprise takes the risks and earns *profits*.

Fair Trading Act 1973: this Act set up the *Office of Fair Trading* under the Director General of Fair Trading. The Act defined a *monopoly* as an organisation that controls more than 25% of a *market*. The Act gives the Director General powers to take action against any company or group that tries to reduce competition or to fix prices. He or she also gives general advice to the public and the government about consumer matters.

fax machine: see *facsimile machine*.

field research: the collection of new and original information by going out into the 'field'. Its main business use is in *market research*.

Possible methods:

- Using surveys, where a sample of the public is questioned directly through questionnaires and interviews, or by post or telephone.

- Using consumer panels, where a group of people may be asked to discuss a product. Their reactions to products or events may be observed and fed back to the manufacturer.

- Testing the market by placing a product on sale in a small area to see how well it sells.

final accounts is a collective term used to refer to the *trading* and *profit and loss accounts* and the *balance sheet* of a business.

finance is the money needed to run a business or a project.

Explanation: A business must have money to finance, that is, pay for, its day-to-day operations. This will usually be provided from its *working capital*. If a business wants to expand or develop a new product or build new premises it must finance such a project. It may get the money from its *reserves*, by borrowing money, or by asking its shareholders for more money. (See also *sources of finance*.)

finance company: a company that specialises in lending money to the public through *hire purchase* and *credit* sales. Such companies also give financial support to business by financing the *leasing* of equipment.

> **Explanation:** When goods are bought on hire purchase the seller is paid the cash price by the finance company. The buyer then repays the finance company by instalments. A business may lease rather than buy equipment. The supplier is paid by the finance company who will then be paid regular instalments by the business for the period of the lease. When the lease ends the equipment is reclaimed by the finance company.

finance house: the same as a *finance company*.

financial accounting is the recording of financial information in *accounts*. It provides the information required by the Companies Acts. The information is reported in the organisation's *final accounts*. These can be used by *shareholders* and other people interested in a company's finances. Financial accounting should be compared with *management accounting* which is mainly used to control a business's finance.

financial institutions: a collective name given to organisations, which in the UK are mainly based in the City of London. They sell *financial services* to business and the public. Providers include *banks*, *building societies*, *insurance* companies, mortgage and insurance *brokers*, *stockbrokers* and specialist *fund managers*.

financial services: a wide range of money-based services sold to the public by a variety of *financial institutions*. The services include pensions, insurance, various savings plans based on *equities*, such as unit trusts, investment trusts and personal equity plans (PEPs).

Financial Services Act 1986: this act set up a system of self-regulation for companies involved in selling *financial services*. Systems of registration of individuals and firms were introduced to make sure that only those who were fit and proper could sell their services to the public. A number of organisations such as the Personal Investment Authority (PIA), the Investment Management Regulatory Organisation (IMRO) and the Securities and Investments Board (SIB) were established to control their members, usually through a *code of practice*.

financial year: the period over which a business reports its accounts.

> **Explanation:** Limited companies must produce annual accounts (see *Annual Report and Accounts*). The date at which they start and end the year is up to the company; however, once fixed it must be the same each year. By having the same date each year it is possible to compare one year's results with another. The government's financial year runs from 6 April to 5 April the following year. This is also the tax year.

fiscal policy is government policy for raising money through taxes and borrowing and for the spending of money on services.

> **Explanation:** Fiscal policy consists of three parts – taxation, public spending and public borrowing. The government's fiscal policy has an effect on *demand*, *economic growth* and *inflation*.

- **Public spending –** the government spends money on education, defence, transport, foreign policy and many other things. If the government spends more money on public services it will have to pay for them by either raising taxes or borrowing more money.

- **Taxation –** the government collects taxes to pay for services. If the government collects more money in taxes then taxpayers will have less money to spend. Therefore the *demand* for goods and services might fall. If demand is lower, firms are less willing to expand and economic growth will slow down. In a period of economic growth the government's revenue from taxation increases. This allows it either to increase public spending or reduce public borrowing.

- **Public borrowing –** if the services provided cost more than the government collects in taxes, the difference has to be borrowed. This borrowing is called the 'public spending borrowing requirement' (PSBR). There is only so much money available to lend so if the government borrows more money, there is less available for business. This is likely to cause interest rates to rise. Businesses will then be less willing to spend money on expansion.

fixed assets are *assets,* used in a business, that have a long life. They appear in the *balance sheet* over more than one year. Examples are premises, machinery office equipment and motor vehicles. They are usually sold only when they come to the end of their useful life.

fixed costs are costs that do not change when the level of output changes. Rates and rent are examples.

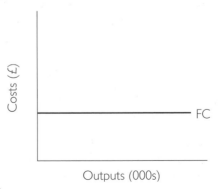

Short term fixed costs

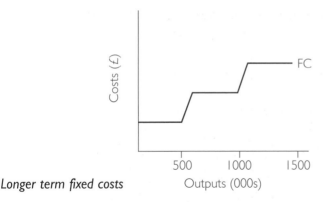

Longer term fixed costs

Explanation: The fixed costs are the same even when nothing is produced. For example, a company will still have to pay the same rent on its premises whether it is producing nothing or 20 000 units a month.

Fixed costs do not stay the same for ever. There comes a point when a firm cannot increase its output any further using the same *fixed assets*. If the firm wants to expand it may, for example, have to have new premises with higher rents and business rates. Its fixed costs will rise, but stay more or less constant, until it again needs to expand its *capacity*.

The average fixed costs will fall as the quantity produced increases.

Example:

Output	Fixed costs	Average fixed costs
	£	£
1 000	20 000	20
2 000	20 000	10
3 000	20 000	6.60
4 000	20 000	5
5 000	20 000	4

fixed exchange rates exist when the *exchange rate* of a country's *currency* is fixed by the government. The main advantage of a fixed exchange rate is that *exporters* can be sure how much they will receive when they sell goods overseas. *Importers* will also be sure how much they will have to pay for overseas goods. Compare fixed rates with a *floating exchange rate*.

fixed rate loan: a loan where the *rate of interest* stays the same throughout the life of a loan or for a certain period of time.

Explanation: Money is usually borrowed at the market rate of interest. The interest goes up and down as interest rates vary. However, it is possible to borrow money at a fixed rate of interest. The interest is fixed at the beginning and stays at that rate for the period of the agreement.

flat rate of interest: is the *nominal rate of interest* that is charged on a loan. It is charged on the whole amount borrowed for the whole period of the loan. It is, therefore, not the true rate of interest, which is shown by the *annualised percentage rate* (APR) of interest.

flat rate wages are wages paid at a fixed basic rate of so much per week or month. The flat rate does not depend on how much work a person has produced in the time nor does it include any bonuses. Flat rate wages may be used to pay highly skilled workers where it is not possible to measure the time a job will take. The main disadvantage is that there is no incentive for a person to work harder or faster.

flexible working: where workers are willing to change their working practices to suit the job in hand. There is no strict *demarcation* of jobs under flexible working. Workers are *multi-skilled* and willing to do whatever needs to be done, at the time, to get a job finished.

Flexitime is a system that allows workers to choose their own working hours within rules laid down by the *employer*.

> **Explanation:** *Employees* are usually expected to work a certain number of hours a week as laid down in their *contracts of employment*. Under Flexitime they are expected to work during a core time, usually between 10 a.m. and 4 p.m. They work the rest of their hours at any time, to suit themselves, but normally between 8 a.m. and 6 p.m. There is usually a clocking-on system, that allows employers and employees to check how many hours they have worked.

Flexitime is usually worked in offices. It is especially valuable for workers who may need to fit their working hours around other commitments.

floating exchange rate: where the *exchange rate* of a *currency* is decided by market forces. The rate varies constantly. The rate is decided by the supply and demand for the currency, and without government interference. The main disadvantage is that businesses are never sure how much they will earn when selling overseas. *Importers* are not sure what price they will have to pay for foreign goods. (See also *fixed exchange rate*.)

flotation happens when a company decides to raise *capital* by selling *shares*. The shares may be sold to the public or to *financial institutions*.

flow production is where products are produced continuously on a production line. The goods being made pass from one stage straight on to the next without a break. This is also called *mass production*.

> **Explanation:** Under this system goods are assembled on a production line. The product is moved along on a conveyor belt. Each worker has a stock of the components and tools needed to do one particular job. It may be adding and fixing a single component. They do the same operation all day, every day. The products do

not have to be identical. For example, cars can be produced, on a single production line, in different colours or with different engine sizes.

Characteristics of flow production:

- A large amount of capital is needed. Flow production needs big factories, with very costly specialised machinery. A car production line may be half a mile long. Because of the high capital cost firms want to work non-stop; they often work three eight hour shifts per day.

- It must be possible to break down the production into a number of separate operations. Many of the operations are suitable for *automation*.

- It is only suitable for making goods that sell in large quantities (e.g. cars, computers, washing machines).

Disadvantages of flow production:

- Workers may become bored doing the same thing all the time. Loss of concentration can create a safety risk.

- The production line sets the speed at which people have to work. This may cause stress.

- Workers become very skilled in one very narrow job. If that job ends, they cannot use their skills in some other job.

forecasting: estimating the effects of factors that are likely to affect a firm's future. For example, sales forecasts will try to estimate a company's own sales, those of their competitors and those for the market as a whole. Forecasts can be used to set targets for managers.

Uses of forecasting:

- Forecasting is an important part of preparing *budgets* and *business plans*. Budgets are themselves forecasts of future income and spending.

- To identify possible problems as far ahead as possible. For example, there may be a change in the law due in two years' time. A business needs to estimate the effects and plan ahead.

foreign exchange market: the market where foreign currencies are bought and sold. The market is made up of specialist dealers, linked by telephone and computer. The main centres are in London, Tokyo and New York. Dealers buy and sell currencies as though they were goods.

Explanation: The demand for foreign currencies depends on international trade. If a country has high exports the demand for its currency will be high, because the foreign buyers of goods will have to pay for them in the exporter's currency. Similarly, a country with high imports will have to sell its own currency to buy foreign currencies to pay for the goods.

foreman: a person who supervises manual workers, probably in a factory. The foreman will be responsible for making sure people are working hard and doing their jobs correctly. The foreman will also be responsible for quality, timekeeping and discipline. It is the most junior level of management.

formal communication is the use of the official channels of communication laid down by a firm. All communication through the official lines of communication will be formal. Contacts do not have to be in writing to be formal.

Formal communication also refers to the way a matter is communicated. Usually, communications in writing, outside the firm, will be formal. (See also *informal communications*.)

four Ps: the four parts of the *marketing mix*. They are *product, price, place* and *promotion*. Sometimes a fifth 'P' is added – *packaging*.

franchise: a business that is licensed to use the name, logo and expertise of an existing, well known and successful business. Examples include: Little Chef, Burger King, Fast Frame, Body Shop and McDonalds.

> **Explanation:** Someone wanting to start their own business may choose to do so by buying a franchise. Under a franchise a company allows another firm (the franchisee) to use its name and logo and to sell its products. The company selling the franchise is called the franchisor.

Features of a franchise:

- A lump sum must be paid to buy a franchise to start the business. In return, a buyer will be given the sole rights to the franchise, within an area. The franchisor is also paid a share of the profits.

- There are strict rules about the way premises are designed and how the name and logo will be used. Shop fittings, staff uniforms and training are standardised.

- All supplies must be bought from the franchisor.

Advantages of buying a franchise:

- The franchisee is given support by the franchisor. This includes marketing and staff training. The franchisee may benefit from national advertising and being part of a well-known organisation.

- A franchise allows people to start and run their own business with less

> risk than normal. The failure rate among new franchises is lower than for other new businesses.

Advantages to the franchisor:

- The business can be expanded without having to take on many of the costs of expansion. The costs of new premises and of extra staff are met by the franchisee, who will contribute to other costs, e.g. advertising.

- Franchisors gain the economies of scale from bulk buying from their suppliers. They also make a profit on the supplies they sell to the franchisees.

- Because the franchisees have a financial stake in the success of the business they are likely to work very hard to make it succeed.

free market: an economic system in which the government does not interfere with the way the market works. Prices depend on the *supply* and *demand* for goods and services. Buyers and sellers make all the decisions. Buyers will only buy the goods and services offered by sellers if they think they are good value for money. Sellers have to sell at the price the buyer is willing to pay or go out of business. This is often described as the 'market economy'.

free trade happens when there are no barriers to trade between countries. That is, there are no *import duties* (*tariffs*) or *quotas*. Goods from other countries are able to enter a country without any restriction.

> **Explanation:** Most countries accept that more trade is good for everyone. Everybody will have a greater choice of goods and there will be greater *economic growth*.

frictional unemployment occurs where people are unemployed because they have left one job and are waiting to start another. It is a short-term, temporary form of unemployment.

fringe benefits are benefits given to employees in addition to their wages or salaries. Although they have a money value they are not given in the form of money. Fringe benefits or 'perks' are liable to income tax. The best known fringe benefit is the company car. Other common examples are free pension and health insurance schemes and discounts when buying the company's goods.

full employment is the level of employment at which there are jobs available for everyone able or willing to work. There will always be some unemployment because people may be unable to work because of ill health or because they are changing jobs. It is also difficult to decide at what age to start, and stop, counting people as being able to work. Students, for example, are able to work but they are not considered to be unemployed.

fully paid-up shares are the *shares* in a company, issued to the public, that have been paid for in full.

> **Explanation:** When a company first sells shares to the public it does not usually ask for all the money at once. It collects the money in three stages.

> **I** **Application –** when the public applies for shares they will be asked to send perhaps half the price of the shares with their application forms.

> **2** **Allocation –** the company tells applicants how many shares they have been allocated. If the shares are popular they may not get all they asked for. They will be asked to pay a second instalment shortly after being told their allocations.

> **3** **Final instalment –** when the buyers are asked to send their final payment. It is only when the third stage has been completed that the shares become fully paid-up.

functional organisation/management is an organisation divided into a number of key departments. Each department is responsible for a specific task or function. The department is responsible for a certain function across the whole organisation. Each function will have a senior manager in charge. Typical functions would include production, marketing, sales, personnel, accounting.

fund managers: companies that specialise in managing funds collected from the public. The money is usually invested in *stocks* and *shares*. Examples include pension funds, investment trusts and unit trust managers.

gap in the market: a niche where there would seem to be a business opportunity because a need is not being met by existing products.

gearing: the proportion of a company's total *capital employed* that is provided by long-term loans.

> **FORMULA *for calculating gearing:***
>
> $$\text{Gearing} = \frac{\text{Long-term loans}}{\text{Capital employed}} \times 100$$

> **Explanation:** A long-term loan is a loan for more than one financial year. The more money that a company has to borrow, the greater the *interest* it has to pay its lenders. Interest is an *expense* deducted in the *profit and loss account*. It lowers the *net profit* and increases the firm's *fixed costs*. This might make a company less competitive.
>
> The higher a company's gearing the bigger the proportion of capital used in the business that is made up of long-term loans. A greater proportion of the company's profits have to be used to pay interest. There will be less money to pay *shareholders* their *dividends*. If a company's gearing is already high it will find it harder to borrow more money.

general union: a *trades union* that draws its members from any industry or trade. Such unions originally drew most of their members from unskilled and semi-skilled workers. As new industries have grown the general unions have provided services to workers of all grades in a wide range of industries. The best known example is the Transport & General Workers Union.

gilt-edged security: a type of government security sold to the public. Gilt-edged securities are a way the government can borrow money. Gilts pay a fixed *rate of interest* and are usually repaid at a certain date. They are very safe because the government guarantees to pay the interest and to repay the loan. They are therefore said to be gilt-edged.

> **Explanation:** If the government spends more money than it collects in taxes it has a *budget* deficit. It therefore has to borrow money to cover the difference between its earnings and its spending. One way of borrowing money is to sell securities (also called *stocks*) to the public. They can be bought and sold on the *stock exchange*.

Giro credit: see *credit transfer*.

going concern: a business that is expected to carry on trading for the foreseeable future.

> **Explanation:** The *balance sheet* of a business is drawn up on the basis that the business will carry on trading. If this assumption was not made the *assets* would

have to be valued differently. The *assets* of a firm that is continuing to trade can be valued on the basis of what they cost. If the business was going to close down, the assets would be valued on the lower basis of what they could be sold for.

The term is also used when a business is sold. A business that is being run by a *receiver* may still be a going concern. The firm may have failed because its *working capital* was too low. With more capital the firm may be able to do well.

goods are physical products that have a money value and can, therefore, be bought and sold. Goods can be classified in several ways, for example, as *consumer goods* and producer or *capital goods*. Consumer goods can be sub-divided into *durable goods* and *non-durable goods*.

goodwill is the good reputation and loyalty that a business has built up among its customers and in a locality. This can be part of a business's *assets* and can be given a value.

> **Explanation:** When a business is sold the buyer expects to take over the firm's customers. It is much easier to take over a business that has regular customers and a good reputation. This is called the goodwill and is sold as part of the price of the business. The goodwill is hard to value accurately and there is no guarantee the customers will carry on dealing with the new owner.

go-slow: a form of *industrial action* where workers work at a slower rate on purpose. They keep working but only at the speed that earns them their *basic rates*, probably losing any bonuses or *productivity* payments.

government intervention happens when a government interferes in the way business operates. The extent to which a government intervenes will depend on the kind of economy. In a *free economy* the government does not intervene at all. All decisions are made by the market. In a *planned economy* most decisions about the economy are made by the government.

Reasons for government intervention:

- To control industries by trying to prevent *discrimination* in the workplace, setting safety standards at work, giving workers minimum rights and protecting the environment through laws that control pollution.

- To keep prices as stable as possible by controlling inflation.

- To help areas where there is high unemployment. The government offers grants and other help to companies if they move to certain areas.

- To make sure trading and pricing methods are honest and fair. There are a number of *consumer protection* laws that help to take care of consumers' interests. Governments try to increase competition by controlling *monopolies* and *mergers* where they are thought to be against the public interest.

grant aid is where the government gives a sum of money to business. This is usually for a particular purpose.

- Regional grants are paid to companies that move into certain areas. These areas may be called enterprise or development areas. They include grants to encourage overseas firms to invest in the UK. Nissan, Toyota and Honda, for example, were given large grants to open new car factories in Sunderland, Derbyshire and Swindon.

- Grants are paid to urban development agencies to encourage the growth of new industries. These are in town and city areas with high unemployment due to the closure of old industries.

- Rural development agencies give grants to firms setting up factories in country areas. Because agriculture no longer needs as many workers, rural areas often have high unemployment. One way to stop people moving away from rural areas is to provide local jobs.

- Grants are given for research and development and to encourage new industries. These grants may be to develop new technologies, for example, microprocessing and fibre-optics, or to extend existing ones.

grievance: when a worker, or group of workers, feels unhappy about their treatment at work. The workers may think the firm has acted unreasonably or failed to take their interests into account. A grievance may give rise to a complaint and, perhaps, to a dispute.

grievance procedure: the system used by a company to settle its workers' grievances.

> **Explanation:** Most large organisations have grievance procedures agreed with their trade unions. *ACAS* suggests that grievances should be settled as quickly and fairly as possible. Firms prefer that a disagreement should be settled quickly. There is then less chance of it growing into a more serious dispute.

gross domestic product (GDP) is the total of a country's economic activity during the course of a year. It includes the output of all goods and services produced in that country regardless of who owns the companies. For example, Britain's GDP includes the profits of foreign firms in Britain. It does not matter, for these purposes, that the profits may be sent abroad. (Compare with *gross national product.*)

gross margin is the gross profit of a business as a percentage of its total sales revenue.

> **FORMULA** *for calculating gross margin:*
>
> $$\text{Gross margin} = \frac{\text{Gross profit}}{\text{Total sales revenue}} \times 100$$

It is a useful indicator of the average gross profit a business is making on each item it sells.

gross misconduct: a breach of company rules on behaviour so serious that it results in instant dismissal. Examples of gross misconduct include theft, vandalism and fighting at work.

gross national product (GNP) is the total income earned by the people of a country. Some of the income will have been earned within the country, some abroad. For example, the UK's GNP will include profits earned by companies and citizens in other countries. The UK's GNP will not include profits earned by foreign-owned firms.

gross pay is total pay before *deductions*.

For workers paid on hourly rates, every week, it will be calculated as:

Total hours worked × Rate per hour

For workers paid an annual salary, but paid every month, it will be calculated as:

Annual salary ÷ 12

Worked examples:

1 **If someone works 40 hours a week, works no overtime, and is paid at £12.43 an hour,**
gross pay for a week will be:
£12.43 × 40 = £497.20

2 **If someone is paid an annual salary of £14 400 a year,**
gross pay for one month will be:
£14 400 ÷ 12 = £1200

gross profit is the difference between the total money earned from *sales* and the *cost of the goods sold*, during a period. The gross profit is calculated in the *Trading Account* of a business.

Example: Trading Account of XYX and Company Limited for the year ended 31 December

	£	£
Sales		20 000
less Cost of sales:		
Opening stock	7 000	
plus Purchases	12 000	
	19 000	
less Closing stock	8 000	
		11 000
Gross profit		9 000

growth occurs when a business becomes bigger.

'Bigger' may mean several things:

- a larger *turnover*
- a greater amount of *capital employed*
- more *employees*
- greater *profits before tax*.

Why firms wish to grow:

- The *directors* wish to gain the power and status from running a very large organisation. They want to increase profits through a larger *market share* and to become the *market leader* in their industry.
- To gain the benefits of *economies of scale*.
- It is easier for a large firm to survive when business is poor. Large companies find it easier to borrow money than smaller ones. They also have greater *reserves*.

Methods of growth:

- Internal expansion and growth by selling more of their products in their existing markets. They may sell in new markets, for example, by exporting. They may also increase the number of products that they sell.
- By buying up other companies, either by *takeovers* or through *mergers*.

guarantee: a promise by a company to repair or replace a product, free of charge, if it should fail or go wrong. Guarantees are usually for one year and cover defective parts and workmanship. A company may refuse to repair or replace the product if the fault is caused by the customer's negligence or misuse. It is often possible to extend a guarantee by paying a fee. The extra guarantee is, in effect, an insurance against the product going wrong. A guarantee is also called a *warranty*.

Health and Safety at Work Act 1974: this sets out the duties and responsibilities of employers and employees to ensure health and safety at work. There is a general duty of care on everyone, including visitors, for their own and other people's health and safety. The Act covers all work places including factories, offices, farms and schools and colleges.

Duties of employers:

- To provide a safe working environment including safe machinery and working practices. All entrances and exits must be safe.

- To enforce safety standards and regulations by, for example, making sure machines guards are not moved. All accidents must be investigated.

- To provide safety instruction, training and supervision.

Duties of employees:

- To take steps to protect themselves and others at work by, for example, wearing safety clothing and keeping work areas clear.

- Not to interfere with anything provided for their own safety and that of others.

- To report defects in machinery, equipment and working areas.

Health and Safety Executive: an organisation funded by the government to supervise the working of the Health and Safety at Work Act. The Executive employs factory inspectors, who investigate serious accidents and carry out regular checks to see that the Act is observed. They can ban the use of dangerous machines or even close down factories that are unsafe.

Herzberg, Frederick: an American psychologist who developed ideas of *job satisfaction*. He identified what he called 'hygiene' factors that are essential for a happy workforce. These basic factors create good working conditions. They include safety, cleanliness, reasonable rest breaks, and the control of noise and fumes. If employers ignore these factors, morale and *motivation* will fall and lead to unhappy workers and a lowering of output.

These four factors should be present, but they do not themselves motivate workers. The things that motivate workers include:

- **Recognition** – having good or hard work recognised, especially by managers.

- **Achievement** – the personal feeling that a job has been done well.

- **Promotion** – a development of recognition and achievement which leads to a more senior job.

- **Responsibility** which goes with promotion and increases the idea of recognition.

hierarchy: an organisation in which power and responsibility are built up in layers. The most powerful will be at the top of the hierarchy, those at the bottom will have the least authority.

Explanation: A hierarchy can be thought of as a pyramid. At the bottom there are a number of employees. They have very little influence on the way the organisation is run. The pyramid builds up in layers. Each layer has fewer people and more responsibility and power than the level below. At the top are the people who make all the 'big decisions'.

Example: different types of hierarchy

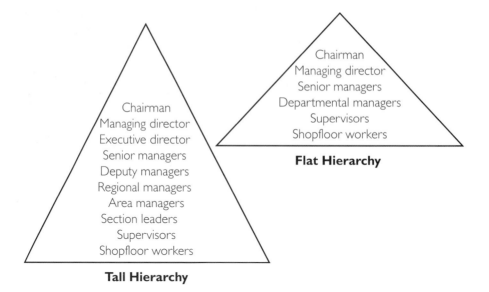

Chairman
Managing director
Executive director
Senior managers
Deputy managers
Regional managers
Area managers
Section leaders
Supervisors
Shopfloor workers

Tall Hierarchy

Chairman
Managing director
Senior managers
Departmental managers
Supervisors
Shopfloor workers

Flat Hierarchy

hierarchy of needs: see *Maslow*.

hire purchase is a method of buying goods and paying for them by instalments. The buyer usually pays the seller a deposit. A *finance company* pays the seller the rest of the price. The goods are therefore owned by the finance company. The buyer hires the goods from the finance company while paying for them by regular instalments. Goods bought on hire purchase are not owned by the buyer until the last instalment has been paid. Buyers must therefore get permission from the finance company if they want to sell the goods before the last instalment is paid.

Features of hire purchase:

- The buyer agrees to make regular payments to the finance company to cover the cost of the goods plus *interest*.

- If the buyer cannot keep up the payments, the finance company can repossess the goods if less than one third of the <u>total</u> price has been paid.

- Once the buyer has paid half the total price of the goods the finance company must get a court's permission to repossess the goods.

Worked example: A buyer buys a car for £10 000 on hire purchase, pays a deposit of £4000 and agrees to pay for it over three years.

	£
Cost of car	10 000
less deposit	<u>4 000</u>
	6000
add Interest at 5% for three years	
(£6000 × 5% = £300 × 3)	<u>900</u>
Total hire purchase price	6 900

Instalments = £6 900 ÷ 36 months = £191 per month

---

histogram: a type of *bar chart* where the information is represented by the total area of the bars. A histogram may be used to measure the frequency of a distribution. The width of the columns may vary as well as their height.

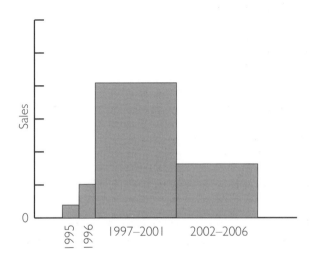

Explanation: At first glance a histogram looks very like a bar chart. In a bar chart the height of the bars shows the differences in the sizes of whatever is being measured. The greater the size of the item being measured the longer the bar. It does not matter how wide the columns are; it is only the height that is significant. In a histogram the width of the bar is also important.

The horizontal ('x') axis shows the classes that are being measured (e.g. years, tonnes). On a bar chart, the class being measured will be the same size all the way along. In a histogram the classes may be of different size. For example, the first two columns might each represent 1 year, but columns 3 and 4 each represent a band of, say, 5 years. In that case columns 3 and 4 would have to be 5 times wider than columns 1 and 2. The total information is represented by the height and the width of the column – in other words, by the area of the column, not just the height.

historic cost: the actual cost of buying an asset. This is the usual way of valuing assets. The value of the asset in the *balance sheet* is calculated on the price at which it was bought, less *depreciation*. The main advantage of the historic cost method is that it is based on an actual cost that can be proven. Assets can also be valued at their *replacement costs*.

holding company: a company that owns other firms which usually carry on trading under their own names. The holding company will be the only, or the main shareholder in the companies. The profits of these *subsidiary* companies will be paid to the holding company. They will be the main source of its profits, since it may not trade in its own name.

horizontal communications: the passing of information between people who are on the same level in a *hierarchy,* for example, between two foremen in a factory.

horizontal integration: see *integration.*

hourly rates (of pay): the wage earned per hour by people who are paid according to the number of hours worked. This wage is paid however much work is done during that time. People who are working in jobs that require a high level of skill may be paid by the hour. This allows them to take as much time as is necessary to do the job properly.

human capital: the people who work for an organisation considered as an *asset* to the business. Like any other form of capital it benefits by *investment.* Investment in this case is in the form of education and training. If the business improves the education and training of its workforce, the business will compete more effectively. Companies may sponsor employees at university or pay for improved qualifications either through in-house training or *off the job training.*

human resources are the people working in an organisation. People are a resource like any other. However, they are different from the other resources in that it is people who make the other resources effective. People are, therefore, an important asset to be valued and looked after. A firm's human resources are a balance of the skills needed for an organisation to work well.

human resource management is the development of people so as to get the most out of them. It is concerned with all aspects of a person's working life.

> ***Explanation:*** *Personnel departments* are mainly concerned with the 'hiring and firing' of staff. They deal with the routine parts of employment, such as record keeping. Human resource management does all that and more. It puts more emphasis on the firm's social and welfare services and the development of people through education and training.

hypermarket: a large out of town shopping store. Hypermarkets usually have very big car parks and sell a large variety of goods under one roof. A hypermarket will be owned by a single company.

import controls include *tariffs* and *quotas* and licences imposed by a government on *imports* of goods and services. They are imposed to try to limit imports. Import controls make imported goods scarcer and more expensive than home-produced goods. This should lead to a fall in demand for imported goods and for more home-produced goods to be sold.

import duty is a tax or duty on imports of goods and services. It is another name for a *tariff*.

import licence: a method of controlling the import of certain goods into a country. The importer must get a licence before the goods are imported. By keeping tight control over licences, *quotas* can be enforced. Licences can also be used as a way of delaying imports.

imports: goods and services bought from another country. Some imports are essential. For example many raw materials of the right quality are no longer available in the UK at the right price. Money goes out of a country when goods are imported. Imports affect the *balance of payments*.

incentives are rewards or promises of rewards to encourage people to reach certain targets. The rewards may be money or they can take the form of some kind of prize. For example, a salesperson may be given a free holiday for having the biggest sales in a year. Workers may be promised a *bonus* if they reach a certain production target.

income is the total amount of money earned by a person or an organisation in a period of time. The income of a business will be mainly from sales. The income of an individual will be made up of wages or salary, bonuses, and money earned from investments.

income and expenditure account: an account for a *non-profit making organisation* that is the equivalent of a business's *trading and profit and loss account*. It is the account where a club or charity's *surplus* or *deficit* is calculated.

income tax is a tax levied by the government on all income received by a person. It is based on all of a person's *gross pay* plus any other income, however it is earned. It is only individuals that pay income tax.

> **Explanation:** Income tax is one of the main ways used by the UK government to collect money to pay for the services it provides. Everyone is given a personal allowance on which no tax is paid. People may have other allowances. Tax is worked out on gross pay minus the allowances. Income tax is deducted from pay by the employer through *pay-as-you-earn (PAYE)*. The more a person earns the higher the rate of tax paid. The tax is collected for the government by the *Inland Revenue*.

incorporation: the process that gives an organisation a separate legal life of its own. In law, it becomes separate from the people that own it. It can sue others and be sued in its own name. It can even commit crimes (such as fraud) and be fined, although it cannot be sent to prison.

Independent Television Commission (ITC): a public body set up by Act of Parliament. All commercial television services provided in the UK are regulated and licensed by the ITC. It has a duty to make sure there is fair and effective competition between the ITV, satellite and cable television companies. It has no responsibility for BBC services.

Independent Television Commission

Scope of the ITC:

- The ITC does the same for television as the ASA does for other advertising. The ITC controls television advertising and sponsorship. Advertisers must follow the ITC Code of Advertising Standards and Practice. Advertisements must not be misleading, encourage or condone harmful behaviour or cause offence.

- It investigates complaints from the public about television advertisements. It can make advertisers change or even withdraw an advertisement. It can also fine the television companies for not carrying out its decisions.

MISLEADING	MCDONALDS HAPPY MEALS
	Advertising agency: Leo Burnett
COMPLAINT FROM	1 viewer
NATURE OF COMPLAINT	An advertisement for McDonalds offered Happy Meals for £1.00 each. A viewer pointed out that she had not benefitted from this special offer at her local branch and that no mention had been made in the advertisement about certain branches being excluded.
ASSESSMENT	The BACC said a genuine mistake had been made. The agency had been unaware that all branches had not participated in the offer. They subsequently amended the advertisement to make this clear. The ITC concluded the original advertisement had been misleading.
DECISION	Complaint upheld.

index numbers are a way of showing how the value of something has changed over a period of time. An index measures the change from one period to the next. It does so by comparing the new value of something with its value at a base period. It is calculated as a percentage of the value in the base period.

There are a number of index numbers issued by the government; the best known is the *retail prices index (RPI)*.

Worked example: Suppose the price of a company's shares over four months is:

> May: 124p   June: 126p   July: 135p   August: 132p

May is called the base period and given a value of 100. All future changes are measured as a percentage of the base period.

$$\text{Index} = \frac{\text{New period figure}}{\text{Base period figure}} \times 100$$

The index for June is 126 ÷ 124 × 100 = 101.6
         July   135 ÷ 124 × 100 = 108.9
         August 132 ÷ 124 × 100 = 106.5

---

index-linked: where the value of something is directly linked to changes in the *retail prices index.*

Explanation: The RPI is the standard measure of inflation in the UK. It is sometimes called the cost of living index. State pensions, for example, are index-linked. Increases in pensions are based on the RPI at a certain date. The idea is that pensions should increase by the same amount as the cost of living so that the real value of the pensions is kept the same from year to year.

indicators: see *economic indicators* and *performance indicators.*

indirect costs are costs that do not relate directly to a particular product. The indirect costs are shared between all the products a business produces. Indirect costs include company vehicles, rent and rates, the costs of the offices and management. They are the general costs of running the business. They are fairly fixed and are often called the *overheads.* A firm will want to keep its indirect costs as low as possible. The more money it has to pay in indirect costs the lower will be its *profits.* (Compare with *direct costs.*)

indirect tax is a tax that is paid on goods and services. Examples include *value added tax* (VAT), petrol tax and all other *excise duties.* Compare with a *direct tax*, which is paid on income.

Explanation: They are called indirect taxes because those who pay them to the government pass them on to their customers. The customers pay the taxes, but only indirectly; they pay them to the seller who pays the government.

induction is a form of training given to someone when they first start working for an organisation.

Induction has a number of purposes:

- To help people to settle down and feel happy in their new work. The sooner they do so the more quickly they become effective workers.

- To help new employees to 'find their way around' the organisation; they often start with a tour of the site. It is to try to save people from feeling lost in a new workplace.

- To introduce new employees to health and safety, security and company rules and to the people they need to know.

industrial action happens when a group of workers decide to take action against their employer. This is normally to follow up some kind of *industrial dispute* or as the result of a *grievance*.

Explanation: When workers 'fall out' with their employers there are a number of actions they can take. The action will be designed to put pressure on the employer.

- **Overtime ban –** refusing to work *overtime*. Instead of taking on new staff many firms ask their workers to work overtime. This happens especially at very busy times. An overtime ban may mean an order cannot be delivered on time. The firm might lose money as a result.

- **Withdraw goodwill –** this includes refusing to attend meetings or refusing to cover for staff that are absent.

- *Go-slow –* when workers carry on working but only as slowly as possible. They lose *bonuses* but still get their *basic pay*.

- **Work-to-rule –** when workers follow the company's rules to the letter. This has the effect of slowing down work.

- **Days of action –** when workers strike for one or two days at a time. Days of action follow no regular pattern. The employer must be given notice but it is as short as possible. Workers make it hard for employers to plan ahead while keeping workers' loss of wages to a minimum.

- *Selective strikes –* where perhaps only one group of workers goes on strike. They may be key workers, so that a few strikers have a very large effect on production.

- *Strikes –* when workers withdraw their labour. This is usually seen as a last resort. Both workers and employers lose money. Before a strike can be called *trades unions* must, by law, hold a secret ballot of workers. Only if there is a majority can the trade union call a strike. They must give the employer notice.

industrial dispute: this occurs when workers (through their *trades unions*) and employers fail to agree. Disputes happen when *collective bargaining* fails to produce a result that both sides can agree upon. Not all disputes are about pay and *conditions of employment*. Other causes of disputes include: victimisation of a worker, closing a factory and moving work to another plant. Both sides want disputes settled quickly and without industrial action.

industrial inertia: the tendency for a firm, or an industry, to stay in the same place, after the original reasons for locating there have disappeared.

> **Explanation:** Many industries were located near the coalfields in the eighteenth and nineteenth centuries. They have stayed in the same places even though they no longer use coal and steam to drive their machines. They have stayed because they are well established in an area. There is a pool of skilled labour available and component suppliers may also be based in such areas. There is no good reason to move and it would be too expensive.

industrial location: see *location of industry*.

industrial relations: the relationship between *employers* and *employees*. This usually means between trades unions representing the workers and the management of a business. It is in the interest of both sides to stay on good terms. Both prefer to settle disagreements before they become disputes.

industrial sectors: a way of classifying industries into groups. Usually industry is classified into three sectors – *primary industry, secondary industry* and *tertiary industry*.

industrial tribunal: a hearing arising from a complaint by an employee of *unfair* or *constructive dismissal*. Tribunals also hear complaints about *discrimination* on grounds of race, gender or trades union membership.

> **Explanation:** When employees think they have been unfairly dismissed or discriminated against they can get help from *ACAS*. If the matter cannot be settled in any other way it may go to a tribunal. Tribunals are made up of three people, the chair (who is always a lawyer), an employer representative and an employee representative.

- Tribunals are more informal than courts. The two sides can be represented if they wish. Employees often have a trades union official to put their case.

- Individuals who 'win' their cases are entitled either to have their jobs back (re-instatement), to compensation, or to the offer of a new job (re-engagement).

industrial union: a *trades union* for people who work in one particular industry. It represents workers in that industry whatever their jobs may be, e.g. BIFU in the *financial services* industry.

industry means two separate things:

> 1   The grouping together of all the producers involved in a common activity. Thus all the manufacturers of motor vehicles, and of the components used in making them, are referred to as the 'motor industry'. All companies involved in selling goods directly to *consumers* form the 'retail industry'.

> 2   Industry is also used to mean all economic activity except the *tertiary* sector. Everyone working in making (*manufacturing*) things and using the gifts of nature (*extractive*) is said to be in 'industry'. This is compared to 'commercial' or 'service' activities.

industry regulator: see *regulator*.

inertia selling: where goods are sent to people although they have not asked for them. Inertia selling is illegal in Britain.

> *Explanation:* Firms using such selling methods hope to frighten people into paying for the goods. Goods are sent with an *invoice*. People are told that if the goods are not sent back within a few days the invoice becomes due for payment. If goods are sent in this way the receiver should write to the sender and ask for either the goods to be be collected or to send the money to pay the return postage. If the sender does not do either, the goods can be kept.

inflation: a general increase in the level of prices. The value of money falls when there is inflation. That is, a given sum of money buys fewer goods. When the rate of inflation is high, prices rise more quickly and the fall in the value of money is faster.

> *Explanation:* There are two causes of inflation.

> 1   **Cost-push inflation** – when prices are pushed upwards by increases in costs. An increase in the price of raw materials increases a firm's costs. Unless it can save money in some other way, it will have to put up prices if its profits are to stay the same. The same thing will happen if wages or any other major cost increases.

> 2   **Demand-pull inflation** – when there is an increase in the *demand* for goods. If, for some reason, people decide to buy more goods, a seller may not be able to increase *supply* quickly. People will want more goods than sellers can supply. Prices will rise to try to make the supply and demand equal.

Inflation can affect a country internally and externally. Internally, people become worse off because the value of their money falls. They can buy fewer goods with a given amount of money. Externally, if the prices of UK goods and services go up, we may buy more from abroad. UK goods and services will also become more expensive abroad and both of these factors will affect the *balance of payments*.

information technology (IT) is the collecting, recording, storing and distribution of information using computers and telecommunications. The term covers both the equipment (the hardware), and the software needed.

> ***Explanation:*** IT is often thought of only in terms of computers. Information is probably recorded and stored on computers but it is often collected and distributed using telephone links. Equipment such as *fax* and video connections is also an important part of IT. Large firms may collect information by connecting branches from all over the country, or the world, to their head office computers. Those connections are made using telephone lines or satellite links. In return, head office will send instructions to its branches.

> ***Example:*** Supermarket chains collect information about the goods sold in their shops by connecting their tills to their head office computers. They are able to collect information on, for example:

- the total sales for each branch for any period of time (e.g. Mondays and Thursdays, or per week, or year)

- the sales of each item in each branch on any day, or week or any other period; this sales information can be used to replace stock levels in each branch.

informative advertising is advertising where the main purpose is to inform the public. Informative advertising is usually factual. It does not necessarily set out to sell something.

> ***Explanation:*** In some ways all advertising informs the public. While giving information it may, at the same time, tell people that a product exists.

> ***Examples:*** Informative advertising includes:

- an advertisement in a trade paper, giving technical information about a product

- an advertisement by a car manufacturer telling the owners of certain models to take them back to their garages to address some problem

- advertisements by a government department telling the public about new services or warning them about health risks (e.g. from smoking, drinking and driving). A local authority may advertise that a certain road will be closed on a certain date for repairs.

infrastructure: the network of essential public services that supports a community and business. It includes roads, railways, air links, telephones and all the public utilities such as electricity, gas and water. Business needs these services to be readily available, cheap and efficient. Areas that have a well-developed infrastructure are able to attract new business more easily than areas where the infrastructure is poor.

Inland Revenue: the government department responsible for collecting *direct taxes*. It collects *income tax*, *corporation tax* and capital gains tax. It is also responsible for the valuation of properties for *business rates* and council tax purposes.

inputs are all the resources put into the production of a product or service. The inputs will include some *direct costs* such as raw materials, components and labour and the running costs of machines. Inputs also include *indirect costs* like capital and the cost of administration and *advertising*.

in-service training is training provided for existing employees of an organisation to help them do their jobs more effectively.

Reasons for in-service training:

- To improve the skills of the workforce by keeping them up to date with modern methods and ideas. For example, staff need to be taught how to use a new machine or a new computer system.

- To prepare staff for promotion or to help them to improve their qualifications. Many firms insist their staff gain qualifications; for example, all staff in the accounts department may have to have an accounting technicians' (AAT) qualification.

- To improve customer relations and sales. For example, instruction may be given in how to answer the telephone or how to deal with customers face-to-face.

It may be delivered through *off-the-job* or *on-the-job* training.

insolvency occurs when a company stops trading because the total of its *liabilities* is greater than its ability to pay.

institutional investors: insurance companies, pensions funds and other large organisations that invest in company *shares* through the *Stock Exchange*.

insurance is a method of covering the possibility of financial loss resulting from certain risks.

Explanation: Insurance depends on the idea of pooling risks. Everyone faces a large number of risks every day. The chances of suffering a loss as a result of those risks is quite small. Those facing a risk pay money (premiums) into a central pool. The few people who actually suffer a loss are paid compensation out of the central pool. The few are helped by the many.

Example: Suppose there are 10 000 people at risk from landslides in a certain area. The insurance company charges a premium of £150 a year against the risk. One year, 20 people suffer a loss of £50 000 each, which the insurance company pays.

The many (10 000) have paid a fairly small amount each (£150) into the pool so that the few (20) who suffered a loss can each be paid compensation (£50 000).

Insurance is based on three principles:

- **Indemnity –** those who suffer a loss will be returned to the same financial position as they were in before the loss. A profit cannot be made from insurance.

- **Insurable interest –** those who take out an insurance must be the ones that would suffer a loss if the event covered by insurance occurred.

- **Utmost good faith –** those applying for insurance must be completely honest with the insurance company. Not telling the whole truth may mean the insurance company will refuse to meet a claim.

The agreement between the insurance company and the insured is called an insurance policy.

Insurance companies depend on statistics to work out the chances of an event happening. Risks whose probability can be calculated are called insurable risks.

Where the probable risk cannot be calculated, the companies will refuse to insure the risk, neither will they insure normal trading risks. These are called uninsurable risks.

insurance broker: a *middleman* who sells *insurance* to the public. (See *brokers*.)

integration usually takes place when a firm expands by either developing into new areas of business using its own resources or when it buys other companies. Integration may be horizontal, vertical or lateral.

- **Horizontal integration –** when a firm expands within the same line of business (for example, the Burton group has a number of different companies, all in the clothing business – Debenhams, Top Shop, Principals, Top Man, Dorothy Perkins).

- **Vertical integration –** when firms expand along the *chain of distribution;* firms can vertically integrate backwards or forwards.

  - When they do so backwards they include the production of raw materials or components used in their business.

  - When they vertically integrate forwards they extend to include the distribution of their product. For example, the British Shoe Corporation manufactures boots and shoes and has vertically integrated forwards to sell its shoes through its own shops.

- **Lateral integration –** when a firm expands by moving into a similar but different area of production using the same skills and techniques as its existing business; for example, a car manufacturer producing vans or lorries or buses.

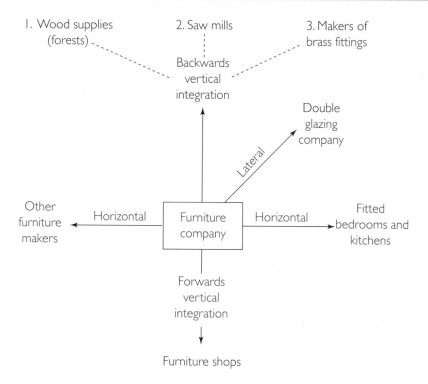

Furniture shops

interest is the cost of borrowing money. It is usually shown as a percentage of the money borrowed.

> **Explanation:** If money is borrowed from a bank or building society, interest is charged on the loan. In the same way, if goods are bought on *credit*, the buyer, in effect, borrows the cost of the goods from the seller. Often the buyer is charged interest as well as the price of the goods, making the goods dearer to buy. The total price of the goods will be:
>
> Cost of the goods + Interest
>
> The total amount of interest paid will depend on how long the money is borrowed for.

interest rate: the percentage rate charged for borrowing money over a period of time. Minimum interest rates are set by the *Bank of England*.

> **Explanation:** The interest rate is the amount of the interest stated as a percentage of the amount borrowed.

FORMULA *for calculating rate of interest:*

$$\text{Rate of interest} = \frac{\text{Total interest paid}}{\text{Amount borrowed}} \times 100$$

Worked example: If the total interest paid on a loan of £1000 is £150, the rate of interest will be:

$$\frac{£150}{£1000} \times 100 = 15\%$$

The monthly repayments will be £150 + £1000 divided by the number of months of the loan. If the loan is for one year the repayments will be:

$$\frac{£1150}{12} = £93.83 \text{ a month}$$

The above example describes the *flat rate of interest* charged on the loan. The interest is charged on the full amount of the loan (£1000) for the full period of the loan (12 months). The flat rate will not be the true rate of interest which is shown by the *annualised percentage rate*.

internal economies of scale: see *economies of scale*.

internal financing occurs when a business pays for *capital expenditure* with money from within the company instead of borrowing the money.

Internal financing may come from a number of sources:

- profits that have not been distributed to the owners, that is, *retained profits*. These may have been built up over time in *reserves*

- the sale of an *asset*; this may be the sale of an old machine to help to pay for a new one or even the sale of a *subsidiary company*.

internal growth is where a company expands because of growth in its sales. It grows because of its own success. It is in contrast to growth by buying up other companies.

internal promotion is where an employee is promoted to a higher grade of job within the same organisation.

internal recruitment is when an organisation recruits from among its existing staff.

Explanation: There may be several ways that companies may recruit from people already working for them:

- Temporary or part-time staff may be invited to apply for permanent or full-time jobs.

- Management jobs may be filled by people from within the organisation, that is, through *internal promotion*.

- People working in one part or branch may be invited to apply for jobs in other parts or branches.

Jobs are advertised within the organisation, details of the jobs will be shown on notice boards or in an internal newsletter. If there is no one suitable internally, the jobs may then be advertised externally.

Advantages of internal recruitment:

- The people being considered for a job are known so the company knows the quality of their work. Some firms take on staff on a temporary basis to try them in the job; if they are good they may then be employed permanently.

- Less training may be necessary because the staff already know where things are and how things are done.

- It is a fast and, therefore, cheap way of recruiting. There is no need for expensive advertisements. Usually the number of people to be considered is small. The successful applicant can start straight away. External recruitment has more stages, takes longer and is more costly.

Disadvantages of internal recruitment:

- There is less choice than there would be if a job was advertised externally. This may mean the quality of the staff taken on may not be as good.

- There is no 'new blood', bringing new ideas to a business.

- Other parts of an organisation may suffer if people are transferred from one part of the firm to another.

international trade is the importing and exporting of goods and services. Countries benefit from international trade.

Benefits of international trade:

- To consumers:
  - Greater choice of goods and services. People do not have to depend on those things that can be produced within a country. Without international trade there are some goods that would

> never be available to us. For example, many kinds of fruit cannot be produced in the UK.
>
> – More competition may lead to lower prices for consumers.
>
> • To producers:
>
> – Access to raw materials which may be unavailable or too expensive in the home country.
>
> – Larger markets. They do not have to depend on the home market for all their sales. Because firms can *export* they may be able to produce more and provide more jobs.
>
> – *Specialisation* by countries who can produce those things they are best at or can make most cheaply.

Internet: a worldwide network of *databases* that can be accessed through computers. Access is through the telephone system via a *modem* to a specialist Internet provider. The system allows messages and information to be sent to, and received from, anywhere in the world.

interview: the asking of questions in a face-to-face situation. In business it is a method used in *job selection* and *market research*.

Explanation: In job selection an interview is one of the last stages in the process of *recruitment*. It comes after the advertisement, application, and *shortlisting*. The number of interviews and the number of interviewers will depend on the company and the kind of job. For a junior job there will probably only be one interview with one person. A more senior job may have separate interviews with a number of different people and with a panel of interviewers.

In market research the interview is widely used to collect *primary data*. It is usually based around a carefully structured *questionnaire*. *Closed questions* are usually used because it is easier to collate the answers into useful statistics. *Open questions* are rarely used.

investment: using money to buy an *asset*. When a business makes an investment it usually means buying a fixed *asset*. This may be new machinery and equipment or possibly moving to a new factory or expanding the existing one.

An individual may invest by buying a house. It can also mean using money to gain an income. This may be in *shares* or *equity*-based funds, such as unit trusts or *investment trusts*.

investment trust: a company whose only income is through investing its *capital* in buying *shares* in other companies. Investment trusts are managed by *fund managers*.

INVESTORS IN PEOPLE

Investors in People: a UK national standard that has been developed by industry and sponsored by government. It sets a level of good practice for the achievement of organisational goals through the good management of people. Investors in People UK manage, promote and quality assure the Standard. It is delivered in England and Wales by the *Training and Enterprise Councils (TECs)*, in Scotland by Local Enterprise Companies (LECs) and in Northern Ireland by the Training and Employment Agency (T & EA).

invisible exports: the selling of services to people overseas.

invisible imports: the buying of services from suppliers from overseas.

invisible trade: the importing and exporting of services. Britain has a *surplus* of *invisible exports* over *invisible imports*.

> ***Explanation:*** Invisible trade includes banking, insurance and financial services; shipping services and tourism. Every time we go abroad and spend money, this spending becomes part of this country's *invisible imports*. If a foreign firm hires a British ship or a foreign passenger uses a British airline, the money earned becomes part of Britain's *invisible exports*.

invoice: the document sent by a seller of goods to tell a buyer the amount owed. It contains all the details of a transaction. It is the 'bill' for the goods.

> ***Explanation:*** When goods are sold on credit a seller sends the buyer an invoice. The invoice is a request for payment. It shows such things as the quantity sold, price per item, any *discounts*, total amount due and terms of payment.
>
> The invoice may be included with the goods or, more likely, sent through the post after delivery of the goods. When the buyer receives the invoice it is checked against the goods. This is to make sure that the quantities shown on the invoice match the goods received and are the same as the buyer ordered.
>
> ***Example:*** A typical invoice is shown on the next page.

issued capital is the same as the *issued share capital*.

issued share capital: that part of the *authorised capital* of a company that has actually been issued to shareholders. The amount of the issued share capital will be shown in the *balance sheet*.

ITC: see *Independent Television Commission*.

XYX & COMPANY LIMITED

The Industrial Estate, Anytown, Midshire RE9 4PH
Telephone: 0123 987 4561
Fax: 0123 987 6544
VAT Registration No.

Invoice No. 01468

Date

To:

Your Order No.

Date of Order

Ref/Cat	Quantity	Description	Unit Price	VAT		Total Price

GROSS PRICE	
Less Trade Discount	
NET PRICE	
Plus VAT @ 17.5%	
INVOICE TOTAL	

E. & O. E.
Terms: 2% 14 Days
        1% 28 Days

A typical invoice

JIT: see *just-in-time.*

job advertisement: an invitation to apply for a stated job. It is a form of *informative advertising.* Job advertisements may be internal or external.

Internal:

Job advertisements are placed on notice boards within an organisation, in a company newsletter or magazine.

External:

Advertisements may be placed in several different places:

1	*Job centres,* usually locally.
2	Local newspapers are used for fairly junior jobs or jobs for which people are unlikely to move house. Some management jobs may be advertised locally.
3	National newspapers are used when an organisation is hoping to recruit from as wide a field as possible. The 'heavy' Sunday newspapers advertise jobs for directors, managing directors and chief executives.

> **4** Trade magazines are widely used to recruit specialist staff.
>
> **5** *Employment agencies* may be notified of vacancies; they may have someone on their books who would be suitable.

The job advertisement should give all the details that a person wanting to apply for the job will need.

It should, at least, contain:

- the job title and location (where the person will work)

- age, qualifications and experience wanted

- details of pay and conditions of work

- details of how to apply (e.g. by letter or application form); the name, address and telephone number to contact for an application form and more details of the job; this will not always be the employer, for example, if an *employment agency* is used.

A selection of job advertisements is shown on the previous page.

job analysis: the breaking down of a job into its various parts. This helps managers to see what the job consists of and whether the work merits a new person. The information may be used to prepare a job description and to decide the qualifications and experience needed, and whether the post should be part-time or full-time.

job application: the formal request to an employer to be considered for a job vacancy. There are several ways of making a job application.

- Usually, an application form is sent by the employer. The form will ask for personal details, education, qualifications and experience, including part-time work. The names and addresses of two job referees will also be asked for.

- The applicant may send a *curriculum vitae* (CV); it contains the same kind of information as that asked for by most application forms.

- A letter of application may be sent with a CV. Applicants may also give reasons why they think they are the right person for the job.

job centres are government run offices that advertise local job vacancies notified to them by local employers. They are to be found in most towns.

Explanation: Job vacancies are displayed in the centre on cards. If someone is interested in a job he or she makes a note of the number and takes it to the reception desk where staff will try to arrange an interview straight away.

Job Centres also help unemployed people to look for and find jobs. People are given 'client advisors' who work with them to draw up a 'Back to Work' plan. Whether benefits are paid or not depends on working with the client advisors.

JobCentre

job description: a list of the tasks, duties and responsibilities attached to a particular job. A job description may be sent, with the application form, to a person applying for a job. It spells out the duties of the job and helps applicants to decide whether or not they want the job.

Explanation: A job description is important because it states exactly what the job consists of, including:

- the job title and the grade of the job and to whom the job holder is responsible
- the day-to-day tasks of the job in detail
- whether the job holder is responsible for other people and if so, how many, and their job titles.

job interview: asking questions of a person who has applied for a job to decide whether that person is suitable for the job.

Explanation: The purpose of an interview is to select the most suitable person for the job. The interviewers will try to assess the candidates:

- by their physical appearance; for example, many companies think that jobs that deal with the public need people who dress well
- by their social and communication skills; the interviewers will try to judge whether the person is polite and can put what they mean into words clearly. These skills which will be more important in some jobs than others
- by whether they have the right level of knowledge or skill for the job
- in terms of whether they will fit in with the people with whom they are going to have to work.

The interview is not just a one-way process. It is also important for the interviewee to decide whether or not to work for the company.

job production is where a single product is produced in response to an individual order. It is a 'one off' made to a customer's specification.

> **Explanation:** Goods produced using job production are usually made to a special order. They are often made by craftsmen. The goods may be made by one person working alone, or they may be made by a team of people.

> **Examples:**

> - Making a piece of furniture to fit a particular space in a person's house.
> - A tailor making a 'made to measure' suit for a customer.
> - An architect designing a building or an artist painting a portrait.
> - Building a bridge.

job references are comments from two or three people who know an applicant for a job, and can give an opinion about the person and their ability to do the job.

> **Explanation:** When applying for a job it is usual to be asked for the names and addresses of two people. These people are known as referees. A referee should never be a relative.

> - One of the referees should be the last employer.
> - Another one may also be a previous employer, or a school teacher, or someone who knows the person well.

When a firm is thinking of employing someone it may write to the referees.

> - The employer may send the referee a form asking very specific questions.
> - The employer may instead invite the referee to express a general opinion about the person. Sometimes they ask for comments on certain things like reliability, honesty and absence record.

job satisfaction: the extent to which a job makes a person feel fulfilled. It consists of the positive aspects of a job that people like.

> **Explanation:** It is difficult to measure the extent to which a job satisfies a person. Most people are unhappy with some parts of their job. Some of the things that have been suggested that give job satisfaction include:

136

- **Levels of pay** – although pay is important some people are prepared to work for lower pay than they could get somewhere else.

- **Working conditions** – this does not always depend on the physical environment. It is concerned more with the general atmosphere being nice to work in. Working hours, and the way they fit in with a person's family may be one such factor. People are more likely to be satisfied with their jobs if they like the people they work with.

- **Job security** is important because people feel they can plan for the future.

- **The level of responsibility** – for some people having a lot of responsibility makes a job satisfying. Status either within the firm or within the eyes of friends may also be important,

The factors that motivate people and give them job satisfaction vary from person to person.

job security is the extent to which a job is 'safe'. That is, there is a reasonable certainty that the job will continue for the foreseeable future.

> **Explanation:** In the past certain jobs were thought to be safe for the whole of a person's working life. More recently, the growth of technology, especially of *automation*, has reduced job security. Poor job security may lead to poor *motivation* and low morale. Being willing to change and to learn new skills through training improves job security.

job selection is the process by which the people who apply for a job are chosen to fill a job vacancy. It is the last stage in *recruitment*. (See also *selection*.)

job sharing is where one job is split between two people. The people job sharing can usually decide how they are going to divide the hours. The usual pattern is for each person to do half the job. Each person may, for example, work two and a half days or one of them may work mornings and the other afternoons.

job specification is a list of the personal qualities, experience and qualifications needed for a job. The job specification is also known as the *person specification*. It gives details of the qualifications and experience needed to do the job. It may also detail expected attitudes, e.g. towards equal opportunities; and qualities such as the ability to make judgements and to show initiative. The *job description* gives details of the task and responsibilities required.

joint stock bank: a bank that is owned by shareholders. All the high street banks are joint stock banks. They were called joint stock banks to distinguish them from local savings banks owned by their members. The distinction is no longer an important one.

joint stock company: a company that is owned by shareholders. It is another name for *limited liability* companies. There are two kinds of joint stock company, *private companies* and *public companies.*

joint venture: when two or more independent companies join together to carry out a business project.

> **Explanation:** There are business projects that can be too expensive or too technically demanding for one company to undertake on its own. One way of carrying out such projects is to set up a joint venture. The companies in the joint venture usually set up a separate 'joint venture company' in which they own all the shares. The size of each company's share holding will vary. The member companies will also supply finance and probably staff and expertise.

A joint venture company is run quite separately from the companies that own it. The member companies stay independent of each other and carry on their business normally and may even compete with one another on other projects. Many joint ventures are international.

Examples:

- European aircraft manufacturers found it hard to compete with the large American aircraft makers, like Boeing. The cost of developing a new aeroplane is too high for any one of the European companies to manage on their own. They therefore set up the joint venture Airbus Ltd, to produce aeroplanes to compete with the American plane makers. British Aerospace has a 20% share in the company, with other shareholders being French, German and Spanish planemakers.

- Eurotunnel who built, and now run, the channel tunnel, is a joint venture involving a consortium of French and British companies.

just-in-time (JIT) is a manufacturing system for keeping stock levels of raw materials and component parts to a minimum.

> **Explanation:** Keeping large stocks of raw materials, components and work in progress is very expensive. Using JIT, stocks are kept to a minimum to reduce these costs. The aim is to get the parts and materials to where they are used just before they are needed. The production line must not stop because of a shortage of parts and materials. If one of the suppliers fails to get the goods to the firm in time there will be hardly any stock to fall back on. JIT relies on a very highly organised system for ordering parts and materials. It also depends on suppliers being able to get their supplies to the manufacturer at exactly the right time, in other words, just-in-time.

kaizen: a Japanese term that means continuous improvement. Under this policy a product is being improved all the time, especially its quality. Workers are encouraged to put forward ideas on how the quality of their product and methods of production can be improved. The idea is closely linked to *quality circles*.

Kitemark: a symbol issued by the *British Standards Institution*. It shows that the goods carrying the Kitemark are produced according to a *BSI* standard, and therefore of a certain minimum quality. The BSI carries out regular checks on goods awarded the Kitemark to make sure they still meet the standards laid down.

labour: the human resources available for use in economic activity. It includes the people available for work as well as those actually in work. Labour may be a mental as well as physical activity. It is a *factor of production.*

labour intensive: when labour costs are a high proportion of the *total costs* of production. In many industries much of the work that was done by people is now done by machines (e.g. farming and engineering). These industries are therefore less labour intensive than they were in the past. Labour intensive industry can be contrasted with *capital intensive* business.

> **Example:** labour intensive production

> - Restaurants are labour intensive. Very little of the food preparation can be done by machine, neither can waiting at tables be automated.
> - Any business that produces goods by *job production* methods is labour intensive.

labour market: a term used to describe the number of people available for work compared with the number of jobs there are for them to do. If there are more people than jobs the labour market is depressed. If there are more jobs than people to fill them, the labour market is said to be good.

> **Explanation:** When we speak of a labour market we generally mean that unemployment is high or low. In reality, there are many different labour markets. The labour market for professional footballers, for example, is different from the labour market for skilled toolmakers. There are also differences between different parts of the country.

labour mobility: the extent to which people are prepared to move either from one place to another or from one job to another.

> **Explanation:** The extent to which people can move jobs depends on experience, qualifications and the nature of their work. The skills needed in some jobs are easily transferred from one place of work to another. For example, word processing is much the same everywhere.

There are two main types of labour mobility:

> 1 **Occupational mobility –** moving from one type of job to another. It may not be very easy to move from one job to another because of various factors:

> - Some jobs need special natural ability, such as hand or drawing skills. If you do not have that talent then some jobs are not open to you.
> - Long training may be necessary in order to get the right qualifications to do a job (e.g. a doctor). Training is expensive; it is not only the cost of the training but also the wages that may be lost while training.

2 **Geographical mobility** – moving from one part of the country to another for work reasons. People's willingness to move depends on a number of factors:

- Housing may not be readily available at the right kind of price. People are often reluctant to move from a cheap to an expensive area.

- There are costs involved in moving, including estate agents' and lawyers' fees plus things like carpets and curtains.

- Family and friends may live close by and people may not want to move away from them to a place where they do not know anyone.

- Many people do not want to disturb their children's education by moving and having to change school.

3 **Other factors** – both geographical and occupational mobility will be affected by:

- Age, which may be important as it is harder for an older person to move jobs, especially if training is needed.

- The 'benefit trap' means it may pay some people to remain unemployed because they are better off on benefits.

labour supply: the number of people and the variety of skills available for work in a certain area.

Explanation: The total supply of labour in a country, or in part of the country, depends on three factors:

1	the size of population
2	the proportion of that population that is able and willing to work. This will be affected by: the number of children, the number of people over 65 and the number of people in full time education or training
3	the quality and type of skills available in an area.

Some parts of the country have a large supply of available labour. This may be because old industries have closed down and many people are unemployed. One reason why Nissan built a new factory near Sunderland was because of a good supply of labour from the former shipbuilding and mining industries.

labour turnover is the rate at which people enter and leave employment in an organisation. It is usually stated as a percentage of the people employed.

FORMULA *for calculating labour turnover:*

$$\text{Turnover} = \frac{\textbf{Number of leavers}}{\textbf{Total employees}} \times 100$$

Explanation: Labour turnover can be measured for a whole organisation or for a department. High labour turnover can be expensive because of the cost of training new people. It may indicate poor management. It can lead to lower total output because it takes time for new staff to get up to speed.

Labour turnover is affected by:

- rates of pay, compared to other companies in the area
- working conditions, whether the job is, for example, easy or hard, clean or dirty
- whether there are other, local job opportunities easily available.

land: the *factor of production* that includes all the 'gifts of nature' (natural resources such as fertility, fish, minerals and forests) as well as the land surface itself. Land is immobile and in fixed supply.

lateral integration: see *integration.*

launch: when a new product is brought on to the market. This involves planning and *marketing.*

- The marketing department advertises the new product to the trade and then to the public. Usually the trade will be told about a new product well before it is announced to the public.
- Careful planning is needed to make sure there are enough supplies of the product for people to buy. This involves starting production some time before the launch. Stocks will be built up and sent out to sellers beforehand.

A launch may be on a national basis or sometimes companies target one region first. They test *market* in that area with other regions following later.

leadership comprises the personal qualities needed to influence people to perform to the best of their ability. A good leader gains the support, hard work, loyalty, respect (and maybe affection) of fellow workers.

lease: a legal document that transfers property for a definite and fixed period of time. The term is usually used in the context of land and buildings. Land held on lease is said to be leasehold. Leaseholders can use the property as if it were their own. The property will always eventually be returned to the person who grants the lease (the lessor) at the end of the lease. Rent is paid for the use of the property. Goods can also be leased (see *leasing*).

leasing occurs when *assets* are rented from a leasing company for a period of time in return for regular payments.

> **Explanation:** If a business needs new equipment it can either buy or lease it. Leasing works very like *hire purchase*, except the hirer does not own the goods at the end of the lease. If the firm decides to lease equipment, it is obtained from a supplier in the normal way.

- The supplier is paid by a *finance company*.
- The firm leasing the goods (the *lessee*) has a contract with the finance company. The lessee agrees to lease the goods for a fixed time (say three years) and pays the finance company a fixed sum over those three years.
- At the end of the contract, the finance company takes the goods back, or extends the contract for another fixed period of time. Sometimes the finance company will give the firm the chance to buy the goods cheaply.

Advantages of leasing:

- It saves having to find all the money for a large item of *capital expenditure* at once. The capital can be used for some other purpose.
- It avoids *cash flow* problems that might result from having to pay out a large sum for the equipment.
- Usually all maintenance costs are included in the lease fees; these would have to be paid in addition if the equipment were owned.

Disadvantages of leasing:

- The goods are never owned by the firm leasing the equipment.
- The total cost of the equipment will probably be greater than that of buying it outright. This is because the finance company is effectively lending the price of the equipment. The cost of leasing includes the cost of the goods plus interest and the finance company's costs and profits.

ledger: the main accounting book in which all transactions are recorded using the *double entry* system of *bookkeeping*.

ledger accounts: the individual accounting records kept in the *ledger*.

legislation is law that is made by Parliament. This is usually by means of an Act of Parliament. Legislation also includes regulations, called Statutory Instruments, issued under Acts of Parliament.

liability is a debt owed by a business. The liabilities of a business are shown in the *balance sheet*.

There are three types of liability:

- **Current liabilities** – the short-term debts of the business; these are debts that must be paid within one year. Examples are *trade creditors* and *bank overdraft*.

- **The long-term debts of a business** – these are debts that will not be paid off for more than one year. Examples would include *debentures* and a *bank loan*.

- **The capital** – what the business owes to its owners. In the case of a *limited liability* company this will be the *issued capital* of the business.

limited company: a company the owners of which have *limited liability*. Limited companies have a legal existence separate from their owners; they have been *incorporated*.

There are three types of limited company:

- **Private limited companies** – those where shares in the company cannot be sold to the general public. The name of the company always ends with 'Limited' or 'Ltd.'

- **Public limited companies** – those where the shares are sold to the general public and dealt on the *Stock Exchange*. The name of the company must end with 'plc'.

- **Companies limited by guarantee** – whose members promise to pay a sum of money if the company is wound up. Their liability is limited to the sum agreed. Such companies are usually non-profit making companies, for example, examination boards, clubs or charities.

limited liability: when the liability of the shareholders in a company is limited to the amount of their original investment if the business should fail.

> **Explanation:** Many people will not want to invest in business if they could lose everything they own if the business failed. This is especially true if a person is providing *capital* but has no say in the day-to-day running of the business. The idea of limited liability was developed to encourage investment in business, through the buying of shares.

Advantages of limited liability:

- People know the size of the risk they are taking. All they can lose is the amount they invested in the business. Because the amount they can lose is limited, people are more willing to invest in firms.

- The risk of loss can be spread over a large number of people.

- Small amounts of capital can be collected together. Separately the amounts might be too small to use in business, but they become important when gathered together and controlled under one management.

(Compare with *unlimited liability*.)

limited partnership is a form of *partnership* where at least one of the *partners* has *limited liability*. Such partners just invest money in the business and are paid a share of the profits. They are not allowed to take part in the running of the business. In a limited partnership there must be at least one partner with *unlimited liability*. Limited partnerships are rarely found. They have to be registered with the *Registrar of Companies*.

line manager: the manager responsible for all the people and activities that are on lower levels in an organisation's *hierarchy*. Instructions from above will be passed 'down the line' through the line manager to the people lower down the organisation. The line manager is a worker's immediate boss.

line organisation is a form of organisation where there are direct lines of authority to each level of management. The levels of responsibility can be traced downwards from the top through each level to the shop floor.

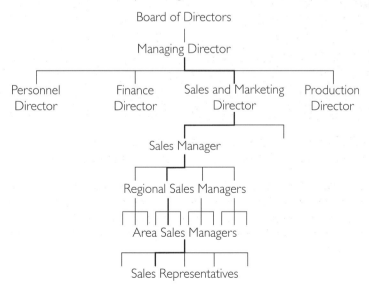

Explanation: The traditional way of drawing an organisation chart is on a line diagram showing the *chain of command*. An example of this is shown overleaf.

At each level it is clear for whom and what the person in charge is responsible. At each level the person in charge is answerable to the person above. Everyone knows their own and other people's positions in the organisation.

liquid asset: an *asset* that can be easily changed into *cash*. The most liquid asset of all is cash, followed by cash in the bank, debtors and stock, in that order.

liquidation: when a company stops trading and its assets are turned into cash.

Explanation: A business may 'go into liquidation' either voluntarily or because it is forced to.

- It will go into voluntary liquidation when either:
  - the owners want to retire
  - or directors of a firm see that it is going to become *insolvent* and take action to close it.
- It may be forced into liquidation if creditors decide to stop it from building up more debts. They will petition the courts to *wind up* the company.

When a firm goes into liquidation the court appoints a *liquidator* whose job is to sell the company's assets for the best possible price. The money from the sale of the assets is used to pay the debts. An individual becomes *bankrupt* but a company goes into liquidation.

liquidator: a person appointed by a Court to close down a company. A liquidator must sell all the company's assets and use the money to pay its debts.

Explanation: A liquidator is usually an accountant. All the assets are sold and creditors paid in a certain order. First will be any tax due, followed by secured creditors; these are creditors who have some kind of security for money lent to the firm (e.g. debenture holders). Trade creditors come next with shareholders being the last people to be paid. Often there is not enough money to pay all the debts. The *creditors* will then be paid a percentage of what they are owed.

liquidity is the ability of a business to pay its short-term debts as they become due. The liquidity of a firm will depend on how easily it can turn its *current assets* into cash.

liquidity ratio: a measure of a firm's ability to pay its debts. It is also known as the *current ratio* and as the *working capital ratio*.

listed company: a company whose shares are listed on the *Stock Exchange*.

Lloyds: a market for insurance based in London. Lloyds is not an insurance company. It has members called *underwriters* and *brokers*. The underwriters do not deal directly with the public. It is Lloyds brokers who deal with the public. Lloyds underwriters take on insurance risks from all over the world. They will accept any risk of any size, from a small car to the world's largest building. It is important to Britain's *balance of payments*.

loan capital consists of the long-term loans of a business. It will include *bank loans* and *debentures* and possibly company *bonds*. Not every business has loan capital.

local government consists of a range of locally elected councils. England and Wales are divided into either county councils (e.g. Dorset and Cumbria) or into metropolitan districts (e.g. Birmingham). The counties are further broken down into borough or district and parish councils.

> ***Explanation:*** Local councils get their money from the council tax, business rates, government grants, borrowing and fees from, for example, leisure centres, market rents and cemeteries. They spend the money on providing services. Not all local councils provide all services. Some services are provided for local authorities by private firms. These are services they used to provide themselves. Many have had to be offered for compulsory *competitive tendering*. Examples include refuse collection, road maintenance, school cleaning.

local pay bargaining is where pay negotiations are carried out in an area, or in an individual company or branch of a business. Local pay bargaining has replaced national negotiations in many industries.

location of industry: where firms decide to site their businesses geographically.

> ***Explanation:*** Firms do not always have all of their business in the same place. Large companies have branches in many places, often abroad as well as in this country. There are a number of factors that may influence a firm's decision on where to locate its business.

- **Industrial tradition** means that some industries are found mainly in one area. Originally the industries settled in that area because they were near their raw materials, or near a port. Examples of such industries are cotton in Lancashire, woollen cloth in Yorkshire and the potteries in Staffordshire. New firms entering the industry will often settle in the same area.

- **Proximity to raw materials** — firms used to locate near their raw materials. The industrial Midlands developed around coal and iron ore. Oil refineries are on the coast because crude oil can either be piped ashore from the North Sea or brought by ship from abroad. Where raw materials are bulky and expensive to transport, firms locate near to them. Brickworks are built near the clay; cement is produced around Rugby because the raw materials are close at hand.

- **Natural resources** are very important for some industries. Flowers are grown in the Scilly Isles because it has a mild climate. Fruit and vegetables are grown in Kent and in the Vale of Evesham because the growing conditions are right. A hydro-electric power station can only be built where there is plenty of water and a steep hill.

- **Proximity to the market** – some goods can be produced anywhere so they are made near the market to keep transport costs as low as possible. Many component suppliers are found close to their customers, for example, firms supplying car components to Midlands car makers are also in the Midlands. Some goods like bread have to be made on the day they are sold and must therefore be close to their market. Many service industries have to be near to the customer (e.g. hairdressers, banks and retailers).

- **Good transport links** – firms want to be able to get their supplies as quickly as possible. They also want to get their finished goods out efficiently. They try to avoid towns because of traffic problems and locate near good transport links, especially motorways. Many distribution firms are sited just off motorway junctions.

- **The cost of land** – this varies between areas. Land is expensive in large towns, which is one reason why there are so many out-of-town shopping centres. Land is cheaper in the north of England than in the south-east. Firms needing large sites are attracted to the cheaper areas.

- **Availability of labour** will attract firms to an area. Many firms have been attracted to areas of high unemployment because there is plenty of labour available.

- **Grants** are offered by local and central government to attract firms to certain areas. Regional Development Corporations have been set up to attract new industries to Wales and the north-east and Scotland. They have been able to offer very large grants to companies locating in their area. Sometimes they offer other things, like factories that are rent-free for a time.

- **Proximity of other firms** in the same industry will attract firms to an area. There may be some external *economies of scale* as a result. There may be a supply of labour with the right kind of skills or local colleges which have training courses geared to the needs of the industry. Component suppliers will also be close at hand.

lock-out: when a firm locks out workers from the premises. This may happen in a dispute when a firm believes that the workers may try to take over the premises or there is some security risk.

logo: a symbol used by a business so that it can be easily identified. It is part of *marketing*. The company hopes that when people see the logo they will recognise it, and think of their product. Many logos are registered as *trade marks*.

loss occurs when a business sells its goods or services for less than it cost to make them. The *total revenue* of the business will be less than its *total costs*. This cannot be allowed to carry on for long but a firm may make a loss for a short time or while the sales of a product are building up.

loss leader: a product that is deliberately sold for less than its *cost price* to attract customers. It is a part of *marketing*. Retailers heavily advertise one article at a loss hoping that once people are in the shop they will also buy other, normally priced goods. Supermarkets often use bread and sugar as loss leaders.

Maastricht: the treaty which led to the *European Community* being widened into the *European Union*. The treaty took Europe further towards political union. The timetable and terms for *European monetary union* were also laid down in the Maastricht Treaty. Maastricht extended the Treaty of Rome. The treaty is named after a small Dutch town where it was signed.

mail order: a form of *retailing* that depends on *orders* received by post, telephone, fax or e-mail.

> **Explanation:** Mail order is a popular way of selling goods. There are three main types of seller:

- The large, specialist catalogue firms, like Great Universal Stores, Littlewoods and Freemans. They sell a similar variety of goods to department stores. The people who take a catalogue are called *agents* who are paid a *commission* on the goods they sell.

- Manufacturers and wholesalers that sell direct to the public. They advertise in the press and magazines and issue a catalogue to display their goods. Examples include Racing Green, Cotton Traders, Innovations and some of the garden seed and bulb sellers.

- Small manufacturers and shops that advertise their goods in the press and magazines. They may be specialist manufacturers and shops selling handmade goods such as light fittings and furniture. Some specialist businesses, such as model shops or antique dealers, advertise in specialist magazines.

Selling by mail order saves having expensive showrooms. It is a fairly easy and cheap way for small firms to reach a wider public.

Mail order can widen the range of goods available to people living in remote areas and the housebound. The disadvantage is that the goods cannot be examined before they are sent for. Having to send back goods that are not wanted can be expensive and a nuisance.

management accounting is the part of accounting that gives managers the information they need to run the business. It provides the financial data needed for day-to-day decision making and future planning. Most of the information is about the costs of each department or product. Past results may be used to predict what will happen in the future. Compare this with *financial accounting*.

management buy-in: this happens when the majority of the shares of a company are bought by outside managers in order to gain control. The buyers believe that they will be able to run the business more profitably.

Usually the managers in a buy-in have financial backing from *banks* and *venture capital* firms. It is not the same thing as a *takeover* where a company may be bought unwillingly. In a buy-in and a *buyout* the firm is willing to sell and may even want to sell.

management buyout: this happens when the majority of the shares in a business are bought by the existing management in order to gain control. They become the owners of the company they are already working in. This may happen when a large company decides to sell off the parts of its business that do not fit in with the rest of its activities. As with a *management buy-in*, the managers have to get financial backing from *banks* and *venture capital*.

manager: a person responsible for the control and supervision of an activity or group of activities. Every department in a firm will have its manager who makes the decisions about the day-to-day running of the department. All the people working in the department will be answerable to the manager. Each manager is accountable to the next tier above in the organisation.

manpower planning is forecasting the number and type of people that will be needed by an organisation. There should be plans for each of the next three to five years.

> **Explanation:** Companies should plan ahead and estimate the skills and the number and kind of people they need. If they have too few staff, or people with the wrong skills, they may not be able to meet their orders. If they have people they cannot fully employ, their costs rise and may make them uncompetitive.

manual workers are people who work with their hands. They usually work in factories and are sometimes referred to as 'blue collar workers'.

They can be classified as:

- skilled; for example, toolmaker, electrician, qualified fitter

- semi-skilled; for example, electrician's mate, driver, machine operative

- unskilled; for example, cleaner, labourer.

margin is the amount of gross profit a company is making as a percentage of its sales. It is also called the *gross margin*.

> **FORMULA *for calculating margin:***
>
> $$\text{Gross margin} = \frac{\text{Gross profit} \times 100}{\text{Sales}}$$

The greater the margin, the more money a business has available to pay its expenses. When the margin is 'tight' (small), firms have to control their costs carefully if they are to make a *net profit*. Margins tend to be tight when there is fierce competition. Firms are not able to pass on cost increases by putting up their prices. If they did so their goods might become uncompetitive.

marginal cost is the cost of producing one extra unit of output. *Fixed costs* stay the same so the marginal cost is therefore made up of *variable costs*. Marginal cost is equal to the increase in total *costs* resulting from producing one extra unit.

> **Example:** If the cost of producing 49 units of a product is £99 but it only costs £100 to make 50 units, the marginal cost of producing the 50th is £1. The *average cost* of making 50 units however, is £2.

> It costs the firm £2 each to make the first 50 units. But if a customer offered to buy a further 10 units at £1.50 each the firm might accept the order. It will do so because it knows that the marginal cost is only £1 for each of the extra units.

market: the place where buyers and sellers meet. It is where the consumers wanting to buy a product or service make contact with those that have goods to sell.

The term 'market' is also used for the group of people willing to buy a product or service. A particular product may have more than one market. For example, a certain model of car will be bought privately or as a company car. These are two separate and different markets. Each market has different needs and different characteristics.

market economy: an economy in which the allocation of resources is decided by *market forces* only. The system works automatically and governments do not interfere in its working. It is the same thing as a *free market*. Hong Kong, Singapore and Taiwan are examples of market economies.

> **Explanation:** In a market economy it is *supply* and *demand* that determine where and how resources are used.

- Resources are used for those goods for which there is a demand, at a price. If people no longer want certain goods the resources will be transferred to those things for which there is a demand.

- Sellers of goods and services have to sell at a price that buyers are willing to pay. If the prices are too high there will be no demand for the goods. Prices must be cut to a level people are prepared to buy at, or the firms go out of business.

- When the price is right all the goods supplied will be demanded.

Benefits of the market economy:

- It encourages initiative. Successful people and businesses do well, the unsuccessful ones fail. The businesses that develop new ideas and methods and keep prices low, will prosper.

- Economic growth is encouraged and the economy is more efficient. Only the most successful firms survive. They produce what people want at the right price. They keep their prices low by being efficient.

- Competition is encouraged and gives consumers a wider choice. New companies can enter the market. Companies do not want to raise their prices because it would give their competitors an advantage.

Weaknesses of the market economy:

- It is a very harsh system. Economic power may be concentrated in a few hands. Those with most money will have the greatest power. The weakest parts of society may be exploited. People with poor education and no skills can only get lower-paid jobs. This leads to big differences in income between the very highly paid and the low paid.

- It is a wasteful system. Competition may result in more firms than necessary, all doing similar things. Valuable resources may not be used because there is no demand for them (e.g. coal).

- The *social costs* of production may be ignored. Because profit is very important the effects of production on the environment may not be taken into account.

market forces: the operation of *supply* and *demand* in an economy. These two forces work together to decide what is produced and at what price goods and services are sold.

Explanation: If *producers* try to sell goods at a high price the demand may be very small. If they drop their price, demand will increase. This will carry on until a price is reached at which supply and demand are equal. The market forces of supply and demand, therefore, decide how much is produced and at what price.

The diagram overleaf shows that:

- price will settle at the point P when the quantity demanded is Q

- at any price less than P, there will be more goods demanded than supplied. Suppliers will either increase the supply of goods or the price will rise until supply and demand are equal

- at any price higher than P, there will be more goods on the market than there is a demand for; suppliers will either reduce the supply of goods or price will fall.

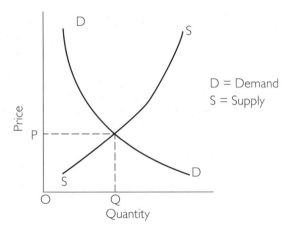

market niche: a gap in the market for a range of products. It is a possible market that is not currently being satisfied. It will probably provide a small but specialised market.

market penetration is the extent to which a firm has been able to gain *market share*. A high market share means greater market penetration. The term is also used for the policy of setting a low price for products in order to increase market share, often described as *penetration pricing*.

market position: the particular part of a market at which a firm decides to target sales of its product. People have different wants depending on their age, or income, whether or not they are married or have children. Many clothes shops position themselves to sell to the young and fashionable. Some set out to appeal to the 25 to 35 age group. Others will aim to sell to the better-off who want designer label clothes.

market pricing occurs when the prices of goods are fixed at about the same level as the prices of other goods in the same market. This may be done to avoid *price wars*.

market research is the collection of information by a firm about existing and potential markets. The firm will use *field research* and *desk research* to collect information about social and economic trends and the attitudes, lifestyles, likes and dislikes of existing and potential customers. It will also try to find out as much as possible about its competitors. A firm's *marketing department* may do its own market research or it may hire a specialist market research company.

Reasons for market research:

- Companies need to know as much as possible about their market. They study trends in population, earnings and the ways people spend their money. They not only look at what is happening now, but at estimates for some years ahead.

- It pays to find out what customers want, and to know the things that make people buy one product rather than another and the price people are willing to pay.

- Companies want to know who their customers are and what they and the public think about the product. If sales are falling they want to know why. Are customers satisfied with the goods or service? How can it be improved?

- A firm may be thinking of launching a new product. It will want to know whether people will buy it, what price they would be willing to pay and whether the name and the packaging are suitable?

- Companies need to know as much as they can about their competitors and their goods.

The information collected is different for different products. For example, colour will be important for some goods, but not for others. Companies use the information collected to make decisions about how to *target* their marketing.

Market research methods:

- **Field research** – the collection of information from *primary sources*, directly or first-hand from the public.

- **Desk research** – using *secondary sources* that are generally available.

market saturation occurs when the market for a product is fully satisfied. It does not mean that everybody has the product, but most people who want it, have. If it is a *consumer durable*, such as a television set or furniture, there will still be a market because it will wear out or become out of date and have to be replaced. If it is a *consumable* there will be a steady sale but the market will not grow.

market segmentation is the breaking down of a market for a product into different groups or types of consumer. Each group or segment of the market can be seen to have different wants. All segments share some common features but each may be targeted differently. The market may be divided into segments in several ways. Firms will choose to segment their markets in the way that is most suitable for their products. The following are possibilities:

- geographically, by region; different regions have slightly different tastes

- by population, by age, gender, or ethnic background

- by income

- by social position and buying habits.

market share is the proportion of the total sales of a product that has been gained by a brand or company. Market share is usually measured as a percentage of the <u>value</u> of the goods in a market. Some products, like cars, are better measured in terms of the share of the total <u>number</u> sold.

Explanation: Companies watch their market share carefully. It shows them how important they are in the 'league table' of producers of a product. If a brand's market share starts to fall, its competitors are winning some of its customers. In that case the company may need to improve its product, change the price or improve the marketing.

market skimming is the result of setting a very high price for a new product. A firm may do this to appeal to the rich. It also tries to attract those people who are willing to pay highly, just to have the latest and newest thing on the market. The product may be given a false scarcity value. The firm will be forced to reduce the price when competitors enter the market. In the meantime it will have made a large profit on each item sold. (See also *skimming*)

market testing involves selling a new product in one area of the country to see how well it sells.

Explanation: It is very expensive to develop and market a new product. A company may prefer to limit the cost of launching a product by having a limited trial. During the trial the company carries out very detailed *market research* to find out what people think of the product. On the basis of the results from this trial they will decide:

- if any changes need to be made e.g. to the product itself or the way it is packaged

- whether to *launch* the product nationally or abandon it.

market value is the price that people are prepared to pay for a product. It is the price decided by the *supply* and *demand* for a product. Something may have cost very little to make, but it may be very rare and therefore have a high market value. The market value of shares will be different from their *nominal value*. If there is a big demand, the market value of shares may be high but the market value may be less than the nominal value if the company is thought to be in difficulty.

Example: Suppose a sheet of stamps is bought at the Post Office which has a mistake in the printing and there is only one such sheet known to exist.

In this case the supply is very small and there is a (relatively) big demand from collectors. Supply and demand determine a high price which does not depend on the nominal value of the stamps or the cost of producing them.

marketing is a range of activities which ensures that customers get what they want, in the right amounts, at the right time and at the right price. Among these activities are:

- identifying the size and type of customers' needs and wants
- deciding which markets to serve
- deciding what products and services to provide at what price
} Market research

- informing customers through *advertising* and *promotion* of the products
- *distribution* – getting the goods to the customer.

marketing department: this function represents the interests of the customer within a business. It acts as a bridge between the customer and the production department.

> **Explanation:** The design, price and the quality of the goods have to be what the customer wants. There is no point in making things that customers will not buy. The marketing department tries to explain the needs and wants of the customer to the design and production departments. So that the goods produced sell it finds out what customers want through *market research*. Once the product is made, the marketing department is involved in the *advertising, promotion* and *distribution* of the product. It may do all these things itself or with the help of an *advertising agency*.

marketing mix: this is the full range of activities that may be used by a business to market its products. The mix is usually referred to as the *four Ps*.

- **Product** – this is the product or service itself; its name or *branding*, its design, its quality, its appearance, its special features, number of models or sizes, after sales service

- **Place** – how the product is distributed, where it can be bought

- **Price** – the price at which the product will be sold; the prices of competing goods will be taken into account

- **Promotion** – the methods used to sell a product including advertising, other publicity, discounts, special offers, point of sale displays, and direct marketing.

Sometimes a fifth 'P' is added for *packaging*; some experts see packaging as part of the product, others think it is part of the promotion.

The marketing mix is different for every product. A new car will be marketed in a different way to a new chocolate bar. The emphasis of the marketing mix depends on the *target market* for the product.

marketing plan: a detailed statement of how the marketing of a product is to be carried out. For example, it shows where the product is to advertised, how often or for how long, and how much each advertising site will cost. The marketing plan shows in detail how the *marketing strategy* is to be carried out.

marketing strategy: a report that sets out the marketing objectives for a business. It refers to the business as a whole, not just to one product.

Marketing strategy is in three parts:

1 **Where are we now?** This part reviews the current marketing of the business, looks at the costs and tries to assess its success. It may also include a *SWOT analysis* of the firm's products.

2 **Where do we want to be?** This part sets out the objectives of the company and shows how the marketing objectives fit in with them. It sets targets, for example, for total sales and market share for the next one, three and five years.

3 **How do we get there?** This part shows how the marketing mix is applied to each of the company's products. It includes the marketing *budget.*

mark-up is the amount added on to the cost price by the seller of an article. The mark-up will be equal to the gross profit.

FORMULA *for calculating mark-up/gross profit:*

Cost price + Mark-up (Gross profit) = Selling price

CP + GP = SP

Therefore:

SP – CP = GP

SP – GP = CP

Mark-up is usually stated as a percentage of cost (cost price):

$$\text{Mark-up} = \frac{\text{Gross profit}}{\text{Cost price}} \times 100$$

Worked examples

1 If a sweater cost £10 to buy and the seller makes £5 gross profit on each item what is the seller's mark-up?

$$\text{Mark-up} = \frac{\text{GP}}{\text{CP}} = \frac{£5}{£10} \times 100 = 50\%$$

2 If a sweater cost £10 to buy and it was sold for £15 what is the seller's mark-up?

$$\text{Mark-up} = \frac{SP - CP}{CP} \times 100$$

$$= \frac{£15 - £10}{£10} \times 100 = 50\%$$

3 If a sweater selling for £15 had a mark up of 50% what would the cost price be?

$$\text{If } \frac{GP}{CP} = \frac{50}{100} \text{ then } \frac{GP}{SP} = \frac{GP}{CP + GP} \times 100$$

$$= \frac{50}{100 + 50} \times 100 = 33.3\%$$

$$\text{Therefore cost price} = SP - \frac{SP}{GP} = £15 - (15 \times 33.3\%)$$

$$= £15 - £5 = £10$$

Maslow, Abraham: an American psychologist who tried to explain why people need to work. He said that people have five types or ranges of needs that they try to satisfy. These form a 'hierarchy of needs'. Maslow believed that each set of needs has to be completely satisfied before people move to the next set of needs. Once the first set of needs has been satisfied, people move on to the next set of needs, and so on, until all their needs have been satisfied.

Maslow's five sets of needs are:

1 **Basic –** the basic human needs are for food, clothing and shelter. People must have these things so that they and their families can survive. They must have an income to be able to meet these basic needs.

2 **Safety –** once the basic needs are satisfied people need to feel safe. People need to feel sure they can survive, and have order and security in their lives. They need to be safe in their homes and at work. If their jobs are secure they will be able to provide security for themselves and their families.

3 **Social –** once people can meet their basic needs and they feel safe, their social needs grow. People need to feel they belong. They want friendship and companionship and to be part of a group.

4 **Esteem –** this is the need to be confident and to receive respect from other people. Most important is to feel the self-respect that comes from being useful and successful.

5   **Self-fulfilment or Self-actualisation** – this is the need for
     satisfaction from realising personal ambition. It is the need to gain
     satisfaction from doing an important worthwhile job and taking
     responsibility.

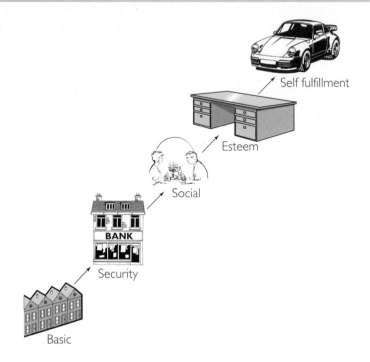

Self fulfillment

Esteem

Social

BANK

Security

Basic

mass production is when goods are produced in large quantities on a
continuous production line. The speed at which people work depends on the
speed at which the line moves. Each person working on the line is responsible
for only a small part of a finished product before it then moves on to the next
person. It is also known as *flow production*.

maturity is the point in the *product life cycle* when the sales of a product are
at their highest. The product is firmly established in the market. It will have
maximised its market share and be at its most profitable. Competitors are then
attracted into the market with more up to date versions of the product.
Beyond maturity the product will go into *decline*, but still make a profit, at least
for a while.

mean: the arithmetic average of a group of numbers. It is the total of a group
of numbers divided by how many numbers there are in the group. Thus the
average of 4, 5, 6, 7, 8, 9 is:

$$\frac{4 + 5 + 6 + 7 + 8 + 9}{6} = \frac{39}{6} = 6.5$$

media: a loose term used to describe radio, television and all aspects of the press. The media are of interest to business because of their use in advertising. Other items and issues they bring to public attention may also influence consumers' buying habits.

memorandum: a form of written communication that is mainly used within an organisation. It is used when written proof of communication is needed.

Features of memoranda:

- they are shorter and not as formal as business letters
- they do not contain a full address
- they are sent to a named person
- they are not signed by the sender, but may be initialled

Example: a typical memorandum pro-forma

> ## MEMORANDUM
>
> **To:**
>
> **From:**
>
> **Reference:**
>
> **Date:**
>
> **Subject heading**

memorandum of association: one of the documents that must be sent to the *Registrar of Companies* when a *limited company* is formed. The memorandum of association must include the following things:

- **The name of the company** – this must be different from that of any other company, and must include the word 'Limited' or 'Ltd' if it is a *private limited company* or limited by guarantee; or *plc* if it a *public limited company*.
- **The address** of the registered office of the company.
- **The objects of the company** – these are very important because they state what the company is allowed to do. A company is not

allowed to do things not covered by the objects clause. For example, if the objects clause said a company was going to produce concrete bird baths, it could not then produce other concrete products. The objects clause should be as general as possible.

- **A statement that the liability of members (shareholders) is limited.**

- **A statement of the authorised capital** – the total amount of *share capital* and the amount of each type of share the company intends to issue. It is the maximum share capital the company is allowed to issue. It is the *authorised capital* of the business. A public limited company must have an authorised capital of at least £50 000.

- **The signatures** of at least two members (who must each hold at least one share) must be on the memorandum.

Changes to any part of the memorandum of association need a special vote at the company's *annual general meeting*.

MEP: see *European Parliament.*

merchandise: a loose term that is often used to describe the goods available for sale by a business. It is usually used in the context of retailing.

merchandising: the methods used by *retailers* to display the goods available for sale in their shops. It may only be a window display but large stores often site display stands in various parts of the store. They may have demonstrations of goods and promotions for a group of products. Manufacturers sometimes provide display materials for shops of all sizes. Merchandising is the *point of sale* promotion of goods. Recently the term has been extended to include the sale of spin off products from copyright material. Examples include the sale of kit by league football clubs, T-shirts by pop groups and items related to films (e.g. Disney cartoon characters or Star Wars).

merger: when two companies agree to join together to form one new company. The new company has one *board of directors* where there were two. There will also only be one management and one department of administration. This may lead to *redundancies*. Mergers are a quick way for companies to expand. Compare mergers with *takeovers* where one company buys another.

Examples:

- Lloyds Bank and TSB merged to form the largest bank in the UK

- Sun Alliance Insurance and Royal Insurance merged to form Royal Sun Alliance Insurance

method study is the procedure used for observing and measuring the way workers perform a job. Each operation is timed and watched to see if the job can be simplified and time saved. The time taken to do a job may also be used as a basis for calculating *piece rates*.

middlemen act as a link in a *chain of distribution* for goods and services. They are *agents*, *brokers* and *wholesalers* who help to bring buyers and sellers together. Manufacturers often prefer to work through a fairly small number of middlemen. Without them, manufacturers would need bigger sales forces. The middlemen *break bulk* and supply the next link in the *chain of distribution* with the smaller quantities required.

minutes are the official record of a meeting. They should state the date and place of a meeting, list the names of the people present, and record any decisions taken at the meeting.

mixed economy: one that is made up of both privately-owned and state-owned enterprises. Part of the economy is thus run by private business, the rest controlled by the state. The amount of private business will vary. In some of the newer mixed economies there is very little privately owned business. It may be little more than selling vegetables in local markets. In others, such as that of Britain, most business is privately run. The state provides services such as health, education, roads and other essential services.

mobility of labour: see *labour mobility*.

modem: equipment attached to a computer to enable one computer to be linked to another via the telephone system.

monetary policy: this is the government policy on the total *money supply* in an economy. It is mainly controlled by the Bank of England, primarily through interest rates, and governs the amount of money available to spend. Changes in interest rates affect the amount of savings, credit and *exchange rates*.

money supply is the total supply of money circulating in an economy. Money is not just cash, it includes deposits in banks and building societies. It also includes the total amount owing on credit. Control of the money supply is important as too much money in circulation can lead to *inflation*.

money transfer services: these are the services provided, mainly by the banks, for transferring funds without the need to use cash. The services include *cheques*, *direct debits*, *debit cards*, *credit transfers*, and *standing orders*.

Monopolies and Mergers Commission (MMC): set up by Act of Parliament, it is independent of the government, although it is funded by it. The job of the MMC is to carry out enquiries into matters referred to it by the

Department of Trade and Industry or by the *Office of Fair Trading*. It is not able to decide for itself what to investigate.

> **Explanation:** One way of protecting consumers is to make sure that competition is as open and fair as possible. Monopolies and mergers reduce the amount of competition. The MMC is asked to advise on whether or not certain mergers or monopolies are in the 'public interest'. The Office of Fair Trading can ask it to report on any matter that may restrict competition. The MMC has no powers to carry out its recommendations. That is left to the Department of Trade and Industry.

monopoly: in theory a monopoly exists when there is only one firm which supplies a product. In practice this does not happen very often. In reality a monopoly is said to exist when one firm, or a small group of firms, is so powerful that it can fix the price of the goods. In this country many of the *privatised* industries used to be monopolies. They were owned by the state and were very carefully controlled to stop them exploiting consumers. Since they have been privatised they are controlled by *regulators* one of whose main jobs is to look after consumers' interests.

mortgage: the signing over of property to a lender as security for a loan. If the repayments on the loan are not kept up, the property can be taken over by the lender and sold. In that way they can be sure of getting their money back. Mortgages are used mainly in the housing market.

motivation: the factors that make a person want to do something. It is quite hard to define because people's reasons for doing things differ. In the business context motivation consists of the reasons that people have for wanting to work, or work harder, or wanting to start up a business. Some of the things that motivate workers are the need to buy food, have clothes and a home. For others it will be conditions at work, ambition or *job satisfaction*. (See also *Maslow*.)

multinational: a company which has its head office in one country but has branches or factories in several other countries.

Advantages of multinationals:

- Multinationals bring in new *investment* to a country. In poor countries they provide investment that the country itself could not afford. They create new jobs and increase total income. There will be more money to spend resulting in more shops, better services and a higher standard of living.

- They may introduce new methods and new technology. Japanese car makers, for example, helped to introduce new technology and management methods in the British car industry.

- They may provide training and so improve the quality of the skills in a country. In some cases they employ local people as managers. They may help to improve roads and other forms of *infrastructure*.

- If the goods they make are exported, they help a country's *balance of payments*.

Disadvantages of multinationals:

- Multinationals can decide to move production to some other branch of their business. They may make such decisions for their own reasons which do not take into account the effects on a country's economy.

- Because of their importance they may have too much power and political influence.

- The jobs they create may only be low-level jobs. They may bring in people from their own country for the skilled and management jobs. A country may not benefit very much from them because all the profits are returned to the country where the head office is based.

multiple stores are shops that have a number of branches selling the same group of products. The shops will all look the same and will be run from a head office which buys all goods centrally. Examples include Boots, Marks and Spencer, Halfords and Next.

multi-skilled: where workers are trained in more than one skill and are thus able to do more than one job. This results in a more flexible workforce. Workers can be moved to where they are needed. It may also mean there are fewer *demarcation* disputes.

national bargaining happens when *trades unions* negotiate with *employers* on a national basis. They may do this for a whole industry or for just one company. There is now much less national bargaining than there used to be. It is slowly being replaced by *local bargaining*. Companies know that average wages are different for different parts of the country. They may therefore be able to save money if pay rates are based on local averages instead of one rate for the whole country.

national debt: the total amount of money borrowed and therefore owed by a country.

> **Explanation:** The government has to borrow money because taxes and income do not come in steadily through the year. In some years the government spends more than it collects. It then has a *deficit* on the *budget*. The government does not just print the money it needs. It borrows the money by selling *stocks* ('gilts') to the *banks*, other *financial institutions* and the public. These stocks may not be repaid for many years. *Gilt-edged securities* can be bought and sold on the *Stock Exchange*.

national income is the total of all incomes earned by people in a country during a year. This income comes from *wages*, *salaries*, *profits*, *dividends*, *rents* and *interest* payments. It is quite difficult to measure accurately. Income is a constant flow of money so any statement of national income is a snap-shot at just one moment.

National Insurance is the means of paying for the system of welfare benefits provided through the government. The benefits include the National Health Service, sickness and unemployment benefits and the state retirement pension. These are paid for from taxes and through compulsory National Insurance *deductions* from the wages and salaries of people in work. The amount paid depends on how much a person earns. Employers also make a contribution.

national pay bargaining: see *national bargaining*.

National Vocational Qualifications (NVQ): a national system of vocational qualifications. NVQs are industry based practical tests of a person's ability to do a specific job at work.

> **Explanation:** Until 1986 there were a large number of bodies that issued vocational qualifications. Each one had its own examinations and decided its own standards. There was no central body to control what they did or to make sure they all used the same standards. This variety of qualifications has been replaced by a single national vocational qualification. It is called the National Vocational Qualification (NVQ). It is based on what employers said they wanted workers to be able to do at each level. All qualifications at a certain level are at the same standard.

The NVQ is now administered by the *Qualifications and Curriculum Authority (QCA)*. It does not set its own examinations or tests or issue certificates. The tests and examinations are set and the certificates are issued by awarding bodies. Before any awarding body can issue NVQs it has to be approved by the QCA. The qualifications they issue have to meet the standards laid down by the QCA.

- NVQs are based on the idea of being able to do a particular job properly at work. This is termed competence. Tests of competence try to find out whether a person can do the job quickly, safely and accurately. NVQ tests are mainly practical and contain very little theory. Higher levels have more theory in them than the lower levels.

- NVQs are set at five levels. Level I is the basic operative level and level 5 is professional standard.

nationalisation occurs when companies and industries are taken over by the state. It happens when *private sector* companies become *public sector* organisations and is the opposite of *privatisation*.

natural wastage occurs when a firm wishing to reduce its *labour* waits for people to leave or retire instead of making workers *redundant*. When a *vacancy* arises the firm does not fill the post. Natural wastage may come about through retirements or people changing jobs. For the firm it is a cheap way of reducing its labour costs.

negotiations occur when two groups work together to arrive at a position that both can accept. Negotiations may be between two or more companies trying to agree the terms of a contract. They may also be between *trades unions* and employers to agree pay and conditions. In negotiations there will be some bargaining. It is rare for any side to get exactly all it hoped to achieve.

net assets are the assets that a company has after all its liabilities, except shareholder capital, have been taken away from the total assets.

FORMULA *for net assets:*

$$\text{Net assets} = \text{Total assets} - \text{Current liabilities} - \text{Long-term liabilities}$$

net earnings are a person's total income from all sources minus any deductions. A person's earnings are composed of wages or salary, plus dividends from shares, plus interest received on bank or building society accounts. The deductions will mainly be tax, National Insurance and any pension contributions.

net income: the same as *net earnings*.

net margin: see *net profit margin.*

net pay is the figure shown on a person's *pay slip* that states what he/she will actually be paid. It is made up of his or her gross pay minus all *deductions* made by the employer. These will usually be *income tax* and *National Insurance.* Other deductions might include superannuation payments and *trades union* subscriptions.

net profit is the gross profit earned by a business *minus* all the expenses of running the business.

> FORMULA *for calculating net profit:*
>
> **Net profit = Gross profit – Running expenses**

The net profit will be calculated in the *profit and loss account* for the business.

Example:

Profit and Loss Account for XYX & Company Limited for the year ended 31 December

	£	£
Gross profit		100 000
Wages	30 000	
Salaries	25 000	
Rent	15 000	
Heating and lighting	11 000	
Telephones	4 000	
Insurance	2 500	
Depreciation	6 000	93 500
Net profit		6 500

net profit margin: the amount of *net profit* a business is making as a percentage of its sales.

> FORMULA *for calculating net profit margin:*
>
> $$\text{Net profit margin} = \frac{\text{Net profit}}{\text{Sales}} \times 100$$

The net margin gives a better idea of how well a business is doing than does the *gross margin.* All the day-to-day running costs are taken into account so that the net margin is the true rate of profit for the business before tax.

Example: Suppose a firm's *trading and profit and loss account* showed the following information over two years:

	Year 1 £	Year 2 £
Sales	5 000	10 000
Cost of sales	2 500	6 000
Gross profit	2 500	4 000
Expenses	1 000	2 500
Net profit	1 500	1 500

If these figures are shown as a percentage of sales it can be seen that sales doubled. However, a 10% fall in the gross margin has had a big effect when combined with a small (5%) increase in expenses. The rate of net profit (the net profit margin) has halved.

	Year 1 %	Year 2 %
Sales	100	100
Cost of sales	50	60
Gross profit	50	40
Expenses	20	25
Net profit	30	15

net worth: the amount a business would be worth if all of its *assets* were sold and all of its *liabilities* paid. If a business went into *liquidation* all its assets would be sold. The money would be used to pay off all its liabilities. Any money that was left would be the net worth of the business and this would be paid to the *shareholders*.

new technology is a term that is mainly used to describe technical changes based on the silicon chip. New technology has resulted in new products, such as computer games and personal electronic organisers. Manufacturing methods have been improved (e.g. through the use of *CAD* and *CAM and CIM*). New technology has brought about big changes in *communications*, for example, in cell phones and *fax* machines.

niche market: a small, probably specialised, *segment* of a market. It may be a very narrow, but specialised, part of an existing market. Niche markets are often filled by small firms since the total turnover may be too small for big firms to bother with.

no strike agreement: an agreement between a *trades union* and an *employer* in which the trades union agrees never to call its members out on strike. In return the employer usually agrees to recognise only one trades union.

nominal capital is the total face value of each type of share actually issued by a *limited company*. If the company has issued all the shares allowed by the *memorandum of association* it will be equal to the *authorised capital*. The nominal capital will be shown in the *balance sheet*.

nominal rate of interest: the stated rate of interest charged on a loan. It is the same thing as the flat *rate of interest*. It is not the true rate of interest which is expressed as the *annualised percentage rate (APR)* of interest.

nominal value is usually used to describe the face value of *shares*; it is also called the *par value*. This will not be the same as the *market value*. The value given to the capital in the *memorandum of association* is based on the nominal value of each type of share. When *dividends* are declared they are stated as a percentage of the nominal value of the shares not of the market value.

> **Example:** Suppose that the balance sheet of a business shows the following:
>
> > Authorised share capital:
> > 50 000 10% preference shares of £1 each
> > 100 000 ordinary shares at 50p each
> > 100 000 ordinary shares at 25p each
>
> The nominal values of the shares are £1, 50p and 25p respectively.

non-executive directors are *directors* who play no part in the day-to-day running of a company. They are usually part-time directors and are paid for their work. They will often be directors of other companies too. Their main job is to make sure that the company is run in the best interests of all the shareholders. They often give specialist and neutral advice. They may be able to provide expert knowledge in an area in which the firm is weak. They also act as a brake on the *executive directors*.

non-financial rewards are the rewards, other than pay, that people get from doing their job. They will be very personal things and may be no more than doing a job they like. They will often be the parts of the job that provide a strong *motivation*. They will be things like status, *job satisfaction* and *job security*.

non-price competition occurs when companies compete in ways other than through price. Examples are the issuing of vouchers, free offers, competitions and *promotions* of all kinds. *Advertising, branding* and *packaging* are other examples of this kind of competition.

non-profitmaking organisations are organisations that exist for some purpose other than to make a profit. They can be very large and are often run like a business. They must not make a loss, and will try to make a small *surplus*. They are usually charities like the Save the Children Fund or social organisations such as social clubs or amateur sports clubs. There are also other kinds, such as examination boards.

notices are a form of written *communication* used to provide information. They are often used as a method of informing people in the work place. They are normally placed on a notice board. They may include things that are on permanent display such as Health and Safety regulations. They are also used to tell people about holiday dates, meetings and social events. They may be used to advertise internal job vacancies.

objectives are the targets that a business sets itself. There may be objectives for the business as a whole and others for each department. A department's objectives will be a more detailed breakdown of those for the whole organisation. The objectives are what drives a business and should have certain features.

- They must be realistic and everyone should know them.

- They should be attainable and measurable. If an objective cannot be measured people will not know when they have reached it. They should be reviewed regularly to check progress and revised if necessary.

- They ought to have a time limit. There is no point in saying the business has a target (for example, to grow by 5%), unless that target has to be reached within a certain time.

(See also *business objectives* for some examples of long-term objectives.)

obsolete describes a process, service, product or machine that becomes out of date. It is obsolete when it is replaced by something that does the same or a similar job more efficiently or more cheaply. Things become obsolete because of technical advances or changes in style or fashion.

OFFER is the office of the *regulator* for the *privatised* electricity industry.

Office of Fair Trading: was set up under the *Fair Trading Act 1973*. It is a government body headed by the Director General of Fair Trading; its main duty is to enforce regulations under various Acts of Parliament.

Functions of the Office of Fair Trading:

- To give general consumer advice to the public but not to deal with complaints about the quality of individual products.

- To look at complaints from the public about the way traders do business. If companies fail to behave within the law, it has the power to make them change their ways.

- To give advice to the Secretary of State for Trade and Industry on whether a planned *merger* or *takeover* should be referred to the *Monopolies and Mergers Commission* to check that the merger is not against the public interest.

- To keep a watch to see that new monopolies do not arise and to carry out enquiries to discover whether there are abuses of monopoly power.

- To stop anti-competitive practices such as price fixing agreements or the setting of quotas to make sure that prices are kept high. The OFT watches out for any practice that works against the interests of consumers. Where it spots such practices, firms can be made to stop them.

- To ensure that only people licensed by the OFT can give credit to the public.

off-the-job training is all training that is done away from the workplace. It may be done by a company itself. More often it will be done at a college on *day release* or possibly *block release*. Sometimes the theory work is done in college while the practical work is dealt with by *on-the-job training*.

OFGAS is the office of the *regulator* for the *privatised* gas industry. It is responsible for British Gas and the new companies allowed to sell gas to the public as a result of its policies to increase competition in the gas supply industry.

OFTEL is the office of the *regulator* for the *privatised* telephone industry. It is responsible for the cellular phone and cable companies, as well as BT.

OFWAT is the office of the *regulator* for the *privatised* water supply industry.

on-the-job training is all training that takes place in the place of work. It may consist of being shown the job step-by-step by an experienced worker, or it may simply be watching someone do a job and trying to copy that person.

- It is easy and cheap to organise and is the most common form of training.

- People are taught to do a job the way the firm wants it to be done. Workers learn only the practical parts of the job they are going to do. They may go for *off-the-job training* to learn the theory of the job.

- A disadvantage is that not everyone is good at showing other people how to do a job. Existing workers may pass on their bad habits to the new worker.

open questions are questions to which there are no pre-set answers. Unlike *closed questions* people can answer them in their own words and give their own opinions. They are often used in job *interviews*. Open questions should be avoided in a *questionnaire* because each answer will be different. Answers will therefore be very hard to summarise and convert into statistics.

opening stock is the amount of stock held by a business at the beginning of the financial year. The opening stock is shown in a firm's *Trading Account*. The opening stock will be the *closing stock* in the previous year's Trading Account.

opportunity cost is that which is done without in order to obtain something else, when limited resources force a *choice* to be made.

Explanation: Most people have more wants than they have the means (resources) to satisfy. They have to make a choice about how to spend their resources. Suppose a person has £5 and wants to go to the cinema but also wants a supper of fish and chips. That person can do one thing or the other, but not both, and has to make a choice. If the cinema is chosen the cost is not the £5. That money could have been spent in another way. The true cost is the opportunity sacrificed, of having the fish and chip supper. The opportunity cost of going to the cinema is the supper that was foregone.

This is an important idea in business. A business only has a limited amount of resources at any one time. Resources can often be used in a number of different ways so a choice often has to be made. A piece of land, for example, could be used for housing, or an office block or a factory. If it is used for a factory, the opportunity cost will be the housing and office block that were not built. The business will choose what to use its resources for on the basis of what it thinks will give it the highest profit. In the same way the government has to choose how to spend *public money*. For every business decision there is an opportunity cost.

order: a definite request to supply a stated quantity of goods or services at a stated price. An order does not have to be in writing. Orders may be given

			Order No. 02403	

XYX & COMPANY LIMITED
The Industrial Estate, Anytown, Midshire RE9 4PH
Telephone: 0123 987 4561
Fax: 0123 987 6544
VAT Registration No.

Date
To:

Please supply the following goods

Ref/Cat No	Quantity	Description	Unit Price	Total Price
Authorised by .... *Purchasing Department*			TOTAL	

A typical order proforma

face-to-face or over the telephone. They are best in writing since there can be no dispute about what was ordered. Telephone orders are often confirmed by following up with a written order. Large organisations use an official, numbered order form, as shown opposite.

ordinary shares are the main type of shares issued by a *limited company*. Each share represents a part of the ownership of the company.

Features of ordinary shares:

- The holders of ordinary shares are paid a share of the company's profits. This is called a *dividend*. The dividend on ordinary shares is paid only after *preference* shareholders have been paid their dividends.

- The dividend on ordinary shares varies. When a company does well there may be a high dividend. If a company does badly no dividend may be paid. There is therefore a higher risk with ordinary shares compared with other shares.

- The ordinary shareholders vote at the *annual general meeting*. They have one vote for every share they hold and also elect the company's *directors*.

- If a company goes into *liquidation* the ordinary shareholders will only be paid after all other claims on the *assets* have been met.

organisation: any body or group that has an identity that is separate from any other body or group. It has a common purpose. There are many different kinds of organisation, for example:

- *public sector* organisations run by central or local government to provide services for which there is no direct charge, for example the health service, street lighting, education, roads

- business organisations of all kinds and sizes that aim to make a *profit*.

- Voluntary organisations, like charities and clubs that depend on people working for them voluntarily (without being paid). There are also big charities and clubs that employ people, as well as using voluntary help.

Most organisations have some business aspect to them; nearly all, for example, will need to keep accounts and buy goods and services.

Some features that are common to all organisations:

- **Objectives** – these set out the overall purpose of an organisation, the reasons for which the organisation exists.

- **Organisation –** the same systems of administration and methods of working are used in all parts of an organisation.

- **Functions –** these are the various roles within an organisation (for example, finance, sales, marketing or personnel). In small organisations all the functions may be carried out by one person. Large organisations will have separate departments for each function.

- **Resources –** they will all have some resources. They will either employ people or have volunteers (*human resources*). Most will have use of land or buildings or machinery (*physical resources*). They will also collect or earn money and use money (*financial resources*).

- **Culture –** the style of an organisation, its ethos, traditions and working practices.

- **External environment –** the things from outside that affect organisations, over which they have no control. They will be affected by their competitors, by the law, government controls and taxation and by what is happening in the economy locally, nationally and internationally.

organisation chart: a diagram that shows the internal structure of an organisation. It shows how an organisation is split up into various parts. This may be into departments, sections or teams. It may show the names of the people in each part. By reading the chart it should be possible to see the following things quickly and clearly:

- the number and type of each function and division

- the levels of *hierarchy* that exist and the *span of control*

- the chain of communication and command.

An example of an organisation chart is shown on the next page.

organisation tree: another name for *organisation chart*.

output: the final product that is the result of a production process. The term is also used in the sense of the total quantity that is produced at a factory or by a company.

over-capacity occurs when there are more resources available than are needed to meet the current level of demand for a product. There may be over-capacity in a particular factory or company or in a complete industry. For example, there is more steelmaking capacity in the world than is needed to meet the demand.

- Over-capacity may be permanent, for example, in an industry that is in decline.

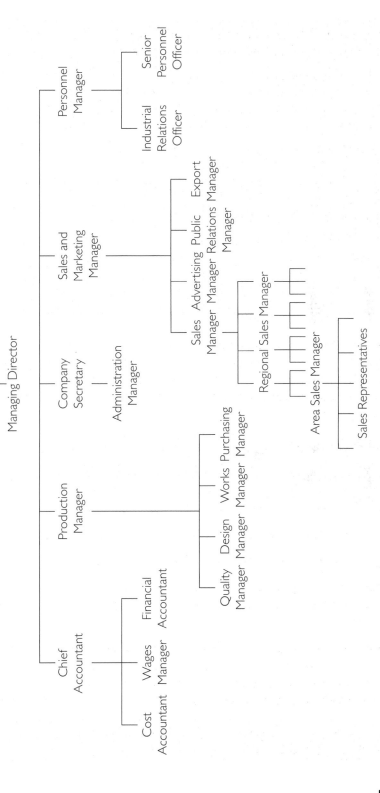

organisation chart

- It may lead to the weakest and least efficient firms having to close.

- It is very common during a *recession* and may mean that companies can expand quite quickly when there is a *recovery*. They will be able to expand without increasing their *fixed costs* so their *unit costs* will fall quickly.

overdraft: an agreement with a *bank* that allows a customer to draw out more money than is in the *current account*, up to an agreed limit. An overdraft is shown as a *current liability* in a firm's *balance sheet*.

> **Explanation:** Normally banks will not let their customers draw out more money than they have in their current account. A firm or individual can, however, agree with the bank that they can draw *cheques* for more money than they have in their current account, up to an agreed amount. It is a kind of safety net that is only used when necessary.

- It is a way of getting over a short-term *cashflow* problem.

- Each time the account is overdrawn the firm is, in effect, borrowing money from the bank. The bank charges *interest* on the amount overdrawn.

- Each time money is paid into the current account the overdraft is reduced, or may disappear. In the same way every time money is withdrawn from the account the overdraft is increased. The size of the overdraft keeps changing, so interest is charged on the daily balance.

(Compare overdraft to a *bank loan*.)

overheads are the general costs of running a business. They are costs that are not directly related to the cost of producing a product. They are often called *indirect costs*. They are likely to be of a fixed nature over the short-term. Examples include office expenses, administration costs, rent, heating and lighting. Overheads are shown in the *profit and loss account*.

overtime is working for longer than the basic working week in return for an extra payment. It is usually voluntary; people do not have to work overtime. Firms often use overtime at very busy times, preferring to use overtime to taking on extra workers. Overtime is usually paid at a higher rate than the basic rate of pay. It is often paid at time-and-a-half, or double-time at weekends or bank holidays.

overtime ban: a form of *industrial action* that allows workers still to be paid their basic wages. It may disrupt the firm, especially at very busy times or when there is a special order that has to be finished quickly. It is most effective in those companies that rely heavily on overtime, for example, the railways which depend on train drivers working overtime.

overtime pay: the payment received by workers for working longer than the basic working week. Overtime pay will be extra to *basic pay*. It will probably be paid at a higher rate than basic pay.

own label: when a *retailer* has its own *brand* and *trade mark* on the goods sold in its shops. The goods are often made for the retailer by firms whose brands are competing with the own label goods.

- The name may be the same as the name of the shop, for example, 'Next' and 'Principles'. Other firms use a different name, for example, Marks and Spencer's own label is 'St. Michael'.

- Some shops, like Marks and Spencer and Next, only sell goods with their own label. The own label clothes are often made to the retailer's own design and *specification*.

- Others, like the food supermarkets, sell their own label goods alongside other brands. Their own label goods are usually cheaper than the other brands.

owner: the individual or organisation that has full legal rights over property.

Explanation: The idea of ownership is important in business. The owners of goods, or other property, can do what they like with them, as long as it is within the law.

- Normally the buyer of goods owns them straight away, even if they have not yet been paid for.

- Goods bought on *hire purchase* are not owned by the buyer until the last payment has been made. Such goods are still owned by a *finance company* and cannot be sold without the finance company's permission.

- Goods bought from places other than shops or showrooms may not be owned by the seller. If the seller does not own them, they are not his to sell, for example, if they are stolen or are still part of a hire purchase agreement. The buyer of stolen goods, or goods still on hire purchase, may have to hand the goods back to the true owner. Buying such goods may mean that the buyer loses the money and the goods. The only way to get the money back would be to sue the dishonest seller for the return of the money.

packaging: the materials used to protect and present a product. It is an important part of the *marketing mix*. Some experts regard packaging as part of the product. Others consider it to be so important that it should be a fifth 'P' in the marketing mix.

Explanation: Packaging is important in protecting goods from damage and also keeps them clean and hygienic. Packaging is also used to present and sell goods to the public.

- Packaging is used to give products an identity. It will, for example, include a *brand* name and a company *logo* or *trademark*. Manufacturers hope that people can recognise their product from its packaging without reading the label. For example, the shape of the Coca-Cola bottle can be easily recognised. Packaging is one method of *product differentiation*.

- Products can be made to look attractive and different through their packaging. The packaging is always in the same colour or colour scheme. Things like perfume and after-shave are often given a very distinctive container.

paid-up shares are shares where the *nominal value* of the shares has been fully paid by the shareholders.

Explanation: When a company first sells its shares to the public (on *flotation*) it does not collect the full price of the shares at once.

The money is collected in three stages:

- **Application** – a stated sum per share must be sent when applying for the shares.

- **Allocation** – a further stated sum has to be sent when the issuing company decides how many shares each applicant can have.

- **Call** – the rest of the money is called for by the company. It usually collects this money in one sum, but not always.

It is only after the company asks for all the money due at the 'call' stage that the shares become fully paid-up. The 'issued capital' section of the *balance sheet* shows which shares are fully paid-up.

par value is the same as the *nominal value* of a share.

parent company: a company that has at least one *subsidiary* company over which it has control. The subsidiaries will either be companies it has set up for a particular purpose or bought. The term 'parent company' is sometimes used to describe a *holding company*.

partner: each person who is a member of a *partnership*. The relationship between the partners should be set out in a *deed of partnership*.

All partners have certain things in common:

- They all have *unlimited liability* except for limited partners, who are quite rare.

- All partners are entitled to a share of the profits. The size of the share depends on the deed of partnership.

- Each partner is entitled to take part in running the firm and is an *agent* of the firm. This means that each partner can make binding contracts without asking the other partners. Partners must therefore trust one another.

- Each partner is liable for the debts of the firm. A creditor can sue the whole firm or choose to sue only one (or some) of the partners. Partners are also liable for the debts of the other partners, if they arise from the business.

- The death of a partner may end a partnership.

partnership exists when two or more people carry on business together with a view to making a profit. The maximum number of partners allowed is 20, except in partnerships involving solicitors, accountants and stockbrokers, which may have more. The relationship between the partners is set out in a *deed of partnership*. There does not have to be a such a deed but if there is not, the law presumes that the partners own the business and share the profits equally. A partnership is often the first step taken by *sole proprietors* who want to expand their business.

Advantages of a partnership:

- They can be set up quickly and cheaply.

- Because there are up to 20 people involved, quite large amounts of capital can be brought into a business.

- Costs are shared, so it will be cheaper, for example, for three doctors to share the same premises than for each one to have a separate practice. Problems and management of a business can also be shared.

- *Division of labour* is possible within a partnership. Each partner can specialise in the part of the business in which they are most interested. For example, a solicitors' practice in which each partner specialises in one branch of the law will be better than one where every partner tries to cover everything.

Disadvantages of a partnership:

- Partnerships can still be short of capital. The money that each partner can invest in the business may be quite small.

- Differences of opinion may cause a business to break up. There can be difficulties if one of the partners is seen by the others as not working very hard.

- Each partner can bind the business and the other partners. A rogue partner may cause financial problems for the other partners.

pay-as-you-earn (PAYE) is the system by which employers deduct *income tax* from an employee's wages or salary before it is paid to them each week or month. The amount deducted is shown on the *pay slip*. *Employers* collect tax from *employees* and pay it to the *Inland Revenue*.

pay roll: a list of all the people who are paid by an organisation. It lists all the *employees'* names and the amounts each person is to be paid in *wages* or *salary*.

pay round: the annual period during which *trades unions* and *employers* negotiate the rates of pay for the following year. *Wages* and *salaries* have tended to be fixed once a year, usually during the autumn. In recent years there has been an increase in two or even three year pay deals. This makes financial planning and *budgeting* easier.

pay slip: a form issued to all employees when they are paid. The form gives details of all *gross pay*, including *overtime*. It also shows details of all *deductions* made, and finally, net pay.

ORGANISATION									DATE	
PAYROLL									21/07/95	
									PAY REFERENCE	
PAY ADVICE FOR						N.I. CATEGORY		X	520291	
DEPARTMENT	039			002/502/520291		TAX CODE		BR	TAX PERIOD	
PAY POINT	4005					N.I. No				
PAY						DEDUCTIONS			TAXABLE PAY	
DESCRIPTION	T/N	UNITS	RATE	VALUE	BALANCE	DESCRIPTION	VALUE	BALANCE		
				273.72	1093.11	TAX	68.50		273.72	
									NON TAXABLE PAY	
									00.00	
									TOTAL PAY	
									273.72	
									TOTAL DEDUCTIONS	
									68.50	
									NET PAY	
									205.22	
									ROUNDING	
					TAXABLE PAY TO DATE	TAX TO DATE	B/FWD	C/FWD		
					1093.11	273.25	00.00	00.00		

payee: the person or organisation to whom a *cheque* is made out. The cheque is an order by the *drawer* to a *bank* to pay the payee.

paying-in slip: a form on which details of *cash* and *cheques* paid into a *bank* current account are entered. The form also includes the date, the account holder's name, account number and the branch where the account is based. There will also be a counterfoil showing the amount paid in, which should be kept in case there is a dispute about the transaction. The money can be paid into any branch of the account holder's bank

payment by results: a system of pay based on a level of output or on results. It is hoped that linking pay to results will act as an incentive to people to work harder. The two best known methods of payment by results are *piece rates* and *commission*. Some people are paid a basic rate and the rest of their pay or their *bonus* payments depend on results. The pay of many managers is partly based on the results (profits) of the business.

payment card is a name sometimes used to describe a *debit card.*

penetration pricing: this occurs when a business sets a low price for a product in order to gain a good *market share* quickly. It is used when a new product is brought onto the market or when a manufacturer is trying to break into an existing, established *market*. Once the market share has been won, the price can be slowly increased to gain larger profits.

pension funds are *financial institutions* that collect the pension contributions made by employees and employers. They are run by *fund managers* who invest the money collected, mainly in stocks and shares. Pension funds are one of the biggest groups of *institutional investors.*

per capita literally means per head or in effect, per person.

performance appraisal: see *appraisal.*

performance indicators are measures designed to show how well a business is doing. They are not exact measures of success or failure but pointers which indicate how well a business is performing. An indicator taken on its own can lead to wrong conclusions. For example, if total sales show an increase it suggests that the business is being successful but another indicator may show that the cost of each sale has risen. The success may not be as great as looking at just one indicator might suggest.

performance-related pay (PRP) is an addition to an employee's salary that is paid when certain targets are met. It is very like a *bonus* and is usually paid to salary earners. The targets may be agreed during the *appraisal* interview. The linking of appraisal with performance-related pay has made appraisal unpopular.

perks: see *perquisites*.

perquisites ('perks') are the *fringe benefits* that go with a job.

person specification: also known as a *job specification*.

personnel is a general term that refers to the people employed within an organisation. It includes everyone from the managing director through to the most junior member of staff.

personnel department: the section that deals with the people who work within an organisation. Large companies will have a separate personnel department and a specialist personnel manager. The department controls the number of staff in a firm, and, through its selection methods, the quality of the staff. The work of the personnel department falls into several parts.

1   Employment matters

- *Recruitment* of all staff from the most senior managers downwards.

- Organising *appraisal* interviews.

- Negotiating *disciplinary* and *grievance* procedures; the department also tries to make sure that procedures are applied correctly.

- *Terminating employment;* the department will handle *dismissals* and *redundancy*. To avoid possible *industrial tribunals* in the future it tries to make sure that the right procedures are used. There will also be people who leave a firm voluntarily either to retire or work somewhere else. The department has to make sure that they have all the correct documents that they may need.

2   Industrial relations

- *Negotiation* of wages and salaries and working conditions with the trades unions.

- Working with the trades unions in *industrial relations* to avoid disputes. If a matter does become a dispute the department works to resolve it.

- Representation of the organisation at *industrial tribunals*.

3   Welfare and training

- Organisation of *training* to make sure all staff have the skills needed to do their job. It is the job of the personnel department to make sure that the training meets the needs of the business.

- Provision of *welfare* by setting up childcare schemes, arranging first aid rooms and perhaps a medical room with a nurse or doctor. In a big organisation the personnel department may organise the sports and social clubs.

4   Record keeping

- Staff records will be kept by the personnel department. These include name and address, qualifications and starting date of each employee. It will also keep details of things that have happened while an employee has been with the firm, for example, training courses attended, extra qualifications gained and promotions.

persuasive advertising is advertising that tries to persuade the public to buy a particular product. Persuasive advertising is linked to *branding*. The advertising tries to create a brand image and to give the brand a separate identity. *Packaging* is also part of that image and identity. They are all part of the *promotion* of a product.

> **Explanation:** The main purpose of persuasive advertising is to sell a product. The advertiser will try to convince people that:

- the product is special and better than other products of the same type

- they need the product and that without it they will be worse off in some way. The advertisement may, for example, suggest that people are inferior without the product.

petty cash refers to small payments that are made in cash or the small fund from which such payments are made. Payments are usually for small items such as repaying bus fares, small items of stationery and stamps. They are recorded in a petty cash book. The petty cash book is usually looked after by an office junior.

Explanation: A firm will make most of its payments by cheque. There will be some small day-to-day payments, say under £10, that are made in cash. Instead of cluttering up its main cash book and ledger with these small payments, they are recorded in the petty cash book.

physical resources consist of things such as the land, buildings and equipment that are used in a business. They usually consist of the *fixed assets* of the business.

picketing occurs when groups of workers who are on strike stand at the entrances to premises where there is a strike. The pickets will try to stop anyone 'crossing the picket line' and so going to work or making deliveries.

Explanation: When people refuse to 'cross the picket line' they show support for the strike. Strikers try to dissuade other workers at the firm from going to work. They also try to stop supplies into or goods out of the premises. The law now limits the maximum number of pickets to six.

pie chart: a circular diagram which shows the relative size of each part that goes to make up a total.

Explanation: A complete circle can be thought of as the whole of something, that is, the complete 'pie'. The pie can be cut up into slices of different size. The size of each slice shows what proportion of the total it represents. For example, if a class is exactly half girls and half boys the pie will be cut in half. The size of each slice represents the proportion of the total.

Worked example: Suppose the local council spends £420m a year.

The spending is broken down:

	£m	%
Education	210	50
Social services	63	15
Police and fire	63	15
Environment, planning, economic development	42	10
Libraries and heritage	8.4	2
Justice	4.2	1
Other services	29.4	7
	420	100

Education is obviously half of the pie.

Social services spend 15% of the money. To show this on the pie chart we must cut a slice equal to 15% of the whole circle. The whole circle = 360 degrees. To make a slice equal to 15% we need to find 15% of 360°:

$$\frac{360 \times 15}{100} = 54°$$

We shall therefore make a 54° angle at the centre and extend it to the edge of the circle. We can do the same for each of the other departments.

The finished circle will look like this:

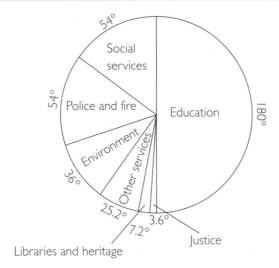

piece rates: the payment for a single item produced/processed when workers are paid according to the amount of goods they produce. Workers will usually be paid a fixed amount for each item they make.

Advantages of piece rates:

- Workers are encouraged to work hard since the more they produce the more they will be paid.

- The system is fairer than flat rate or *time rate* methods of pay as the hard working people are paid more than the lazy workers.

- Piece rates allow workers to work at their own pace if they want to; some may decide they prefer not to have high wages and to work at a speed that suits them.

Disadvantages of piece rates:

- Workers are tempted to produce as many items as they can and ignore quality. (On the other hand, they may not be paid for poor quality work.)

- Firms have to spend more money on *quality control*. They employ inspectors who reject work that is not up to the quality expected. Workers are not usually paid for work that is below the quality standard. This may cause disputes.

- Fixing the rate for the job may be difficult and can lead to disputes. The rate is usually based on work study and has to be agreed with the *trades unions*.

piecework: see *piece rates*.

place: that part of the *marketing mix* that determines where goods are going to be sold and how they are going to get there. Where goods are sold will depend on the nature of the goods.

- *Capital goods*, such as heavy machinery, are sold at specialised *trade fairs and exhibitions*. They are also sold through technical salespeople visiting firms interested in such goods.

- Most goods and services sold to the general public are sold in shops and showrooms. Sellers have to decide in which type of shop to sell their product, that is, how they *target* sales.

  - Many shops specialise in a certain type of product (e.g., furniture, clothes, shoes, toys).

  - Some shops *position* themselves to appeal to a certain 'class' of customer, (e.g. Harrods, Harvey Nicholls, Mark One, BeWise). This usually means they only sell goods within a certain price range. Other shops have a general appeal and stock goods over a wide range of prices.

- Other places where goods may be sold will include:

  - wholesalers

  - *direct sales*

  - *mail order*

  - telephone sales

  - exhibitions (e.g. Ideal Home Exhibition, Motor Show).

planned economy is one in which the state makes most of the decisions about what goods are produced, where they are produced and in what quantity. The state controls all the *factors of production*. The wages of workers and the price of goods are decided by the government. Cuba is one of the few surviving planned economies.

Advantages of the planned economy:

> • Unemployment is very low since everyone is employed by the state.
>
> • The state can decide priorities and make sure only those things that benefit the most people are produced. Resources are used for making necessities first and not wasted in making luxuries.
>
> • There is no wasteful competition or duplication of production. Resources are concentrated where they can be used best. There are no private profits and *economies of scale* can be gained.

Disadvantages of the planned economy:

> • There is usually a very large and inefficient *bureaucracy*.
>
> • Consumers have no choice. All the goods tend to look the same and are made to a standard *specification*.
>
> • There is no reason to improve the system. There is no competition or profit or other incentive to make things better.

planning is the making of definite arrangements for the future rather than leaving things to chance. Every business should plan ahead. There may be several different plans such as a marketing plan, a budget plan and a production plan.

These separate plans are brought together in a *business plan*. Longer term planning should be shown in a 'strategic plan'.

planning controls are the central and local government rules about where new buildings can be put up. The controls are meant to stop anyone building what they like, where they like. Buildings have to meet certain standards of design, quality and safety. The controls are applied by local authorities.

planning permission must be obtained before a new building or an extension can be built. Permission is given by the local authority.

plant-based bargaining is where *negotiations* on pay and conditions of service are carried out on a site by site basis. The negotiations are still between employers and the *trades unions*. In a large company it may mean that conditions and rates of pay for the same job are different at each branch of the company. Plant-based and *local pay bargaining* have largely replaced national pay bargaining in many industries.

plc: see *public limited company*.

point of sale: the place where goods are sold to consumers, usually a shop or showroom. A point of sale display is often therefore a display in a shop. It may be in the shop window or be a free standing display inside the shop.

pollution is the damaging of the environment by infecting the air or water or soil with chemicals, fumes or noise. Companies may have to pay heavy fines for any pollution they cause. They can also be made to install expensive equipment to control or prevent further pollution.

population is the total number of people living in an area, town, region or country. The population provides the supply of labour. The way the population is distributed geographically, and by age, affects the location of industry and the market for goods and services.

In business it is also used in a special sense in *market research*. It is used here to mean a group of people who match certain criteria. For example, a firm may want to know how many men and women, aged 18 or over 'dunk' their biscuits in their tea. Once it knows the total doing so (the population) it can take a sample to test a new biscuit that does not break when dunked.

position: the point in a *market* at which a firm aims its sales. It is the *target market* or *population* for goods. The type of goods a company stocks and the way it markets those goods depend on where the company is positioned. Some companies, for example, may position themselves to target the 16 to 25-year-old age group. Others have changed to the 25 to 35 age group because they are now a larger *segment* in the market.

predatory pricing happens when a company sets its prices very low in order to get a larger share of a *market*. It may try to drive out the competition altogether. Once it has captured most of the market, prices will probably be raised. Supermarket branches have been known to cut their prices to below *cost price* for some goods; fruit, vegetables and bread are favourite targets. The effect has often been to force nearby small shopkeepers to close down.

preference shares: a type of share issued by a *public limited company*. The holders of the shares are part owners of the company. Because they take fewer risks than the ordinary shareholders they have no vote at company meetings. There will usually be fewer preference shares than *ordinary shares*.

Features of preference shares:

- They are issued at a fixed rate of *dividend*. For example, the *balance sheet* may state that the *issued capital* is '100 000 10% preference shares at £1 each'. This means the total dividend is fixed at £10 000 every year, that is, at 10p per share. Preference shareholders are not paid a higher dividend even in those years when the company makes larger profits. Preference shareholders are paid their dividend before the *ordinary shareholders.

- If there is not enough money to pay preference shareholders a dividend in one year they will lose the dividend for that year, unless they hold

> *cumulative preference shares.* They are a special type of share where the dividend may build up. If there is not enough money to pay them in one year, they are paid double the next year if there is enough money to do so.

> - Preference shareholders have their *capital* returned before the ordinary shareholders, if the company goes into *liquidation.* They are only paid if there is enough money left after all *creditors* have been paid.

pressure group: an organised group that shares a common interest, or point of view, which it seeks to promote. It tries to influence others to bring about change through lawful and peaceful methods. Pressure groups may be local, national or international. They may be permanent or set up for a specific purpose, disbanding once the goal is achieved.

> **Examples:** types of pressure groups:

> - **For a specific purpose –** local residents opposed to a new factory estate being built on green belt land near to them may form a group. Once the final decisions are made, they have no other purpose and disband.

> - **Local and permanent –** most towns have a local civic society or a local Victorian society.

> - **National –** *trades unions* put pressure on employers to improve the pay and *working conditions* of their members. They may also try to influence the government and other people about the economy and anything else that affects their members.

> - **National and international –** 'Greenpeace' and 'Friends of the Earth' are examples of international pressure groups.

Prestel is an electronic information system provided by British Telecom. To be connected to the system a subscription has to be paid. A wide range of information is available such as Stock Exchange prices and all kinds of news items. It is widely used by the travel industry to make bookings.

pre-tax profit is the profit made by a company before it has paid *corporation tax*. It is a truer statement of how much profit a company has made than the after tax profit.

price is the money paid when goods and services are exchanged. It is an important part of the *marketing mix*.

> **Explanation:** The sale of a product in a shop is the last stage in getting goods to the *consumer*. The price paid for goods and services by the consumer is built up at each stage in the *chain of distribution*.

The *retailer* buys at a price that includes the costs and the profits added by each of the previous stages. The price paid by the consumer will also include the retailer's profit.

When a price is paid, people expect to receive a commodity or service in return.

price discrimination happens when firms charge different customers different prices for the same product or service.

Explanation: One way of increasing profit is to charge some customers more than others for the same product or service. Firms are able to do this because some people can afford to and are willing to pay more. It is a form of market *segmentation*. A firm often makes some small distinction between what it gives to those paying the lower and higher prices. The company makes more profit per unit from those paying the higher price.

Examples:

- Gas, electricity and telephone companies charge private customers a different rate from that charged to business customers.

- Telephone companies charge different rates at different times of the day. This is done to encourage greater use at the quieter 'off-peak' times, when there is spare *capacity*.

- The railways charge first class and standard class fares on the same trains. It costs a railway company the same amount to run a train if all the seats are the same class but they make a bigger profit on the first class seats. Airlines do the same thing.

price war: this occurs when two or more companies cut their prices, to try to increase their *market share*.

Explanation: In a price war one company cuts its prices. Other companies quickly follow, cutting their prices even further. They get locked into a round of each one reacting to the other. They may get to the point where they are selling below *cost price*. Price wars often happen because there is a surplus of a product on the market. For example, there may be overproduction of petrol. The petrol companies start a price war to get rid of the surplus. Only the customer benefits from the lower prices.

pricing methods are the different ways that may be used to decide at what price goods should be sold. Some methods are based on the cost of the goods and there are others that depend on marketing.

1   **Cost-based methods:**

- **Cost-plus pricing** – when an allowance for *profit* is added to the *average costs* or *unit costs* of goods. Average costs include the *overheads* as well as the cost of materials and labour. In reality it is quite hard to work out the costs exactly.

- **Mark-up pricing** – adding a standard percentage (mark-up) to the *direct costs* of a product. The amount added is *gross profit* and has to be big enough to cover all the *expenses* as well as the *net profit*. The amount added takes into account the prices charged by competitors and what people are prepared to pay.

2   **Market-based methods:**

- **Competitive pricing** – where the prices charged by competitors are taken into account when fixing prices. The supermarket chains employ people to go around rival shops to find out the prices of certain goods.

- **Market pricing** – where prices are fixed at the same level as those of similar goods in the market.

- **Marginal cost pricing** – where a customer may be charged a different price, maybe lower than the usual price. A firm may do this because the price can be based on the marginal cost of making the extra goods.

- **Predatory pricing** – when goods are priced much lower than those of competitors. Firms hope to drive out the competition or win the largest share of a market.

primary industry is made up of the industries that make use of the 'gifts of nature'. It is also called *extractive industry*. Primary industries include mining, fishing, forestry and farming. Once the coal or oil, for example, have been taken out of the ground, they cannot be replaced. Primary industry may also be called primary production.

primary research is the collection of new and original information first-hand. Its main business use is in *market research*. (See *field research* and compare with *secondary research*.)

primary sources are where primary, or first-hand, information is collected. They are the providers of the information in *primary research*. (See *field research* for examples.)

prime cost: the total cost of raw materials and labour directly used in making a product. It also includes any other *direct costs*, such as the running cost of machines and heating and light in the factory. It is the basic cost of a product, before the general *overheads* of the firm are added.

Example:
Manufacturing Account of XYX and Company Limited for the period ended 31 December

	£	£
Raw materials consumed:		
Opening stock	10 000	
plus Purchases	90 000	
	100 000	
less Closing stock	20 000	80 000
Direct labour costs		100 000
Direct manufacturing costs		20 000
Prime cost		200 000

private enterprise is made up of companies that are owned privately. They are owned either by individuals or other companies operating as *sole traders, partnerships, co-operatives* and *limited companies*. Their main purpose is to make a *profit*. It is all business that is not owned by the government or local authorities.

private limited company: a *limited* company in which the *shares* cannot be sold to the public. They are often small companies with all the shares owned by members of a family. The company name must end with 'Limited' or 'Ltd'. To become a private limited company the owners must apply to the *Registrar of Companies*. The Registrar will need to see a *memorandum of association* and *articles of association* before the business can be *incorporated*.

Features of a private limited company:

- Each shareholder has *limited liability*. There must be at least two shareholders but there is no maximum number. There must be at least one director.

- Shares can be issued but they cannot be sold to the public. Transfers of shares can only take place with the agreement of the other shareholders.

- Each year the company must hold a general meeting of shareholders and send a copy of its accounts to *shareholders* and the *Registrar of Companies*.

Advantages of private companies:

- They have limited liability. No one can lose more than the *capital* they have put into the company. This makes people more willing to invest in them than in a sole trader or partnership. This makes it easier for the company to obtain extra capital to expand.

- The owners can keep control and choose the shareholders.
- Such companies have a separate legal existence from the owners.

Disadvantages of private companies:

- Because shares cannot be sold on the open market, it can be hard for investors to get their money back when they want to.
- There is a limit to the amount of capital that can be raised from friends and family.

private sector: that part of an economy that is made up of business organisations that are not owned by the state and are run by *private enterprise*.

privatisation is the sale or transfer of enterprises and services to the *private sector* from the *public sector*. The term is mainly used in two ways.

1 the sale to private shareholders of companies such as British Telecom, British Gas and the Electricity Boards

2 the *contracting out* of services, such as school cleaning and rubbish collection to privately-owned companies.

Explanation: During the 1980s and the early 1990s a number of organisations that had been owned by the state were sold. Most of them were run by *public corporations* and provided services, like gas, telephones and water. Usually they were the only suppliers of the service. They had a *monopoly*. Other state monopolies like British Rail, British Coal and British Steel were thought to be so important that it was better if they were state owned. Other privatised companies, for example, British Sugar, Cable and Wireless, British Petroleum and British Leyland (now Rover), had come into state ownership for various reasons.

The companies were sold in two ways:

1 by offering shares to the public (British Gas, British Petroleum, electricity and water companies are examples)

2 by asking other companies to bid for state-owned companies. This was how Ford bought Jaguar and British Aerospace bought Rover and how parts of the railways were sold.

Arguments for privatisation:

- The companies will be more efficient. Governments and civil servants are not very good at running businesses as they are too bureaucratic.

- There will be greater competition. As a result the public will get better, more efficient and therefore cheaper services.

- They are able to attract investment from the *financial institutions* whereas the government could not afford to invest in them.

Arguments against privatisation:

- It is not right to make a profit out of the supply of basic services like water, light and heat.

- It means selling off the nation's assets.

- It is substituting a private monopoly for a state monopoly. The state ran the services for the benefit of the consumers. Private monopolies will want to make a profit. They are thought to be more likely to exploit consumers. This has been recognised, which is the reason for having *regulators* for the privatised *utilities* companies.

producers are those people engaged in any part of the process of production.

> **Explanation:** All the people involved in supplying goods and services for money are producers. Producers meet a want for which people are willing to pay. This includes people like ballet dancers and actors. The term is also used as a general title for all firms that are in any way involved with supplying goods and services.

product: that which is made or supplied at the end of the production process. In the *marketing mix* it refers to the design, quality and size of the product being marketed. Product will also include things like *branding*, *packaging* and *guarantees*.

product differentiation happens when firms try to make the public think that their products are different from similar products made by other firms.

> **Explanation:** Firms want to make their products special and different in the minds of consumers. To do this, they try to give those products a special identity. Firms usually do this in two ways:

1. They give their products special names, that is, by *branding* them. They will protect these names by registering them as *trade marks*.

2. They also try to make the products different through the *packaging*. They identify the products by using combinations of colour, design, containers and styles of writing that are easily recognised by consumers.

Once a product is differentiated it is much easier to advertise and promote. It is easier to promote 'Palmolive' than it is to promote soap in general.

Example: Pepsi Cola changed the colour and style of its cans in order to differentiate its product more sharply. A number of other cola makers had cans that looked too like the Pepsi can. The public might mistake the rival product for Pepsi so the packaging was changed to make the product more distinctive.

product life cycle is a theory stating that all products go through a number of similar stages before they come to an end or are withdrawn from the *market*. The length of the cycle will be different for each product.

There are five stages in the product life cycle:

1   **Research and development stage –** this stage can last for several years.

- The stage when a new product is being designed, developed and tested. Design and development costs will be high. These will include the 'tooling up' costs which are the costs of buying or preparing the machinery and equipment needed to produce the product. There will be no sales and there is a loss.

- There is also *market research* and there may be *test marketing* at this stage.

2   **Introduction –** when the product is launched and placed on the market.

- There will be heavy advertising and promotion of the product. Costs will still be high, probably higher than *sales revenue*.

- It will depend on the type of product as to how quickly it sells. Sales may be slow because people are careful about buying new goods. It may take time for people to get to know about the product.

3   **Growth –** when sales are growing quickly.

- Heavy advertising will probably still be necessary.

- Sales revenue will be building up. It will probably be greater than production and marketing costs. The product moves into profit.

- There may now be a growth in competition.

4   **Maturity –** this stage will probably be longer than the introduction and growth stages.

- The product is well established in the market. It may have reached maximum *market share*. It may be at *market saturation* point.

- Sales will be good, but growing only slowly, if at all.

- The manufacturer must still advertise to keep market share.

- The product is making a good profit.

5 **Decline** – this stage can be quite long. A firm may carry on producing because the product is still making a profit, even if this is falling. The 'Mini' car is a product in decline but is still produced because there is a market for it.

- Sales and market share are falling. The speed at which they fall will depend on the type of product. Rival products are more up to date and attractive.

- There is little or nothing spent on advertising

- Unit costs will be low and the product may still make a profit.

- The product may become *obsolete*. The firm will eventually decide to withdraw the product.

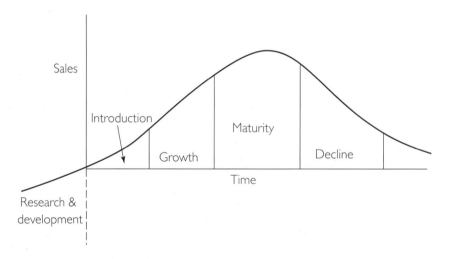

Explanation: All products have a limited life that will vary in length according to the nature of the product. The length of each stage, and the total length of a product's life, depend on a number of things. They make it hard to predict the length of each stage.

- Technical changes affect some goods so that they become *obsolete*.

- External factors may affect the demand and therefore the product life cycle. For example, health warnings and high taxation have affected tobacco products.

- The durability of the product will affect the product life cycle.

- Fashion is one of the greatest factors in a product's life cycle. Clothing sales are obviously affected by fashion. Goods that are 'in fashion' grow and mature very quickly and then go into rapid decline to be replaced by the next fashion.

For goods that have a long life and change only slowly, the diagram shows them as having both a long time axis and a long sales axis. Fashion goods, such as clothing, have a short life. Clothes firms have at least two fashion changes a year. The product life cycle for clothing may, therefore, have quite a high sales axis but only a short time axis.

The length of a product's life cycle can be extended by claiming that the product has been changed in some way. Car manufacturers do it every year through small changes in design or specification.

product mix: the range of goods made by a firm. Each product is probably aimed at a different *segment* of the market. Most car manufacturers have models that aim at the small car, family car and executive car markets. They have a number of different engine sizes, colours and body styles for each type. By having this variety of choice they hope their product mix will appeal to most segments of the market.

production is the creation of goods and services to satisfy human wants. It is organising all the resources needed to meet consumer *demand.* The term covers every stage of getting goods and services to the *consumer.* Production is more than just making things. It includes shops, banks, transport, hospitals, theatres and any other activity that helps to satisfy what people want. Production can be classified into three types.

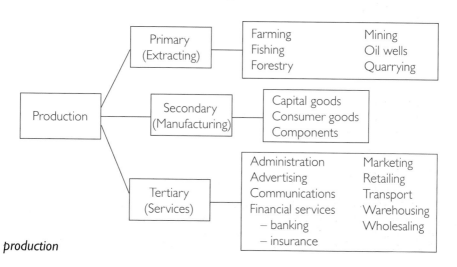

production

productivity is the quantity of goods produced by a worker in a given amount of time.

> **Explanation:** Productivity always relates the quantity produced to time. It is one way of measuring how hard people are working. It is usually measured as the average number of units per worker, produced in an hour. The more goods made each hour, the higher the productivity. This method of measurement is best used for gauging output in factories and cannot be applied to all jobs.

productivity bonus is an extra payment for producing more than a target output. Workers are paid a basic wage to which the productivity bonus is added.

profit is the part of a firm's total revenue that is left over after total costs have been deducted.

> FORMULA *for defining profit:*
>
> **Profit = Total revenue – Total costs**

Profit can also be calculated for a single product, when it will be

> **Profit = Sales revenue – Product costs.**

There are a number of different types of profit: *gross profit, net profit, pre-tax profit* and profit after tax.

profit and loss account is a statement that lists all the running expenses, or *revenue expenditure* of a business. The total of the *expenses* is deducted from the *gross profit* to give the *net profit* for a given period. The gross profit will have been transferred from the *Trading Account*. The main purpose of the profit and loss account is to work out the net profit for the business. The net profit is what the business 'makes' in a year, before it pays tax.

> **Example:** typical profit and loss account

Profit and Loss Account of XYX & Company Limited for the year ending 31 December

	£000	£000
Gross profit		120
less Expenses:		
Salaries	50	
Heating and lighting	15	
Rent and rates	12	
Depreciation	8	
Bad debts	5	90
Net profit		30

profit centre: a department or division of a business given the task of making a profit. It will usually be given a target profit and the power to make the decisions necessary to reach the target. It will, for example, be allowed to fix prices and hire staff. In this sense it is like a business within a business. A car dealer may have three profit centres – new car sales, used car sales and service departments. *Subsidiary companies* will usually be profit centres.

profit distribution is the division of a firm's profits between the owners. In a *limited company* the profits will be distributed to the *shareholders* in the form of a *dividend*. In a *partnership* the profits will be divided according to the *deed of partnership*.

profit margin: the amount of *profit* a business is making as a proportion of its *sales revenue*.

FORMULA *for calculating profit margin:*

$$\text{Profit margin} = \frac{\text{Profit}}{\text{Sales revenue}} \times 100$$

The profit margin can be shown either as a percentage of total sales or as the profit per item sold.

Worked example: A shop sells 500 items at £50 each. Its profits on the sales are £15 000. Show the profit margin as a percentage of a) total sales and b) per item.

a) $\dfrac{\text{Total profit}}{\text{Total sales revenue}} \times 100 = \dfrac{£15\,000}{£25\,000} \times 100 = 60\%$

b) $\dfrac{\text{Profit per item}}{\text{Selling price}} \times 100 = \dfrac{£30}{£50} \times 100 = 60\%$

Notice that the margin is always calculated as a percentage of sales. Mark-up, on the other hand, is a percentage of the *cost price*.

profit sharing happens when firms set aside part of their profits to be shared by their employees. It is paid out as a *bonus* either at the end of the financial year or every half year.

Explanation: Profit sharing is based on the idea that all workers play a part in the success of a firm. If workers feel they are valued by having a share in the profits they will feel much more a part of the firm. They may work harder because they will feel that are sharing directly in the profits they help to make. Some firms also issue *shares* to their employees on which they get a *dividend* in the same way as other *shareholders*.

profit-related pay is a method of *remuneration* where part of employees' pay is linked to their firm's *profits*. If the profits go up then the employees' total pay will also rise. If the profit goes down so will the employees' total pay. It is not a bonus but a part of a person's wages or salary.

promotion (job) occurs when a person is appointed to a more senior or responsible job. It will probably mean higher status and pay. When a person is given a higher grade of job by their existing employer it is an internal promotion. If the higher level job is with a new employer it is an external promotion.

promotion (marketing): the part of the *marketing mix* where it is decided how a product should be marketed or sold. Promotion is itself a mix of methods. The main methods of promotion are as follows:

- **Advertising**

- **Sales promotion –** including discounts, coupons, free offers, competitions, demonstrations and displays such as window and *point of sale* displays.

- **Direct marketing –** through personally addressed mailing, telephone sales and teletext.

- ***Sponsorship –*** of a person or an event.

- **Personal selling –** through sales representatives (who are mainly used for selling to business) also trade fairs and exhibitions and party sales.

- ***After sales service* and customer care –** designed to build up customers' loyalty so that they keep coming back.

prospectus: a document that has to be produced by a *limited company* wanting to sell *shares* to the public. Any company that wants its shares listed on the *Stock Exchange* must have a prospectus. The law and the Stock Exchange lay down what it must contain. The prospectus gives the sort of information that someone needs to have before deciding to invest in a company, in particular:

- what the firm does

- what its profits have been for at least the past three years

- estimates of the firm's future prospects and profits.

The firm must not make claims that it cannot support. There are very severe penalties if the claims made are dishonest.

protectionism happens when a country tries to restrict *imports* of goods and services by using *import duties* (*tariffs*) and *quotas*. Many developing countries try to protect their home industries from foreign competition, so as to give them a chance to develop.

psychological pricing is the fixing of a price to make it look more attractive; for example, when goods are priced at £9.95 instead of £10.

public corporations are a form of organisation and control of state-owned enterprises, that is, *public sector* organisations. They are not government departments. They are trading bodies, selling a product or a service. Most of the nationalised industries were set up by Act of Parliament and run by *incorporated* public corporations. Most of them no longer exist because they have been *privatised*. The BBC, the Post Office and the Bank of England are among the few that are left.

public enterprise is made up of trading organisations that are owned and run by national or local government. It is the part of the *mixed economy* that is publicly owned. There are not many public enterprises left since most of them have been *privatised*. Public enterprises that are still run by local councils include leisure centres, council housing and catering. The Post Office and the BBC are the largest of the nationally owned public enterprises.

public liability insurance is a form of *insurance* taken out to cover the risk that a member of the public might suffer some harm while on an organisation's property. It covers such things as slipping on a polished floor or a stand collapsing at a football match.

public limited company (plc): a company having *limited liability,* whose *shares* can be bought, and sold, by the public. The company has no control over who buys its shares. The ownership (by the shareholders) of the company is separated from the control (by the *board of directors*). Plcs are formed only after the *Registrar of Companies* has approved the following:

- the *memorandum of association,* which includes the company name which must end with 'plc'
- the *articles of association*
- a list of the names and addresses of the first directors and of the company secretary
- a statement that all the legal requirements have been met
- a copy of the *prospectus* or offer for sale when shares are to be sold.

Features of a plc:

- The shareholders have *limited liability*. There must be a minimum capital of £50 000.
- The company can be set up by two or more people; the memorandum has to be signed by at least two people.

- The company is *incorporated*, which means that it has a legal existence that is separate from its shareholders.
- *Directors* must be elected to run the company at an *annual general meeting* when the directors present the *Annual Report and Accounts*. A copy must be sent to the *Registrar of Companies* which can be inspected by anyone.

Advantages of public limited companies:

- The market for shares is highly organised through the *Stock Exchange*. Shareholders can normally get their money back very easily. This means that people are willing to invest in plcs.
- They enable very large amounts of *capital* to be gathered in one organisation. Very large companies can be formed that are able to compete on a worldwide basis. Banks are more willing to lend to companies with large share capital.
- They are able to gain *economies of scale*.
- Anyone wanting to do business with a plc is able to check their *annual report and accounts* to see if they are financially sound.

Disadvantages of public limited companies:

- In practice, the small shareholder can do very little to influence the way the company is run.
- They are subject to takeover bids. Other companies can buy big blocks of shares, and there is no way of stopping them.
- Their activities are very closely controlled by company law.
- When a private company becomes a public company the original shareholders may lose control of the company.

public money is money collected from the public that is spent by the government or local councils. Most of it will have been collected from the public in taxes. Some will be from loans, selling goods and services and government or EU grants.

public relations (PR) is the management of every aspect of a firm's relationship with outside bodies. This includes its customers, suppliers and the public generally. The firm tries to make sure that all publicity is good by managing all references to it in the press and media to make sure they show the company in a good light.

public sector: all activity carried out by either national or local government. It is made up of two parts:

- trading bodies set up to sell a product or service to the public. These are the _public enterprise_ organisations. Since _privatisation_ they have become a fairly small part of the public sector

- the part set up to provide services to the public.
  - This includes those services that are provided by _central government;_ for example, law and order, defence, the National Health Service and Social Security.
  - Services that are provided by local councils, often with the help of government grants; for example, education, social services, housing, libraries and museums, police and fire services.

public spending is spending by government departments, government agencies and local councils. Most of the money for this is collected from taxpayers. It also includes money that has been borrowed by both local and national government.

purchases: the buying of all supplies needed by a business. These can be divided into two groups:

- the purchase of raw materials and components or finished goods. These are a part of the _cost of goods sold._ They are shown in the _Trading Account_ and their value deducted with net stock from the _sales,_ to find _gross profit_

- other supplies, such as stationery and heating and lighting fuel. These are shown as expenses in the _profit and loss account._

QCA: see *Qualifications and Curriculum Authority*.

Qualifications and Curriculum Authority: a *statutory* body that came into being in October 1997. It advises the government on curriculum, assessment and qualifications across the whole of education and training. It acts as the *regulator* for all school and vocational qualifications, including the *National Vocational Qualification (NVQ)*. It approves the NVQ awarding bodies and monitors the standards of their tests and qualifications.

quality assurance (QA): the steps taken by a firm to make sure that there is a known standard of quality built into all its products. It is the process that a firm uses to ensure that the standards of quality it sets are met in all aspects of its work.

> **Explanation:** The quality of a product depends on the price at which the product is to be sold. Quality assurance tries to make sure that all those working in a firm know the level of quality that is expected. The job of QA is to make sure the firm has the right procedures to ensure quality.

- Quality is part of every stage in production, from design to the finished article, including *after sales service*.
- All components used must meet the set quality standard.
- BS 5750 and ISO 9000 and *Investors in People* are quality assurance standards. If a firm has these standards or the *BSI's Kitemark*, it can display the *logos* on its letterheads and publicity to help in marketing.

(See also *total quality management*.)

quality circles are groups of workers and managers who meet to discuss quality problems in their area of work. They suggest ways of getting over the problems. It is part of *quality assurance*. The circles try to make the people doing the job take responsibility for the quality of their own output. Originally a Japanese idea, it is now widely used all over the world.

quality control is the methods used by firms to make sure that their products are of the right quality. This is usually done by inspecting the product at every stage during production. It may also be done by testing the goods at regular intervals. Goods with faults are either scrapped or put right before they move on to the next stage. (Compare with *quality assurance*.)

questionnaire: a list of questions designed to produce answers about a defined set of issues. In business, questionnaires are used mainly in *market research.* They are designed to find out customers' attitudes to one or more products. They need to be very carefully designed.

- The questions should be *closed* rather than *open questions* and be easy to understand, in the right order, and not flit from point to point.
- The answers should be easy to summarise and convert into statistics.
- The questions should not be biased (loaded questions) or lead people towards a particular answer, for example, 'Do you think it would be a good idea if …'.

quota: a limit on the quantity of a product that can be dealt in. There may be several reasons for having quotas:

- to limit the quantity of a product being imported into a country
- to avoid producing too much of certain products. The European Community, for example, sets quotas on the amount of milk and wheat that should be produced
- to conserve stocks of a product. There are worries that some types of fish could become extinct. To stop overfishing the EC has agreed quotas for the number of certain types of fish that can be caught.

quotation: an offer to supply goods or services at a certain price and on stated conditions.

Explanation: If a firm wants to buy some specific goods or services it may ask a number of possible suppliers how much they would charge. This is known as an enquiry. The reply to an enquiry is a quotation. A quotation is a definite offer to supply services or a named quantity of named goods at a specified price. A quotation includes certain information:

- **The specification for the goods** – their catalogue number, size, colour, the price for each item, the date for delivery.
- **Terms of payment** – these state when the goods have to be paid for and whether there are any discounts.
- **The time for which the quotation is open** – if an order is not placed within that time, a new quotation would have to be obtained.

quoted company: one whose shares are listed on one of the *Stock Exchange* markets.

Race Relations Acts 1968 and 1976: these make it unlawful to discriminate on the grounds of colour, race, nationality or ethnic origin. Discrimination in employment, training, housing, education and in the provision of goods, facilities and services is unlawful. In work it covers such areas as recruiting, promotion and the choosing of people for *redundancy* or *dismissal*. Anyone who thinks he or she has been discriminated against can ask the *Commission for Racial Equality (CRE)* for advice and support. The commission may help to take the case to an *industrial tribunal*.

radio advertising promotes goods and services using commercial radio. It is a form of indirect *advertising*. It is the only form of advertising that is not visual, relying entirely on sound. There is a wide choice of national and local radio stations. Radio advertisements are fairly easy and cheap to make and to broadcast.

random sample is a group of people, chosen by chance, without taking age, sex or income into account. The information they give will be taken to represent the views of a *population*.

> **Explanation:** In *market research* it would take too long and be too expensive to ask everyone who might buy a product what they think about it. Instead, a *sample* is asked. Ideally they would like to find a sample that is exactly like the product's target population. Again it might take too long and cost too much. Instead a random sample may be taken, where everyone has an equal chance of being questioned. In fact, it may only be every tenth person passing who is questioned. Random samples are not very accurate. This is because the make up of the sample will be different each time, according to where and when it is taken.

rate of interest: the percentage rate charged for lending, or paid for borrowing, money over a period of time.

> **Explanation:** Money deposited in a building society or bank is, in effect, being lent to it and it will pay a stated rate of interest. In the same way, when money is borrowed, a rate of interest is charged. It is always stated as a percentage.

FORMULA for calculating rate of interest:

$$\text{Rate of interest} = \frac{\text{Total interest paid}}{\text{Amount of loan}} \times 100$$

This will give the *flat rate of interest*. This should be compared with the true rate of interest which is shown by the *annualised percentage rate (APR)*.

rate of stock turnover is the number of times the *average stock* is turned over during a year. It is a way of measuring the speed at which goods are sold.

FORMULA *for calculating rate of stock turnover:*

$$\text{Rate of turnover} = \frac{\text{Cost of goods sold}}{\text{Average stock}}$$

Explanation: The rate of turnover is important for all businesses. Holding stocks increases a firm's costs. Some goods, like perishable foods, have to be sold quickly. Other goods, like sheet steel or furniture, will tend to sell more slowly. By working out the rate of turnover a firm knows the average time goods are kept in stock. The information needed to work out the rate of stock turnover is found in the *Trading Account.*

Average stock = Opening stock + Closing stock ÷ 2

Cost of goods sold = Opening stock + Purchases – Closing stock.

Worked example: What is the rate of stock turnover of the business with the following Trading Account?

Trading Account of XYX & Company Limited for the year ended 31 December

	£000	£000
Sales		185
less Cost of goods sold:		
Opening stock	24	
plus Purchases	120	
	144	
less Closing stock	32	112
Gross profit		73

$$\text{Rate of stock turnover} = \frac{\text{Cost of goods sold}}{\text{Average stock}} = \frac{112}{28} = 4$$

Stocks are sold four times a year. That is, goods were kept in stock, on average, for three months.

rate of turnover is another name for the *rate of stock turnover.*

ratio analysis is the use of accounting data as a method for analysing the success of a firm during a given time. As with all ratios one piece of data is related to another.

Examples:

* The *current ratio* relates current assets to current liabilities, thus:
    Current assets
    Current liabilities

- The *net profit margin* relates the net profit to the sales turnover:

$$\frac{\text{Net profit}}{\text{Sales turnover}}$$

Ratios can be used to compare one year with another, or one department with another.

Ratios may be useful to a number of people:

- **shareholders:** to see how well their investment is doing, or how safe it is. People thinking of buying shares in a firm may look at, for example, the *dividend yield*, the *gearing* and the *return on capital employed*

- **managers:** will want to compare their results with those of previous years and other departments. Senior managers may want to see who has met their targets and who has not

- **creditors:** or firms thinking of giving a company credit will look at its accounts and probably work out its *liquidity ratio* or *gearing*.

rationalisation happens when a business reorganises in order to be more efficient. This means cutting costs, by closing down branches or departments. Alternatively it may reduce the size of its management through *de-layering*.

raw materials are goods bought by a manufacturer to be used in the production of another product. Sometimes they will not have been processed – iron ore brought into an iron making factory, for example. Often the finished goods of one firm will be the raw materials of another. For example, steel plate will be the finished goods of a steel factory but the raw material for a firm pressing car bodies.

real income is the value of incomes after taking changes in prices into account. People are only better off if incomes rise by more than prices over a period of time. If real income rises it means a person can buy more with the same amount of money. If real income falls then the same amount of money will buy fewer goods.

Example: If wages have gone up in one year by 5%, then money incomes are said to have risen by 5%. If, in the same year, prices have gone up by 3%, real income will have risen by 2% (5% – 3% = 2%).

receipt: a document issued by a seller to a buyer when the buyer has paid for goods. It is proof that payment has been made. Receipts should be kept by the buyer. Often shops will only take back or exchange goods if a buyer has the receipt for them.

receiver: a person appointed to run a company that goes into *receivership*. It will be the receiver's job to try to sell the company's *assets* so as to get enough money to pay the *creditors*. The receiver tries to sell the company as a *going concern*. If the business can be sold as a going concern the receiver is usually able to raise more money than by selling the assets separately.

receivership is the period during which a company is being run by a *receiver* who will manage the company while trying to find a buyer for it. The company carries on trading while the receiver tries to sell it as a *going concern*.

recession: a phase in the *business cycle* when economic activity is falling. There will be a fall in spending on goods and services. *Gross domestic product* will fall.

Features of a recession:

- There is a lack of business confidence and firms reduce *capital investment*.

- Sales of goods and services fall and therefore profits also fall. Prices and *profit margins* may fall as firms try to tempt people to buy goods.

- As sales fall, firms will cut *capacity*. Unemployment will increase. There is an increase in business failures.

recommended retail price (RRP): this is the price at which manufacturers suggest retailers should sell their goods. Manufacturers cannot make the retailers sell at the suggested price. In practice the prices should vary from shop to shop.

recovery: the phase in the *business cycle* when economic activity begins to rise. It comes after a *recession*.

Features of a recovery:

- Consumer spending on goods and services and capital items begins to rise.

- Business confidence starts to pick up. Firms start to invest in new *capital equipment*.

- Firms start to make bigger profits. Unemployment begins to fall.

recruitment is the whole process involved in taking on new employees. Some firms recruit all jobs through their *personnel department*. Other firms may use *employment agencies*, at least for some jobs. There are a number of stages to recruitment:

1. Deciding that there is a vacancy. This may mean filling a job that has become empty because someone has left or *job analysis* may have shown the need for a new job. At this stage it will be decided whether a job is permanent or temporary, full-time or part-time.

2 A *job description* and a *job specification* are drawn up.

3 A *job advertisement* is prepared. A firm must decide where to place the advertisement. This depends on whether it is going to use *internal* or *external recruitment*. If external, the firm will have to decide whether to advertise nationally or locally and in which papers.

4 The *selection* stage involves:

- deciding on a *shortlist* of candidates to interview. *References* will be taken up at this point

- deciding when to *interview* and how the interviews will be organised

- carrying out interviews, and perhaps second interviews after further selection.

5 The appointment stage is reached when a letter of appointment is sent to a successful candidate. The letter sets out the terms of the appointment and may give a starting date. A formal *contract of employment* usually follows later after a person has accepted a job.

redeployment is the transfer of employees to a different job within the same firm. It may be an alternative to *redundancy*. There may be several reasons for redeployment.

- A branch or department may have closed. This may mean moving staff to a new department, maybe at a different branch or even in a different part of the country.

- A firm may decide that a job is no longer necessary. This happens when there is *rationalisation* or *delayering* in a firm or sometimes when *new technology* is adopted.

- An employee may not be coping with the demands of his or her job. The firm may redeploy instead of sacking the person. The new job may be a sideways move or even a demotion.

reducing balance: a method for calculating the *depreciation* of a *fixed asset*. Under this method a fixed percentage is deducted from the net value of the asset, as it was shown in the last *balance sheet*.

Worked example: A machine is bought for £12 000. It is to be depreciated at 25% per year using the decreasing balance method. What is the value of the machine at the end of three years?

	£
Purchase price	12 000
Depreciation, year 1: £12 000 × 25%	3 000
Value at end of year 1	9 000
Depreciation, year 2: £9 000 × 25%	2 250
Value at end of year 2	6 750
Depreciation, year 3: £6 750 × 25%	1 688
Value at end of year 3	5 062

Under this method the depreciation is high in the first year but goes down each year afterwards. It is a good method to use with assets such as motor vehicles which tend to depreciate very quickly when they are new.

redundancy happens when employees are dismissed because their jobs are no longer needed by their employer. For redundancy to take place a job must come to an end. There is no redundancy if a person is replaced by someone else doing exactly the same job. There may be several reasons for redundancy:

- the business or a branch is closing because of *rationalisation*

- the introduction of *new technology* may result in people being replaced by machines

- the business no longer needs, or needs less of, a particular kind of employee.

The recognised *trades unions* have a right, in law, to be consulted by an employer about likely redundancies. They will try to negotiate other ways of dealing with the problem. Failing this, the unions will try to get the best financial deal possible for their members.

Employees who have been made redundant are able to claim redundancy payments. Firms will often offer special terms to try to get people to volunteer for redundancy. If there are no special terms then workers made redundant are entitled to statutory redundancy pay. This takes into account the worker's:

- age

- number of years worked for the firm

- rate of pay.

However it only applies to workers who work more than 16 hours a week and have worked for the same firm for two years without a break.

references: see *job references*, and *trade references*.

Registrar of Companies: the individual made responsible by *statute* for three main things:

- approving all documents that are needed when setting up a *limited company*. They have to be agreed before the *Certificate of Incorporation* can be issued. The Registrar also officially dissolves companies that are wound up and cease to exist

- keeping copies of all the documents needed to form a company. The Registrar also receives and keeps copies of all the annual accounts and returns that companies must make

- making sure that all the information is available to the public. Anyone can go to Companies House, in Cardiff, to inspect the information.

regulator: a person appointed to supervise and control the activities of an industry. There are three kinds of regulator.

- Regulators appointed by the government under statute.

  - There are separate regulators for each of the *privatised* utility industries such as water, gas and electricity. Their main function is to protect the interests of the consumer. They try to control prices by having strict rules on the way prices are fixed. They also have to bring competition into the industries. Any new companies entering the industries also come under their control. (See *OFFER, OFGAS, OFTEL, OFWAT.*)

  - A regulator may also be needed for new industries where there is a risk that the public could be exploited. The Regulator for the National Lottery (OFLOT) and the *Independent Television Commission (ITC)* are two examples.

- A *private sector* industry may be indirectly controlled by the government. The *Bank of England* acts as the regulator for the banking industry.

- Private industry has set up its own regulators. Industries often do so under the threat that if they do not control themselves the government will impose external regulation. The *Advertising Standards Authority* and the Press Complaints Commission are examples.

remuneration is the full package of rewards received by an employee as payment for work. For most people it is just their wages or salaries. For others, remuneration may include *fringe benefits, bonuses* or share options.

rent is the payment made for the use of land or property. Normally a business or person will *lease* property for a fixed period of time. A rent is paid for hiring the use of the property during that time.

repeat order: this is when exactly the same goods are ordered again. A business making a repeat order for goods may earn an extra *trade discount*. A *consumer* who buys a *branded* product several times may be said to be developing a brand loyalty towards that product.

replacement cost: the value of an *asset* in the *balance sheet* based on the cost of replacing that asset.

> ***Explanation:*** The value of assets in the balance sheet is usually based on their purchase price (*historic costs*). Some people say it would be more realistic to value assets at the cost of replacing them. Valuing assets at their replacement cost may not be very accurate since it can only be an estimate. The real replacement cost cannot be known until an asset is actually replaced.

reports are a form of *communication* about a specific subject. Reports may cover a very wide range of topics and may have several purposes.

- Simply to give information e.g. minutes of meetings, monthly sales figures.

- To give an account of detailed research into some aspect of a firm. For example, a firm may be thinking of buying new equipment or changing its accounting software.

- To comment upon or make suggestions about a specific topic. For example, a department's manager may put forward ideas on how to develop the department.

Reports may be either internal or external. Internal reports will be written by someone within the firm. An external report is prepared by someone from outside the firm, for example, a consultant or an auditor.

Reports can be verbal but they are usually in writing. Exactly how a report is presented will vary according to the 'house style' of a firm. The format of all reports will have some common features.

1. **Title** – this should state clearly what the subject is and be as brief as possible.

2. **Introduction** – this should set out any terms of reference and relevant background information.

3. **Sub-sections and sub-headings** – the subject should be broken down into parts, each part being a sub-section. Each sub-section should be given a clear sub-heading.

4. **Conclusions/recommendations** – these should be based on what has been written earlier in the report.

5. **Originator's name** – this is often written at the end, but it may be at the beginning. If it is at the beginning, it is best included after the title

with a phrase like 'A report prepared by …'. Care must be taken not to make the report look like a *memorandum*.

6   **Date –** this, too, is often written at the end of a report. If at the beginning it should follow the originator's name.

7   **Whom the report is prepared for –** this should be shown at the beginning. Avoid 'To…'; it looks too much like a memorandum.

8   **Reports are never signed.**

research and development (R & D) refers to the technical development of new or existing products. This may need scientific as well as technical research and will include testing. Investment in research and development is very important for the future for many firms.

Reasons for research and development:

- To develop new products. For example, chemical companies may take years to develop a new drug. Car manufacturers spend years developing new models.

- To develop new, perhaps cheaper, manufacturing processes.

- To improve existing products and solve any problems they may have.

(See also *product life cycle*.)

reserves are the *retained profits* of a firm that have been built up, perhaps over several years. They will be shown in the *balance sheet* as part of *shareholders' funds*. They are not usually kept as cash but will be invested. They are an important *source of finance* for long-term *investment*.

residual value is an estimate of what the value of an *asset* is likely to be at the end of its useful life. It is hard to guess the secondhand value of a piece of equipment in, say, ten years' time. The residual value is used in working out *depreciation* by the *straight line* method.

resource allocation is to provide the financial, physical and human resources needed to produce goods and services. When a firm decides to produce a product it has to make sure there are enough resources. This will mean having a *budget*. The budget allocates money for every stage of development, marketing and production. The money will be used to buy the physical and human resources needed.

resources are all the means necessary for the production of goods and services. They are the land, labour and capital used in production. Most of a firm's physical resources can be given a money value and will be shown as *assets* in a firm's *balance sheet*. Human resources, especially things like flair, initiative and skill cannot be shown in a balance sheet.

restrictive practices (in the marketplace): any practice that in some way reduces competition, restricts or distorts a market. Such practices include any attempt to insist that goods are only sold at a certain price or when suppliers of goods share out a market between them. A restrictive practice is unlawful unless it has been registered with the *Office of Fair Trading*. Very few have been registered.

restrictive practices (in the workplace): a *trades union* agreement that stops managers deciding who should do which job and where. Such agreements are mainly things of the past. They often led to *demarcation* disputes. The closed shop was an example of a restrictive practice. It is now illegal.

restructuring happens when a firm reorganises. It will mean changing the *organisation chart* of a firm. It is supposed to lead to more efficient working but often leads to *redundancies*. *Delayering* is an example of restructuring.

Retail Co-operative Society: one of the societies that owns and runs a 'Co-op' shop. Each Society is separate and covers a local area. The Societies are owned by their members who will, in the main, also be their customers. They are run by a management committee elected by the members. (See also *co-operatives*.)

retail margin is the amount of profit made by a retailer as a percentage of selling price.

FORMULA *for calculating retail margin:*

$$\frac{\text{Selling price} - \text{Cost price}}{\text{Selling price}} \times 100 = \frac{\text{Gross profit}}{\text{Selling price}} \times 100$$

This is the *gross margin*. It is the profit before *overheads* have been paid. It can be worked out for each separate item or as the average profit on total sales.

retail prices index (RPI): an *index number* that shows how much the price of the average shopping basket has changed. The index is published every month by the government. The RPI is the main way of measuring *inflation* in Britain. It is sometimes called the 'cost of living' index.

Explanation: The index is based on a 'basket' of goods and services that the average household buys. It includes housing, food, motoring costs, fuel, drinks and tobacco. Some things, (e.g. food) are more important than others. Such items are given a bigger weighting. A change in the price of goods with a high weighting will have a bigger effect on the index than that for goods with a low weighting. A change in food prices, for instance, will have a bigger effect than a change in the prices of leisure services.

retailing: the selling of goods directly to the public. Retailers are the last link in a *chain of distribution*. They sell goods to consumers in the small quantities they want. The term not only includes shops, but also market stalls, mail order and vending machines.

retained profit is the part of a firm's *profits* that is not taken out of the business by the owners nor is it paid to the shareholders as *dividends*. The retained profit is kept in a business as *reserves*.

retraining occurs when a person who is skilled at one job is trained to do another. This may be necessary for a number of reasons:

- because of reorganisation some jobs in a firm have ended. Instead of making those people redundant, the firm may offer retraining so that they are able to do different jobs

- there is no longer a use for an employee's skills. So that such workers can work again they have to be taught new skills. This happened to people who worked in the shipbuilding industry, for example

- a person's skills may need to be brought up to date. For example, typists may need to be retrained to wordprocess.

return on capital employed (ROCE) is the *profit* made by a business as a percentage of the *capital* invested in it. It is a measure of the amount the owners of a business earned on the capital invested in the business.

> **FORMULA *for calculating return on capital employed:***
>
> $$\text{ROCE} = \frac{\textbf{Net profit for the year}}{\textbf{Capital at the start of the year}} = \times 100$$

Explanation: This is an important figure because it tells the owners how worthwhile their investment has been. Money invested in a business by the owners can always be used for something else. It could, for example, be invested to earn interest. If the ROCE is less than could have been earned elsewhere their *investment* was not a good one.

Someone thinking of buying shares can look at the *annual accounts* of several companies. By comparing their ROCE, potential buyers are able to judge where they could make the best return.

> ***Worked example:* A company that started the year with a capital of £600 000 made a profit of £120 000. What is the return on capital employed?**

$$\text{ROCE} = \frac{\text{Profit}}{\text{Opening capital}} = \times 100 \ \frac{£120\ 000}{£600\ 000} = \times 100 = 20\%$$

This means that for every £1 invested in the company the shareholders would earn 20p. That is a good rate of return that would be difficult to match by investing elsewhere.

revenue is the income earned by a business. The main source of revenue for most companies will be *sales revenue*. There may be other income, such as rents from land or dividends from subsidiary companies, that would go to make up *total revenue*.

revenue expenditure is spending that is paid for directly out of income. It is spending on the things needed in order to earn an income for a firm. It is the firm's expenses. In effect, it is money that is spent on anything other than buying *fixed assets*. Examples include buying materials and paying expenses, like wages and salaries.

ROCE: see *return on capital employed*.

RPI: see *retail price index*.

salary: a method of paying *employees* for their work. Salaries are normally stated on an annual basis but are usually paid monthly. They are often paid by *credit transfer* directly into employees' bank accounts. Salaries are paid to managers and 'white collar' workers. Compare with *wages*.

Sale of Goods Act: this sets down the legal framework between the buyers and sellers of goods. The Act applies only to the sale of goods by a business to members of the public. The Act does not cover private sales or the sale of services. The general rule of *caveat emptor* – ('let the buyer beware') still applies. The Act is an important part of *consumer protection*.

Features of the Sale of Goods Act:

- Contracts for the sale of goods can be either in writing or made orally.

- Goods bought from a trader who normally deals in those goods are assumed to be of 'merchantable quality'. That means the goods must be fit for ordinary use. Merchantable quality partly depends on price. More expensive goods are expected to be of higher quality. There are two exceptions to this rule; namely:

  - if a seller draws any defects to a buyer's notice when the goods are bought or

  - if a buyer examines the goods and is satisfied with them.

- Goods are assumed to be fit for the purpose for which they were bought, especially if a buyer has asked the seller for advice.

- When goods are bought on the strength of a description, the goods must match the description. For example, a sweater described as being 100% wool must not contain any other fibre.

A buyer only has a contract with the seller of the goods. If there is a problem, the buyer must complain to the shopkeeper, not the manufacturer of the goods. A buyer does not normally have a contract with the manufacturer. Sellers cannot take away a buyer's rights under the Sale of Goods Act, e.g., by displaying notices or through special guarantees.

sales: providing goods and services in exchange for money. When goods are sold, the buyer obtains ownership of the goods. Sales are shown in the *Trading Account*.

sales department: the department that plans, organises and administers the sales of a firm's products. It is the department that communicates with customers. The sales force will be members of the sales department.

Main functions of the sales department:

- Receiving *orders* for goods, acknowledging them and passing them on to the production department or the warehouse. It will also receive all customers' communications, including complaints, and should make sure replies are sent.

- Making sure that all sales documents are sent out:

  - advice, delivery or dispatch notes that tell customers that the goods are on the way

  - *invoices* showing the right price and terms of the sales

  - *statements of accounts* to remind customers of how much money they owe.

- Receiving payments from customers and passing them on to the accounts department.

- Receiving reports from the sales representatives on customers' complaints, suggestions about new products or changes to existing ones.

sales forecast: an estimate drawn up by a *sales department* of probable sales for the coming year. It is an important part of the normal planning of a firm. It may be the basis upon which production is planned and may affect the firm's employment policy.

sales promotion: a special event or other short-term attempt to persuade people to buy a product or service. It includes special offers, money-off tokens, free gifts, offers on packs, competitions, *discounting,* special displays and price cuts. A sales promotion lasts only for a limited period.

sales revenue: the total value of a firm's sales in a given period. It includes sales on *credit* as well as any cash sales. At the end of the year it will be the figure that is shown as 'sales' in the *Trading Account.*

> FORMULA **for calculating sales revenue:**
>
> **Sales revenue = Sales volume × Price**

sales turnover is another term used to describe *sales revenue.*

sales volume is the quantity of goods sold in a stated period of time.

sample (statistical): a small group of people, taken as being representative of a much larger group. Sampling is a method widely used in *market research.*

> **Explanation:** In market research it would cost too much and take too long to interview the whole of a *population.* A smaller group is interviewed instead. What

those people say is taken to represent the views of all people with similar characteristics. It is assumed that if, for example, 15% of a sample responds in a certain way, then 15% of the whole population will respond that way. The way the sample is chosen will partly depend on what the research is trying to find out. If the views of pensioners are wanted there is no point in asking 18-year-olds.

sample (trade): the term 'sample' or 'trade sample' is used when sellers show an example of their product to buyers.

sandwich course: a type of training course made up of attendance at college or university and practical experience working in a firm. It is usually spread over four years. At the end of the time, trainees will earn a degree or other qualification. Sandwich courses enable trainees to apply the theory learnt at college to a practical situation in a work place.

savings: the part of a person's income that is not spent. Savings are not usually just hoarded up under the floorboards. They are placed in a *bank* or *building society* or invested in some way. The banks, building societies and *financial institutions* lend this money to private borrowers or to finance business *growth*.

scab: a term of abuse used against someone who does not support fellow workers during an *industrial dispute*. A scab is someone who is prepared to cross a *picket* line.

scale of production describes either the quantity produced or the size of the plant used for production. Thus 'large-scale production' means that goods are produced in very large quantites, which needs very large factories.

scarcity is an important idea in economics. Human wants are almost without limit. The resources available to satisfy those wants are scarce. This is true of individuals and of society. Because resources are scarce, choices have to be made. When a choice is made there is a sacrifice – an *opportunity cost*. Scarcity is also important in deciding price. The more scarce a product, the higher the price people will be prepared to pay. This is why some firms limit the amount they produce.

secondary action happens when *trades unions* taking *industrial action* at one firm also take action at other firms that have little or nothing to do with the dispute. For example, workers at a supplier's are called out on strike 'in sympathy' when there is a dispute in a car factory. Such action is now illegal.

secondary industry: industry that manufactures or processes goods. It includes the construction industry and the providers of public utilities like gas, water and electricity.

It receives raw materials produced by primary industry and changes them into something different.

> **Example:** Farmers produce milk (a primary industry) that manufacturers of dairy goods (secondary industry) change into butter or cheese.

Secondary industry may also combine several manufacturers' products to make some thing else.

> **Example:** A car manufacturer buys components from very many manufacturers. It combines those parts to make something different, that is, a car.

secondary research makes use of existing information that has been published. It is an important part of *market research*. It is the same thing as *desk research*.

secondary sources provide the information that is used in *secondary research*.

For examples of possible sources see *desk research*.

securities: the general name given to all types of *stocks* and *shares*.

security (loans) is the *collateral* required by banks and other lenders of money. The security is normally at least equal to the value of the loan. If the loan is not repaid the security will be sold. In that way the lender is sure to recover the amount lent.

Examples:

- A bank may ask for part of a firm's *assets*, probably a *fixed asset*, as security for a loan, to be signed over to the bank, giving it the power to sell the asset if the loan were not repaid. The bank has a *mortgage* on the asset.

- When a building society lends money to buy a house the title deeds are signed over to the society. There is a *mortgage* on the house which means the society can sell the house if the loan is not repaid, or if the payments get too far behind.

security (data) refers to the steps taken to protect computer files and other data from either being lost or from unauthorised access. Anything that may be of interest to other firms, especially commercial rivals, will be a security problem for all firms.

segmentation: see *market segmentation*.

selection is the last stage in the *recruitment* of a new employee. Selection should be based on the *job specification*. In practice, firms use other factors such as appearance, personality and a person's ability to 'fit in' with the rest of the staff.

The stages in selection:

1 *Shortlist* – there may be a large number of applications for a job. These applications have to be cut down in number to make the interviews manageable.

2 Make arrangements for the interviews.

- Who is going to do the interviewing?

- Dates have to be agreed that are suitable for everybody involved.

- Letters asking for *references* should be sent.

3 Invite the shortlisted candidates giving the dates, times and locations of the interviews.

4 *Interview* – the purpose of the interviews is to choose one person for the job.

5 After the interviews:

- inform the successful candidate. This must be confirmed in writing if the job was originally offered by telephone or face to face. The unsuccessful candidates must also be informed but not usually until the successful candidate has accepted

- arrange a starting date with the appointed person. If that person is working he or she will have to resign from their present job. It may be several months before he or she can start the new job

- prepare a *contract of employment*

- organise an *induction* programme for the new employee.

selection tests are used by some employers to help them in the selection of new staff. They are used to measure intelligence, personality and aptitude (having the right skills). It is common, for example, to ask secretaries to take a keyboard test.

self-employed: a term describing people who work for themselves. They may work freelance or run their own businesses. The majority of such businesses are quite small but may employ several other people.

self-regulation happens when industries set up their own systems to try to control their activities. Usually they issue a code of practice or a code of conduct which they expect their members to follow. The schemes are usually voluntary and there is no method of punishment, other than publicity. Examples include the *Advertising Standards Authority* and the Insurance Ombudsman Bureau.

semi-skilled worker: a worker who has some, but not all of the skills of a skilled worker. Unlike skilled workers, semi-skilled workers will not have completed an apprenticeship. They may not have qualifications, although they might have the necessary hand skills.

service department: the department which provides a firm's *after sales service.* This may be a repair service, or, in many firms, regular maintenance under contract.

service industries are the industries that are in the *tertiary* sector. They do not sell a product but a service. It is provided directly to the client. Examples include; insurance, banking, retailing and shipping. In well developed economies they are the main source of employment.

Sex Discrimination Acts, 1975 and 1986: these Acts make it unlawful for anyone to discriminate on the grounds of gender when advertising a job, employing people or in setting the age of retirement. Men and women must be treated equally in matters of training, promotion and dismissal. People who feel they have been discriminated against can get advice from the *Equal Opportunities Commission.* It may help to take a case to an *industrial tribunal.*

share capital is the total value of the shares that have been issued to the public. The share capital is made up of *ordinary shares* and *preference shares.* The share capital is shown as part of the *shareholders' funds* in a firm's *balance sheet.*

share certificate: a certificate that shows how many shares are registered by a firm as being owned by a shareholder.

share issue: the issue of shares to the public. They are advertised through a *prospectus* or an offer for sale.

share premium: the issuing of shares at more than their *nominal value.* A popular company may know that there will be a big demand for its shares. It expects the *market price* to be higher than the nominal value of the shares. It tries to get some of that profit for itself by selling the shares at a premium.

share price: the price at which shares are sold on the *stock exchange.* The price can vary from day to day. The share prices for the companies quoted on the Stock Exchange are listed in the 'heavy' newspapers every day. Firms watch their share price carefully. It tells them how outside experts and the *financial institutions* think they are performing.

shareholder: someone who holds shares in a *limited company.* Shareholders are part-owners of a company. Shareholders may buy and sell shares through the *Stock Exchange.*

Reasons for buying shares:

- To earn a regular income. *Savings* can be used to buy *shares* in order to obtain income from *dividends*. In most years the income from share dividends will be higher than interest from building societies or elsewhere.

- To gain capital growth. Shareholders hope that the prices of shares will rise on the Stock Exchange and that they will be able to sell shares for more than they paid for them. They will then make a capital gain. The general trend of the prices of shares on the Stock Exchange is to rise.

Reasons for selling shares:

- A shareholder may need the money for some reason and so decides to cash in any capital gain.

- Investors may think they can gain even more by investing the money somewhere else.

- The price of the shares is expected to, or has already started to, fall. Shareholders may decide to 'cut their losses' by selling the shares before they fall any further.

shareholders' funds: the part of a firm's capital that is owned by the shareholders. It is shown in the *balance sheet*. It is the capital that would be paid back to the *shareholders* if a company were wound up. It is made up of a firm's *issued capital* plus its *retained profits* held in the form of *reserves*.

shareholders' rights are the rights given to ordinary shareholders by law.

- Shareholders are entitled to a share of the company's profits.

- They are entitled to copies of the *Annual Report and Accounts*. Shareholders usually get a shortened version of it unless they ask for the full report.

- They can attend and speak and vote at the company's annual general meeting. They are then able to: propose resolutions; appoint and dismiss the company's directors and auditors and approve the company's *final accounts* and proposed final *dividend*.

shares are the units into which the capital of a *limited company* is divided. The total value of the shares equals the *issued capital* of a firm. Shares are of two kinds: *preference shares* and *ordinary shares*.

Explanation: A firm divides its capital into units. Those units are usually £1 each but they can be of any value (in fact £10 shares and 1p shares have both been issued). This will be the *nominal value* of the shares, not their *market value*.

shift work involves working regular hours that are outside the normal working day. It is widely used in services such as the police and fire service where there has to be 24 hour 'cover'. It is also used in the manufacturing industry. Its use avoids stopping and starting processes, and ensures the best use of costly *capital equipment*.

> *Explanation:* When a shift system is worked the day is divided into equal parts. The pattern of shifts might be: 6 a.m. to 2 p.m. (morning shift); 2 p.m. to 10 p.m. (afternoon shift); and 10 p.m. to 6 a.m. (night shift). Some people may work the same shift every week. Others may have to change shifts once every week or every fortnight. Shifts are used in factories especially if they have very expensive equipment and use *flow production* methods. A three shift system will only be used when the *demand* for the goods is high.

shop steward: a *trades union* official elected at the place of work by members of a trade union to give their views to a firm's management.

> *Explanation:* Shop stewards are ordinary workers who have been elected by their fellow workers from the same trade union. Shop stewards do their union duties voluntarily. Firms may allow them some paid time off for their union duties. In a small firm there may only be one shop steward. In large firms each recognised trade union will have its own shop steward.

Duties of shop stewards:

- They recruit new members, collect union subscriptions, and pass on information from the union to their members. They also pass members' views back to the unions.

- They act as links between firms and their workers. They take up members' problems and try to sort them out with the management. They try to avoid disputes by dealing with problems quickly.

- They may be members of shop stewards' committees that negotiate with firms on matters that affect all workers, for example, *local pay bargaining*.

shortlist: the list of applicants for a job that have been chosen for *interview*.

> *Explanation:* There may be a large number of applications for one job. It would be very expensive and probably a waste of time to interview everybody. The applications are considered by the relevant *personnel department*. A list is drawn up of perhaps six suitable people to interview.

- Every application is considered against the *job description* and the *job specification*. The department looks for people with the 'right' qualifications and experience needed for the job.

- Those with poor, careless applications and those without the right experience or qualifications are eliminated first.

single market: this came into being on 1 January 1993 when the *European Community* became one market. This has meant that people, goods, services and capital are able to move as freely between EC countries as they can within their own country.

single union agreement: this arrangement exists when a firm only recognises one *trades union* as representing all its employees. Workers can join other unions, but a firm will only deal with one union. All *collective bargaining* is therefore between the firm and that one union. This makes negotiations much simpler. Single union agreements often also include a *no strike* clause.

skilled worker: a worker who has both knowledge of theory and practical ability in a particular job. The worker will have obtained *NVQ* qualifications, probably up to level 3. In the past a skilled worker would have completed an apprenticeship.

skimming is said to occur where the price of a new product is set very high. It may be a policy used for products for which people are prepared to pay a high price because they are new. Such products will probably have a high prestige value. The price will probably fall later after 'skimming the cream'.

small firms are defined by the government as those having fewer than 200 employees. Such firms can, however, be quite large in terms of turnover, especially 'high tech' firms. Small firms are very important in the UK economy. For example, 40% of those working in manufacturing industry work in firms with less than 20 employees.

Why firms stay small:

- The owners may lack ambition. They like being their own boss. They do not want the firm to become too big for them to manage themselves.

- Firms can provide specialist or luxury items or services for which there is only a limited demand.

- The market may be very local. For example, those businesses which provide direct services to the consumer, such as dentists, hairdressers, plumbers and decorators.

Strengths of small firms:

- They may be able to do jobs that the big firms cannot do. Small firms may have skills and equipment the large firms only need occasionally. These jobs are *sub-contracted* to the small specialist firms.

- They are more flexible than large firms. They can change very quickly to suit the needs of the market. Decisions can be taken quickly; the boss can make decisions 'on the spot'.

- They often have good labour relations because the owners work side-by-side with their employees.

Weaknesses of small firms:

- Costs of borrowing and of buying materials and components are higher. They cannot gain any of the *economies of scale*.

- They have limited capital and find it hard and expensive to get the finance to expand.

- They may depend very heavily on their owners. There may be no one to take the owner's place if (s)he is away or ill for any length of time.

social benefits are the positive effects that a firm or an industry has upon its locality.

> ***Explanation:*** The main benefit that firms bring to their area is employment, which will have 'knock-on' effects. The workers spend money in local shops and other businesses. The social effects will be most obvious when a firm starts up in an area where there has been high unemployment.

Some firms also provide facilities in an area, such as sports grounds and clubs. Other firms have built good quality houses for their workers. The best known examples are Rowntree in York, Cadbury in Bournville and Lever Brothers at Port Sunlight.

social costs are the negative effects that a company has upon its locality.

> ***Explanation:*** Decisions made by a firm may affect the locality, and create costs felt by the community where the firm has its business. These costs are external to the company, and do not directly increase its costs. The costs are carried by the community.

> ***Example:*** typical social costs

- If a firm closes down or makes a number of people *redundant* it will affect the local economy. If it is the main employer in the area it may have a very big effect.

- A firm may cause traffic congestion in an area at certain times of the day.

- A firm may cause pollution through smoke or noise or unsightly spoil heaps.

sole proprietor: the individual who owns and controls a business. Sole proprietors have *unlimited liability* and are to be found in a wide range of industries.

Features of a sole proprietor business:

- All the *capital* is provided by the owner. That person will run the business and make all the decisions. The sole proprietor takes all the risks of the business, receives all the profits and carries any loss.

- It may employ other people. It is very rare that the owner works without any help. Quite often the family works in the business.

- It is well suited to providing specialist, local services, e.g., hairdresser, plumber, market gardening.

Advantages of sole proprietors:

- It is easy to set up in business. There are very few formalities. Large amounts of capital may not be needed to start up a business. The amount of capital needed will to some extent depend on the kind of business. Owners are hard-working because the success of the businesses and their profit depends on their own efforts.

- Owners can easily control the businesses. Decisions can be made quickly as there is no need to spend time consulting other people.

- They are very flexible and can adapt to their customers' needs very quickly.

Disadvantages of sole proprietors:

- *Unlimited liability* places all of their personal possessions at risk if the businesses should fail.

- Shortage of *capital* makes expansion difficult. Borrowing money will tend to be expensive. Getting extra capital may mean having to take a *partner*. That will lead to some loss of control because decisions will have to be shared. They do not benefit from *economies of scale* through *bulk buying*.

- Owners are always tied to their businesses, often working long hours with few holidays.

sole trader means the same as a *sole proprietor*.

solvent: when the value of a company's assets is greater than the total of its external debts. This means that if a company closed and all of its assets were sold it would be able to pay off all of its debts. It is illegal for a company to *trade* if it is *insolvent*.

sources of finance are the places where a company can get money for use in the business. It may need the money for extra *working capital*, or to pay its short-term debts, or for extra longer term *capital*.

Short-term finance:

This is for periods of up to one year and is used to pay for wages, materials and running expenses.

- **Sales revenue** is the main source of finance for every company. Firms hope to be able to pay for most of their running costs from sales. However, money does not always come in regularly. Firms therefore need to have other sources of money they can use if they need to.

- **Trade credit** is used when a firm buys its supplies on credit. During the period of credit the firm is, in effect, using its supplier's money. The firm can use the goods supplied and may even sell the goods before paying for them.

- **Overdrafts** are agreements whereby banks allow firms to overdraw their *current accounts* up to an agreed limit. Most firms will have such 'arrangements' but may not use them. They are a fairly cheap way to borrow money. *Interest* is only paid on the amount actually used.

- **Factoring** debts is a way of raising money fairly quickly. A firm may prefer to have 75% of the money owing to it now, rather than have to wait for it all.

Medium-term finance:

This is for periods of up to five years to cover such things as buying equipment or paying for *research and development.*

- **Bank loans:** where fixed sums of money are borrowed for stated periods of time. They tend to be expensive. *Interest* is charged on the full amount for the full period of the loan.

- **Trade credit:** some sellers of large equipment will offer a credit package as part of a deal.

- **Hire purchase** may be used to buy machinery and equipment, including vehicles. The credit is at a fixed *rate of interest* and for a fixed period of time. The cost can be spread rather than having to pay for the equipment in a lump sum. It can also be used and may create enough extra income to pay for itself.

- **Leasing** is another way of spreading the cost of equipment over several years. It saves having to make a large capital outlay. It is a fairly cheap way of keeping equipment up to date. Leased goods are never owned by the user who may be able to buy them very cheaply at the end of the lease.

- **Retained profits** are probably the main source of finance used by companies for buying equipment and for expansion.

> • **Government grants** may be available for buying equipment and to fund growth, especially in certain geographical areas.

Long-term finance:

Long-term finance is for periods of longer than five years.

> • **Debentures** are a form of loan at a fixed rate of interest. They may be repaid either on some fixed date or at a date chosen by the issuing firm.

> • **Equity** capital is raised in the form of *shares* by *limited companies*. This will be the main form of long-term capital. The shares will either be *ordinary shares* or *preference shares*.

span of control: a measure of the number of people over whom a manager has *direct* control.

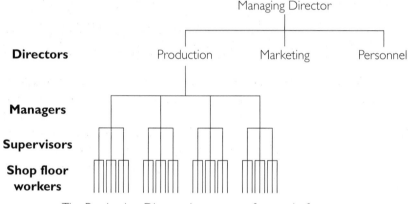

The Production Director has a span of control of
4 managers but is responsible for 56 people

Explanation: The span of control refers to the people <u>directly</u> controlled by a manager. There may be other people for whom the manager is responsible but under the *direct* control of someone else, to whom the manager has *delegated* control. The number of people over whom a manager has control will vary. It will depend on:

> • the nature of a job. If the people below a manager need a great deal of careful supervision the span of control will be very narrow. Another job may need very little supervision and the span of control can then be wide

> • the kind of structure of organisation in a firm. A flat structure, with only a few layers will tend to have a wide span of control. If the structure is tall and has a large number of layers, each manager may control only a few people.

specialisation is the breaking up of a job into separate parts. Each part is carried out by someone who specialises in that function. Specialisation leads to the *division of labour*. It also leads to dependence. When a firm specialises it will depend on other firms to provide supplies and to distribute and sell the product.

Specialisation can be classified in many ways

- **By product (or service)** – where a firm only produces one product or service.

- **By process** – where the job of making the product is broken down into a number of small parts. Each of the parts of the process is carried out by different people, e.g., in *flow production*.

- **By country** – where a country uses its resources to produce the things it is best at making. It imports the goods which it may not have the resources to provide itself.

- **By function** – where a person specialises in a job or aspects of a job, e.g., a plumber or a solicitor specialising in company law.

sponsorship is the support given by firms to events, teams or individuals, by providing finance, goods or other materials or services. It is a form of *promotion*. Local firms may sponsor local events and local sports people or teams. National events are sponsored by large companies. Firms provide sponsorship because they hope to obtain good publicity from being involved with major events and teams. They hope that the team or person they sponsor will win. Firms wants their names to be linked to winners and success.

spreadsheet: a computer-based program designed to handle numerical information. Data are entered and displayed in columns and rows. By putting in formulae it is possible to make the machine carry out calculations automatically. By changing the data it is possible to see the effect that a small change might have. For example, a firm would be able to see the effect on its profit of a 5% or 10% increase or fall in its sales. This is known as the 'what if' facility.

staff development is another term for staff training. It should be linked to the needs of the company, and also meet the needs of the person and help their personal development at work.

stakeholder refers to everyone with an interest in a company. This includes individuals or groups of people. Each one has a stake in the success of the company and will benefit in some way. Equally, they would suffer some kind of loss if the company failed. The main stakeholders are as follows:

- **Employees –** success may mean that their jobs will be safer. It may mean higher pay. This applies to all employees at all levels within the company.

- **Customers –** success may lead to better quality and cheaper goods. They may have less choice if a business failed.

- **Suppliers –** the more successful a company becomes the more supplies it will need. The success of suppliers partly depends on the success of the companies they sell to.

- **Lenders –** if a company fails there is less chance of lenders getting their money repaid.

- **Shareholders –** if a company is a success the value of its shares will increase. Shareholders will also be paid higher *dividends*.

- **The community –** successful firms benefit their communities by providing more and safer jobs. The people in those jobs will spend more money in the local shops and on other services.

standing order: a method of transferring money from one bank account to another. It is used for the payment of fixed amounts of money at regular intervals.

> **Explanation:** When regular payments have to be made there is always the danger of forgetting to send the money. A standing order is an instruction to a bank to pay a stated sum of money on the same date at regular intervals. A bank will automatically transfer the money to the payee's bank account and this is shown on the *bank statement*. Standing orders can be used to pay bills where the amount to be paid is the same each time, e.g. insurance premiums, mortgage or hire purchase repayments.

start-up costs are the costs of starting up a new business. They are paid only on that one occasion. They include the costs of buying or renting premises and new equipment, getting stationery printed and the legal costs of registering the company.

statement of account: this is sent by a supplier to a customer and is a summary of the trade that has taken place between them since the last statement. A statement is usually sent every month. It shows details of all purchases, returns and payments made in the month. At the end it will show the amount still owed by the customer. It acts as a reminder that payment is due. Be careful not to confuse this with a *bank statement*.

> **Explanation:** A statement is, in effect a copy of a customer's account as it appears in the supplier's books. A customer should use the statement to check that all the details are right in the supplier's accounts. Some firms prefer not to pay for goods when they receive an *invoice*, waiting until they get the statement. This gives them more time before they have to pay for the goods.

Example: a typical statement of account

			Statement of Account				
			XYX & COMPANY LIMITED				
			The Industrial Estate, Anytown, Midshire RE9 4PH				
			Telephone: 0123 987 4561				
			Fax: 0123 987 6544				
			VAT Registration No.				

To:

Date	Invoice No.	Order No	Details	Debit	Credit	Balance
					BALANCE DUE	

statute is another name for an Act of Parliament.

statutory organisations are bodies that have been set up under the terms of an Act of Parliament. Examples include the *Office of Fair Trading*, the *Equal Opportunities Commission* and the *regulators* of the *privatised* industries such as *OFFER* and *OFTEL*.

stock is the supply of goods and raw materials held by a firm. It is used by firms either to produce goods (stocks of raw materials and components), or to sell to customers (stocks of finished goods). All organisations hold stocks of some kind. They should not be too big. Holding large stocks ties up capital. Firms hold stock for a number of reasons:

- to meet orders from customers without delay

- to keep production running by having enough supplies of materials and parts

- to spread production evenly throughout the year if sales are seasonal. Stocks are built up over quite a long time and released over a short period.

stock brokers are people who buy and sell *stocks* and *shares* on the *stock exchange* on behalf of clients. They also give advice on what shares to buy. They are paid a *commission* for their services.

stock control is the management of the level of stock held by a company. It is the systems used to make sure that stocks are ordered and delivered and held in the right amounts.

> **Explanation:** Manufacturers must have plenty of raw materials and parts so that production is not held up. They must also have enough finished goods to be able to meet orders straight away. A shop must make sure it has enough of every item that it sells. Firms therefore have to keep records of their stock. It is these records that provide the stock control system, which should:

- keep a record of the date of all deliveries of goods received and of when goods are taken out of stock

- make sure that stock is used in the right order, usually the oldest first

- include a method of making sure new stock is ordered before stock runs out.

Stock Exchange: a market where *stocks* and *shares* are bought and sold. The main Stock Exchange in the United Kingdom is in London. Only 'members' are able to trade on the floor of the exchange. Only *listed* stocks and shares that have been approved by the Stock Exchange can be dealt in there. The London Stock Exchange is one of the main stock markets in the world, dealing in foreign as well as British securities.

- Only stocks and shares that are already owned by someone are sold. It is a market for 'second hand' stocks and shares. New securities are not sold on the stock exchange.

- It helps companies to raise new capital because it enables shareholders to sell their shares if they need the money. People would be less willing to buy shares if there were no way for them to get their money back when they needed it.

- There are strict rules that have to be followed by firms before their shares can be *listed*. This helps to give the public confidence that the companies whose shares are listed are financially sound.

stock turn is the speed at which the *average stock* of a firm is sold. (See also *rate of stock turnover*.)

stock turnover is the same as *stock turn*.

stocks are securities, other than *shares*, that may be issued by the government, by local authorities or by companies. They are, in effect, fixed interest loans. They may be dated, which means that the capital will be paid back on a certain date. If they are undated the issuer will decide when they are to be repaid. Stocks can be bought and sold on the *stock exchange*.

store cards are cards issued by retail stores. Most of the large *retailers* issue such cards hoping to encourage people to shop at their stores. The cards, which can only be used at branches of the stores that issue them, are of three types:

1   **Credit cards –** these work in the same way as Access and Visa cards. They have a credit limit on the card and a statement is sent every month. A customer can either pay all the debt or pay it off monthly. *Interest* is charged on the balance due after a certain date.

2   **Budget cards –** these are used by some retailers. A customer agrees to pay the retailer a fixed amount every month, perhaps by *direct debit* or *standing order*. Customers can save up for goods by building up a balance on the card. Every time goods are bought they can be charged against the card. Interest is charged only if customers owe more than they have paid in. Customers are sent a monthly statement.

3   **Loyalty cards –** these are issued free by most of the large supermarkets. Every time a customer buys goods at a branch of the store, points are earned. In return the customer may be sent vouchers giving price reductions on certain goods. Other supermarkets allow points to be built up and redeemed against a bill whenever a customer chooses.

straight line method: a method for calculating the *depreciation* of a *fixed asset*. Under this method an asset is depreciated by a fixed sum every year during its useful life. The amount to be deducted is found by estimating the *residual value* of the asset. This is subtracted from its original cost and divided by the expected life of the asset.

> FORMULA *for calculating depreciation by straight line method:*
>
> **Original cost of asset – Estimated residual value**
> **Number of years of useful life**

Worked example: An asset is bought for £10 000 on January 1. It is expected to have a useful life of five years and a value of £1500 at the end of the five years.

$$\frac{\text{Original cost} - \text{Residual value}}{\text{Estimated useful life}} = \frac{£10\ 000 - £1500}{5\ \text{years}} = \frac{£8500}{5\ \text{years}}$$

$= £1700$ per year

The asset will be depreciated by £1700 each year in the *profit and loss account*. The depreciation each year will be:

	Price/Value £	Depreciation £	Net value £
Year 1	10 000	1 700	8 300
2	8 300	1 700	6 600
3	6 600	1 700	4 900
4	4 900	1 700	3 200
5	3 200	1 700	1 500

The asset has been *written off* over the five years up to its estimated residual value. It is better to under estimate the residual value. If the asset sells for less than £1500 it will not have been depreciated enough.

strike: a form of *industrial action* in which workers withdraw their labour. They do so during an *industrial dispute* to put pressure on their employers in pursuit of a claim. *Trades unions* see strikes as a last resort as their members as well as the employers lose money.

There are several types of strike:

- **Official strikes** are called by trades unions. The union has to hold a secret ballot before it calls a strike. There must be a majority in support of the strike. A union must give notice to an employer when a strike will start.

- **Unofficial strikes** occur when groups of workers go on strike without the support of their trades unions. They are sometimes called 'wildcat strikes'.

- **Token strikes** happen when groups of workers go on strike for a day or even a half-day. They are supported by their trades unions and usually called as a protest.

- **Selective strikes** take place when trades unions call out their members for perhaps one day every week, but on a different day each week. They may strike in certain areas only instead of having full-scale strikes. This is a great nuisance to employers but reduces workers' loss of earnings to a minimum.

- **Sympathy strikes** are called by groups of workers that decide to support those on strike by 'coming out in sympathy'. Such strikes are now considered to be *secondary action* and are illegal.

strike pay is a payment made by a trades union to its members who are on official *strike*.

structural unemployment is unemployment caused by a change in the structure of industry. Such changes in the industrial structure are the result of changes in demand.

> **Explanation:** The demand for labour depends on the demand for the goods that labour helps to produce. If there is a permanent fall in the demand for a product, there will be a fall in the demand for labour in that industry. There has been a change in the structure of the industry.

Reasons for structural changes:

- A product may become out of date. The coal mining industry is an example. Coal has been replaced by oil, gas and electricity as a fuel leaving only a small demand for coal. The change in demand has resulted in a decline in the mining industry.

- The growth of foreign competition may make a home product more expensive. Demand switches to cheaper imported goods. The textile and clothing industries are examples.

- Changes in technology may result in people being replaced by machines. The change means that demand switches to the products made by the new, cheaper methods.

sub-contracting happens when the holder of a contract finds another supplier to do all or part of the work. The main contractor is still responsible for the overall work. Sub-contracting is widely used in the engineering and the building industries. There are two main reasons for sub-contracting:

1   A firm may be very busy and cannot deal with a new order within the time stated. It is better to get someone else to do the work than to turn down an order.

2   A firm may not have the specialist skills to do part of the job. It therefore sub-contracts that part of the work to a specialist firm.

Examples:

- Very often building firms do not employ their own workers in all areas of skill. They will usually sub-contract things like the electrical and heating installation work.

- An engineering firm may sub-contract work that needs an expensive specialist machine they do not have.

subsidiary: a business that is owned by another company. That means that the *parent company* owns at least 51% of the shares in the subsidiary. The firm, however, carries on trading under its own name. It will have its own managers who can make everyday decisions but only within policy set by the parent company.

subsidies are payments made by the government to producers of goods and services. They have the effect of reducing the costs of production. This gives the subsidised industries an advantage over their competitors. Countries may pay a subsidy to their home industry to make home produced goods cheaper than *imports*. Subsidies may be paid for social reasons. The railway companies, for example, are paid a subsidy to keep open lines and run services on routes where they would otherwise lose money.

supervisor: an employee who manages the workers on the shopfloor. It is the most junior grade of manager in a firm. Supervisors have very limited powers to make decisions. They see that the operatives are doing their work correctly and meeting targets. They have to make sure that quality standards are met. Supervisors are usually experienced operatives who can give technical advice when it is needed. They can solve problems on the spot, as they arise.

supply: the quantity of goods and services that producers are both willing and able to put on the market at a particular price.

> **Explanation:** There are three important parts to the definition; willingness to supply, quantity and price.

- Producers will not normally be willing to supply goods unless the price is high enough:
    - to cover all the costs of making the goods and
    - to provide them with a reasonable profit in addition.
- Price is therefore the thing that decides whether producers are willing to supply goods and services. Price also helps to decide what quantity of goods and services producers will supply. The higher the price the more producers will be willing to supply.

- The lower the price the fewer goods and services producers will be willing to supply. Only the most efficient firms will be able to make a profit and the less efficient firms will leave the market.

The relationship between the amount of a product that is supplied and its price can be shown on a supply curve. The graph below shows that as price rises the amount supplied also increases.

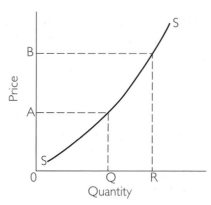

When the price is A the quantity Q will be supplied
When the price is B the quantity R will be supplied

surplus: where *income* is greater than *expenditure*. It is a term that is used instead of *profit* in the *accounts* of *non-profitmaking organisations*, like clubs and charities. The term is also used in government accounts. A surplus is the opposite of a *deficit*.

survey: a study in which information is collected directly from a *sample* of the population. It is a *primary research* method used in *market research*. Surveys can be carried out by personal or telephone interview, or by questionnaire. To make the information collected easy to handle it is changed into a statistical form.

SWOT analysis is a review of the whole or part of an organisation in terms of its strengths, weaknesses, opportunities and threats. It is a method widely used in *marketing* and strategic planning.

> ***Explanation:*** A SWOT analysis is a part of a firm's planning. It can be done for a whole firm or a department. It can also be carried out on a product-by-product basis. The actual content of the boxes will vary according to the firm or the product.

- **Strengths** are the things that a firm is good at. They will also include any new or very good resources it has. For example, it may have a very good design team.

- **Weaknesses** are the things in which a firm is not as good as its competitors. Its resources may be out of date or it may not have any new products coming out, while rivals have.

- **Opportunities** are the ways a firm can use its strengths to improve its position in the market.

- **Threats** will come mainly from competitors. A firm may know that rival firms are bringing out new products. In a strategic plan, a firm may take into account the possibility that it could be the target for a *takeover bid*.

Internal	Strengths	Weaknesses	Present position
External	Opportunities	Threats	Future possibilities

Strengths and weaknesses are a firm's present position. They are also internal; that is, the firm has some control over them; it can try to do something about the weaknesses and develop the strengths.

The opportunities and the threats are external factors. They are things over which the firm has no direct control. The opportunities and threats do affect the firm's future possibilities. It has to spot those possibilities and try to change things in its favour.

takeover is said to occur when control of a firm is bought by another company. A buyer gains control by buying more than 50% of the *ordinary shares* in the target company. The business is then managed by the new owners. Takeovers are a method used by companies to expand.

takeover bid: an attempt by one company to gain a controlling interest in another company. This is achieved by offering to buy the target company's shares.

Takeover bids may be of two kinds:

> 1   **Agreed –** where a firm's *board of directors* recommends that the *shareholders* accept the offer made by the buyer. The price offered will probably be above the *market price* of the *shares* at the time.

> 2   **Hostile –** where a buyer's offer is not welcome. It will be turned down by the *board of directors*. The bidder then has to buy shares on the open market and appeal directly to the shareholders. It can cost a firm a great deal of money to defend itself from a hostile bid.

target market is the *market segment* at which a firm aims its *marketing*. The exact part of the market targeted will depend on the results of the firm's *market research*. The *marketing mix* used will depend on the *target market*. (See also *place*.)

> **Explanation:** It is rare for firms to try to target the whole population. There are very few goods that are suitable for both young babies and the very old. Firms therefore choose a particular part of the market at which to aim their products. A new brand of fashion goods, for example, may be targeted at young working mothers between 25 and 35 years of age.

tariff: a tax on imported goods. The effect of a tariff is to increase the price of imported goods. It is intended to make them dearer than the home produced goods. Tariffs are based on either the quantity or the value of goods.

taxes are the main method used by central and local government for raising revenue.

Reasons for taxes:

> •   To provide revenue to pay for the goods and services provided by the government. Some services are provided directly by the government. Others are provided by local councils. Much of a local council's income comes from grants from central government. The rest of its income comes mainly from the Council Tax.

> •   To reduce consumer spending, as part of economic policy.

- To discourage the sale of goods that the state considers to be bad for people (e.g. tobacco).

Types of taxation:

- Taxes on income are the biggest source of revenue. The main taxes are *income tax* which is paid by individuals and *corporation tax* which is paid by companies. *National Insurance* contributions are also a form of tax on income and firms.

- Tax on expenditure is mainly through *value added tax (VAT)* and also *customs and excise* duties.

- Taxes on wealth that has been built up are of two kinds in the UK: capital gains tax and inheritance tax.

TEC: see *Training and Enterprise Council.*

telebanking is a personal banking service where all contact with a bank is by telephone. Customers have a cheque book, cheque guarantee and cash cards and are able to have loans and overdrafts in the normal way. All the other services offered by banks are also available. First Direct was the first telebank in the UK.

Advantages of telebanking:

- There are no branches which saves a bank a great deal of money. Instead of visiting a branch with a query, the customer telephones.

- They are open 24 hours a day and every day of the year.

- They make no bank charges, but interest is charged when the account is overdrawn.

telesales is the selling of goods and services over the telephone. The first contact with customers is made by telephone. There are a number of agencies that specialise in telesales. They may also do market research by telephone.

teletext is an information service that is based on a large central *database*. The database is made up of pages that are kept up to date by providers such as Ceefax. Access is through an ordinary television set equipped with an adapter.

television advertising is the use of television for the advertising of goods and services. Only commercial (ITV and Channel 4), satellite and cable television stations carry advertising. It is mainly used by large companies that are selling goods on a national scale. Larger regional firms may use local commercial stations.

Features of television advertising:

- It is a very good way of bringing a product to the notice of a very large number of people at the same time.

- It is visual, so the product can be seen in the home. Brand images can be built up so that people know exactly what to look for in the shops. The adverts can be made to suit the audience at a particular time. For example, products that appeal to children are broadcast around teatime.

- The adverts are expensive to make and to broadcast, especially at peak viewing times.

teleworker: a person who works from home using computer links through a modem to keep in touch with their office. Many experts think it is a method of working that will grow. If it does, there may be fewer large offices in the future. Working at home saves on travelling costs and is environmentally desirable. Those who look after families can carry on with their careers more easily.

terms of employment: see *conditions of employment*.

tertiary industry is the part of the economy that supplies services to other industries and to the public. It is the third or 'tertiary' stage in production. It is made up of firms that sell and distribute goods produced by the *extractive* and manufacturing industries. It also includes all other services, like *banking* and *insurance* and *transport*. They all help to make *trade* and the *distribution* of goods run smoothly.

test marketing: the testing of a new product in a small, well defined part of the *market*. This usually happens in one, fairly small area of the country. Firms may test market because they want to test their products in operation. A national *launch* is very expensive and the producers will want to make any changes shown by the test to be necessary before a general launch. Firms may also test market because they do not fully trust their own *market research*.

time rate: payment according to the length of time worked, rather than according to the amount of goods produced. People paid on a time rate are paid so much an hour, or week, or month. *Basic wages* are often worked out on a time rate.

total cost is all the costs involved in the *production* of a product or service. It can be calculated in two ways:

FORMULAE **for calculating total cost:**

Fixed costs + Variable costs = Total costs or

Cost of goods sold + Expenses = Total costs

Cost of sales is found in the *Trading Account* and expenses from the *profit and loss account*.

total quality management (TQM) aims at making all employees, at every level in a firm, responsible for the quality of the firm's products. Everyone is responsible for the quality of his or her own work and is expected to treat the people they deal with as customers, including fellow employees.

TQM: see *total quality management*.

trade is the exchange of goods and services for money. Trade in most modern societies is carried out for money. Trade may be home trade, between firms and individuals within a country, or foreign trade, when goods and services are bought and sold overseas. Trade in more primitive societies may be through *barter*.

trade advertising is advertising to firms that are members of a trade or industry. Most trades have magazines that specialise in their industries. A new product is advertised in the appropriate *trade magazine* before it is advertised to the public. This way the trade knows about the product, and has a chance to get goods into stock before the product is launched to the buying public.

trade associations are organisations whose members are drawn from a particular industry. They are a way of sharing information and of promoting the industry. They may form a *pressure group* to put forward the industry's point of view to the government and others. Examples include the National Farmers' Union and the Road Haulage Association. Others, such as the Association of British Travel Agents (ABTA), also act as *regulators* for their industries.

trade credit is credit given by a firm to other firms, usually within the same line of business.

> **Explanation:** Firms may have different terms for trade customers to those given to the public, where they deal with both. For example, a builders' merchant may only sell to the public for cash but give credit to people in the building trade.

- The length of credit will vary. It will usually be between one and three months.
- Giving credit is expensive so, firms may offer *cash discounts* to trade customers to persuade them to pay promptly.
- Trade credit is an important part of the *working capital* of all companies, large and small. By not paying cash for goods companies can help their *cashflow*. The credit they receive is *interest* free.

trade creditors are firms that are owed money by a company. They are shown as a *current liability* in a company's *balance sheet.*

trade debtors are firms that owe money to a company. They are shown as a *current asset* in a company's *balance sheet.*

Trade Descriptions Act 1968: this Act makes it an offence to give a false description to goods or services or to make a misleading statement about prices. The Act applies both to written and oral statements made 'in the course of trade or business'. The Act is enforced by a local council's *trading standards department.*

> **Explanation:** False trade descriptions include 'clocking' the speedometer on a car or saying that something is 100% wool when it contains other fibres. The Act covers false statements of any kind, for example, about a product's size, quantity, purpose or manufacturer. The Act also applies to false statements in advertisements. Even a photograph that gives a wrong idea about the goods may be a false statement. Misleading claims about prices are some of the more well known parts of the Act. Examples include:

> - a false claim that a price is less than the maker's recommended price

> - false comparison with a previous price; for example, at sale time saying goods were £50 and are now £25 when they have been £25 for the last three months

> - suggesting that the price is less than the goods are actually being sold for; for example, there are hidden extras such as delivery, or packing.

trade directories are books listing details of providers of goods and services, classified according to their trade. They are widely used in business as a source of information about possible suppliers.

trade discount: an amount taken off the selling price of a product when goods are bought by one trader from another. Sellers may list goods at the recommended retail price and deduct the trade discount when they sell to the trade.

Features of trade discount:

> - A trade discount will normally be equal to the buyer's *gross profit* when the goods are re-sold at the *recommended retail price.*

> - Trade discount may vary when buying in bulk. For example, buying 1000 units may earn a 20% trade discount, while 2000 units attract a 30% trade discount.

> - Some customers may gain a higher discount than others. For example, a new customer may get a smaller discount than a firm that has been a customer for a long time.

trade fairs and exhibitions are events where the suppliers of a particular group of products gather under one roof. Products are put on display and promoted to trade buyers and other members of the trade or industry. Members of the public will normally not be admitted.

trade gap: the difference between the total *exports* of goods and the total *imports* of goods. It is the same as the *balance of trade*. The term 'trade gap' tends to be used to describe a *deficit* in the balance of trade rather than a *surplus*.

trade magazines and papers specialise in matters that are of interest to a trade or industry. They contain articles on developments, and things of general interest to the trade. There are advertisements for new products and for supplies of specialist equipment and services and for job vacancies in the industry. Examples include 'Fashion Weekly' for the clothing industry and 'The Grocer' for the food retailing trade.

trade mark: a name, *logo* or symbol used to distinguish a product; for example, 'Mars' and 'Coca Cola' are trade names and trademarks. Trade marks are an essential part of *branding*. They are part of making a product different from any other and part of the image of a product. To stop anyone else from using the trade mark it has to be registered (at the Patent Office in the UK).

trade reference: a letter, or testimonial, supporting a trader's request for credit. This is supplied by another trader at the request of a company being asked to provide credit.

> **Explanation:** When new customers apply for *credit* they may be asked to provide the names of two or three trade references. The company will write to the firms named asking about the applicant's credit record and how promptly the applicant pays bills. Trade references are part of a firm's *credit control*.

trade war happens when one country imposes a *tariff* on another country's goods and that country then responds with a higher tariff in return.

trades union: an association of workers formed to promote the interests of its members with their employers. Workers who are members of trades unions pay a subscription which they can have deducted from their pay by their employer.

Types of trades unions:

- **Craft unions** – the first unions to be formed. The members all share a common set of skills. At one time membership depended on learning the craft through an apprenticeship. This meant that unions could control entry into a trade. Many craft unions are quite small.

- **Industrial unions** – unions formed to represent the workers in one industry. They usually represent people at all levels of the industry.

Examples include USDAW (Union of Shop Distributive and Allied Workers) which represents workers in the retail and wholesale trades.

- **General unions** – these unions originally represented semi-skilled and unskilled workers drawn from every industry. They now represent workers at all levels and are quite strong in the newer industries. They are very large unions. The best known example is the TGWU (Transport and General Workers Union).

- **White collar unions** – the growth of trades unions among non-manual workers is fairly recent. Membership is drawn from people within management, administrative, clerical and scientific and professional jobs. Examples include The Royal College of Nursing and The National Union of Teachers (NUT) and BIFU, the bank workers' union.

Functions of trades unions:

- They negotiate with employers on behalf of their members. Through *collective bargaining* they try to get the best deals they can for their members. They aim to:

  - get the highest possible pay

  - improve conditions of employment including hours, holidays, working conditions and pensions

  - gain the best possible terms for members when there are redundancies.

- They represent members at industrial tribunals and other work-related legal action (e.g. compensation claims for injury at work).

- They provide a range of benefits like strike pay, sick pay, injury benefits, retirement homes and convalescent homes.

- They act as *pressure groups* to put forward their members' interests to MPs, the press and the government. They nominate members of joint committees with the *CBI* and *employers' organisations*.

Trades Union Congress (TUC): the central trades union body. It is made up of the separate unions that are its members. Most unions belong to the TUC. It represents trades union interests generally, in this country and internationally. It is where trade unions are able to discuss matters of interest and form joint policies.

Functions of the TUC:

- It puts forward the trade union point of view to government and employers, acting as a *pressure group*.

- It provides education and training for shop stewards and other union officials.

- It tries to sort out disputes between unions.

trading account: the account in which the *gross profit* of a company for a given period is worked out. It is one of the *final accounts* of a business. It always covers a specified period of time, which must be stated in the heading of the account.

Example: a typical Trading Account

Trading Account of XYX & Company Limited for the year ended 31 December

	£	£
Sales		160 000
less Cost of sales:		
Opening stock	12 600	
add Purchases	107 800	
	120 400	
less Closing stock	11 700	108 700
Gross profit		51 300

trading certificate: a document issued by the *Registrar of Companies* to a *public limited company*. It is granted only when a company has raised enough *capital* to begin trading.

> **Explanation:** A public limited company may not have any capital until after it has issued its *prospectus* and sold *shares*. A company that starts to trade without any money will put those it deals with at risk. It must have enough capital to pay its debts and to be able to trade effectively. A certificate of trading is only issued when the Registrar of Companies is satisfied that a firm has the capital it needs.

trading standards department: a local council department given statutory powers for making sure that most of the *consumer protection* legislation is carried out. Examples of acts it enforces include the Food and Drugs Act, Weights and Measures Act and the *Trade Descriptions Act*.

training is the teaching of skills in a work-related situation. It is about applying knowledge to work. Training may be either *on-the-job* or *off-the-job*. Training is usually organised by the *personnel department*.

Reasons for training:

- To improve the level of workers' knowledge and skills and to make them more efficient and effective in their work. There is a national shortage of skilled workers.

- To provide workers with the right qualifications for their job. This may mean retraining or gaining higher qualifications, perhaps several times during a working life.

- To keep up with the changes in technology people may have to learn new skills.

- To train people to cope with new work situations. This will include help for people who may be *redeployed* or promoted in the future.

Training and Enterprise Council (TEC): a locally based body set up to organise government funded training schemes. It also provides support for business, especially small firms.

> **Explanation:** There are over 80 TECs in England and Wales. Each one covers a local area. Each Council is made up of local business people, local council and trades union representatives. Each TEC collects information about the local labour market. The TEC should be able to identify skill shortages and organise training courses to meet local needs. These courses are bought from local colleges, local firms and training companies.

transport is the carrying of goods from the point where they are produced to the user.

> **Explanation:** Transport is an essential part of a *chain of distribution*. It moves supplies of materials and parts between firms. It also gets goods to where the *consumer* can buy them. The quality of local transport links is an important factor when firms decide where to locate.

> The type of transport used by a firm depends on several factors:

- the type of goods; the form of transport will vary according to whether the goods are bulky, liquid, fragile, perishable or very expensive

- the cost, which will vary with the type of load and the distance. Firms use the cheapest form of transport that suits their needs. Road transport is cheap over short distances but rail may be cheaper over long distances and for large, bulky loads

- other factors include the speed with which goods are needed; the security of valuable or expensive goods and the size of the load; is it a lorry or a train load?

Treasury: the government department that is responsible for the UK's economic policy. The minister in charge of the Treasury is the Chancellor of the Exchequer. The Treasury carries out the government's taxation and spending policies.

tribunal: see *industrial tribunal*.

TUC: see *Trades Union Congress*.

turnover is another term for *sales turnover* or *sales revenue*. It is the total value of sales in a period, e.g. a day, month or year.

underwriters are individuals or companies that take on a risk in return for a *commission*.

The term is used in two quite different ways:

1   Underwriters who are members of *Lloyds*. They are people who personally accept an *insurance* risk. They usually form into syndicates to cover a risk. Each member of a syndicate accepts a percentage of the risk involved.

2   *Financial institutions* that agree to buy any *shares* that are not sold when they are first issued to the public.

undistributed profit is the part of the profit of a business that is not paid to *shareholders* in the form of *dividends*. It is the same thing as *retained profits*.

unemployment: the state in which a proportion of the active working population is not in paid work. Not all the people who are not working are unemployed. *Labour* is different from the other *factors of production* because it is provided by people. When *land* and *capital* are not used it is a waste of resources. Unemployment has serious social results.

Types of unemployment:

*   **Frictional** occurs when there are temporary breaks between jobs. It is usually voluntary and happens because people are changing jobs.

*   **Seasonal** – there are some industries that are more active at some times of the year than others. The hotel and catering industries tend to be busier in the summer. Building and some kinds of farming lay people off in the winter. Unemployment in these industries tends to vary with the seasons.

*   **Structural** – this is long-term unemployment brought about by changes in the structure of industry. Some industries have almost disappeared because there is no longer a demand for their goods. The people who worked in those industries tend to stay unemployed for a long time. Their skills are out of date and cannot be used by the newer industries.

*   **Cyclical** – this is unemployment caused by swings in the *business cycle*. During a *recession* there is a rise in the number of people out of work. Firms need less workers as the demand for their goods falls. Unemployment falls as the cycle moves into recovery.

*   **Technological** is unemployment that is caused by changes in technology. People are replaced by machines and new working methods.

unfair dismissal is the ending of a person's employment for reasons that a tribunal may judge to be unfair. Some reasons are automatically unfair. It is, for example, unfair to dismiss someone because of their trades union activities or because of their race or colour. To claim unfair dismissal there are certain criteria that have to met.

- A full-time employee must have worked for the employer for at least two years.
- A part-time worker must have worked more than eight hours a week for five years.
- Police officers and members of the armed forces are not allowed to apply.

Whether a person is judged to have been unfairly dismissed will depend on what happened in each case.

uniform business rate: a tax paid by businesses to local councils. Businesses pay the uniform business rate instead of the council tax that households have to pay. The rate is fixed nationally, but is based on local property values.

unincorporated is any business that has not been incorporated by *statute* or by the *Registrar of Companies*. It is run as either a *sole trader* or a *partnership*. An unincorporated business does not have its own separate legal existence. Its owners will be personally liable for all the debts of the business, that is, they have *unlimited liability*.

unit cost is the average cost of making one unit of output. It is the same as *average costs*.

unlimited liability is where the owner of a business is personally liable for all the debts of the business. *Sole traders* and each of the ordinary partners in a *partnership* have unlimited liability. This means that all of their personal *assets* can be used to settle the debts of the business.

unofficial strike: this happens when a group of workers withdraw their labour without the support of their trades union. Such *strikes* usually happen very suddenly, probably because of very local *grievances*.

unsecured loan: a loan made to a borrower who does not offer the lender any *security* for the loan. A lender is taking a big risk if a borrower cannot offer any *collateral* security for the loan. A lender will therefore charge a very high *rate of interest* on such loans. *Banks* will not normally provide unsecured loans.

unskilled work is work that does not require any qualifications and only very little on-the-job training. Unskilled jobs are usually manual, like cleaning and labouring.

Unsolicited Goods and Services Act 1971: an Act that protects people from having to pay for goods or services they have not ordered. It is a piece of *consumer protection* law to protect people from *inertia selling*.

> **Explanation:** When a person or firm is sent goods or services they have not ordered they cannot be made to pay for them, or to send them back. If the goods are not collected within six months the recipient can keep them. If the recipient writes to the firm asking it to collect the goods, and it fails to do so, then the goods can be kept or sold after 30 days.

utilities are the industries that provide gas, electricity and water services.

vacancy: a job for which an *employer* is seeking an *employee*. A vacancy may arise because the person who was doing the job has been given another job in the firm or has left. It may arise because new work has arisen.

value added: see *added value*.

value added tax (VAT) is a tax on spending. It is a percentage added to the price of goods at each stage in production. The total of the tax is always equal to the rate on the final selling price. The tax can be claimed back at each stage except by the final *consumer* who cannot reclaim it. There are some goods on which VAT is not payable. They are called exempt goods. Other goods are *zero rated*. Fuel is charged at 8% and the standard rate is currently 17.5%.

> **Example:** A manufacturer sells goods to a wholesaler for £100 plus VAT at 17.5% = £117.5. The wholesaler sells the same goods to a retailer for £150 plus VAT at 17.5% = £176.25. The retailer sells the goods on to customers for £200 plus VAT at 17.5% = £235. VAT increases at each stage by 17.5% of the *value added* at that stage.

	Cost price	Selling price	Value added	VAT on value added	Total VAT	Invoice price
Manufacture		£100	£100	£17.50	£17.50	£117.50
Wholesaler	£100	£150	£50	£8.75	£26.25	£126.50
Retailer	£150	£200	£50	£8.75	£35.00	£235.00
				£35.00		

> The wholesaler and the retailer will each be able to reclaim the VAT they have paid. The total VAT paid by the consumer is the sum of the 17.5% of the value added at each stage in the distribution of the goods.

value analysis takes place when a firm looks very carefully at all the parts that go into a product to see if they can be bought or made more cheaply. It may mean redesigning the product or its parts so that they can be made more cheaply. The aim is to get the same results at lower costs but without losing performance or quality.

variable costs are costs that change in direct relation to the *output* of a firm. So, if output increases by 20%, the variable costs also increase by 20%.

> **Explanation:** It is fairly obvious that if the output of a firm increases, more materials will be used, along with more labour. The running costs of machines may also change in exactly the same proportion as output.

VAT: see *value added tax*.

verbal warning is usually the first stage in a *disciplinary procedure*. If an employee's conduct or work is below standard, he or she may be given a formal verbal warning. They may be given six months to improve their ways. This will be entered on the employee's file and will stay there for (probably) up to a year. If the employee's conduct improves it will be removed from the record. If after six months there has not been an improvement the firm will move on to the next stage in the procedure.

venture capital is capital invested in small firms to help them to start or grow. Venture capital may also help to finance management *buyouts* or *buy-ins*. There are *financial institutions* that specialise in providing venture capital.

> **Explanation:** Small firms need extra capital to expand. Management buyouts can be quite big businesses and may need more capital than the managers themselves have. Both are risky types of business. Raising capital through normal methods may be difficult and expensive. Venture capital companies specialise in providing capital for such firms. One of the biggest venture capital firms is Investors in Industry (3i).
>
> A venture capital firm looks at a business idea very carefully. If it decides to invest it will provide a long term loan or may buy shares in the firm or both. The venture capitalist will support a firm with advice and may expect a seat on the *board of directors*.

vertical integration: see *integration*.

video conferencing is the use of telephone links to set up a television and video network. It allows staff at branches far apart to talk to and see one another. It is often much cheaper than setting up a meeting. It saves travelling expenses and the time taken to travel to and from a meeting.

viewdata is a general name for systems that hold information on a central database that users can contact through the telephone system. Information is displayed on a monitor. The main viewdata system in the UK is *Prestel*. It is widely used by the travel industry to get information about holidays and make bookings.

visible trade is the buying (importing) and selling (exporting) of goods between countries. The difference between the total of *exports* and the total of *imports* of goods is called the *balance of trade*.

vocational training is training that is related to work. It may be *on-the-job* training which takes place in the place of work. It can also be *off-the-job* training where training is given in the local college or by a specialist training firm.

voluntary chain: an association of small, privately owned *retailers*. The retailers usually work with one or more *wholesalers*. The best known examples of these chains are SPAR and VG.

> **Explanation:** The large supermarket chains buy goods in very large quantities straight from the manufacturers. In effect they do their own wholesaling. Small

retailers cannot buy stocks on the same terms. Many manufacturers sell directly to retailers and cut out the wholesalers. Both the wholesalers and the small retailers find it hard to survive. One way of being more competitive is to join together. Retailers can then buy in bulk and get similar *discounts* to the supermarkets. They have also developed their own brands. By advertising as a group they are able to advertise nationally.

voluntary codes of practice: a statement of good practice for firms and people working in an industry. Codes of practice are often produced by a *trade association*. The codes are voluntary because they cannot be enforced. There is very little, other than giving bad publicity, that can be done if the code is not followed or is broken. Such codes are a form of *self-regulation*. Examples include the *Advertising Standards Authority*.

voluntary liquidation happens when a company chooses to close down and to sell its assets. The money raised is used to pay creditors and any money left over paid to the owners.

voluntary redundancy happens when a worker volunteers to be made redundant.

> **Explanation:** Firms may need to cut down the size of their workforce. To avoid sacking people they may ask for volunteers. If they choose to be made redundant, workers are usually offered special terms. These terms will usually be better than the statutory redundancy payments.

voluntary sector: the part of the economy that is made up of voluntary organisations. These are *non-profitmaking* bodies such as charities and sports clubs. Making a profit is not their main reason for being in business. They may make money, but it is all used for a good cause instead of being paid out to shareholders. The sector can be divided into two parts.

1   The small, local organisations that rely on volunteers to run them and work for them.

2   The large, international organisations, such as the Red Cross, Oxfam and the Save the Children Fund. They get their funds from donations and by running businesses like charity shops. They have professional managers to run them and employ full-time workers. They also have volunteers working for them who give their time for nothing. They buy services, supplies and equipment that they use for charitable purposes, and may also employ people overseas.

wages: a method of paying *employees* for the *work* they have done for an *employer*. Wages are mainly paid to shopfloor, 'blue collar' workers. They are usually paid weekly.

warehouse: a large building used to store goods. All firms that need to store goods will have a warehouse. The warehouse overcomes the problem of time. There is always a gap between making goods and selling and distributing them. There is also a time lapse between receiving goods and using them. Warehouses are expensive to build and to run so firms try to keep their storage to a minimum. The space does not earn money and stocks of components and finished goods tie up capital. Systems like *just-in-time* have grown to keep stocks as low as possible and warehouse space to a minimum.

warranty: a promise to repair or replace a faulty product, free of charge. It is another term for a *guarantee*.

Weights and Measures Acts: these Acts require manufacturers to show the weight, or other measure, of goods in a package. They also make it illegal to sell less than the quantity stated on the package or in an advertisement.

wholesaler: a *middleman* who provides a link in the *chain of distribution* between manufacturers and *retailers*. Wholesalers also provide a range of services to both manufacturers and retailers.

Wholesale services to manufacturers:

- They buy in bulk from the manufacturers who only have to deal with a few large orders from wholesalers instead of lots of small orders from retailers. This saves on the clerical and distribution costs of goods.

- They store goods so that manufacturers need less storage space thus cutting their costs.

- They reduce the manufacturers' risks. If the goods are not sold it will be the wholesaler not the manufacturer that suffers the loss.

Wholesale services to retailers:

- Wholesalers break bulk; they buy in bulk from many manufacturers. They sell to retailers in the small quantities they want.

- They offer a choice of goods in one place. Retailers can choose goods from several makers at the same time. This saves them work in, for example, writing different orders to each manufacturer.

- They advise retailers about the latest products, and special and profitable lines that sell well.

The traditional role of the wholesaler is breaking down because manufacturers prefer to sell direct to retailers. This enables them to keep control of the *distribution* of their goods right up to the *point of sale*. However, the wholesaling function still has to be carried out. Manufacturers selling direct to shops have to bear all the costs of warehousing and distribution. The large retail chains have their own very large distribution warehouses.

winding up: the process of closing down and selling the *assets* of a company that is in *liquidation*.

work is the employment by which a person earns an income. It is also the physical and mental effort involved in carrying out a task. Work includes the task itself and the output that results from carrying out the task. From the point of view of business studies we are only interested in paid work. There is a great deal of unpaid work such as cooking, cleaning, gardening and childcare in the home.

work in progress is work that is only partly finished. It is work that is still in the process of production. It may be work that is waiting to move on to the next stage of production. Work in progress is an important part of the *stocks* of a company.

work shadowing is a form of training where the trainee follows and observes an experienced member of staff. The idea is that a trainee quickly learns all about the job being observed. It can be used as a form of *induction* training. It is also used to help students to get a better understanding of the world of work.

worker director is a representative of the workers chosen to be a member of the *board of directors*. The person chosen would probably have been elected by the workforce.

> **Explanation:** Worker directors are common in the rest of Europe, especially in Germany. The main advantage is that the workers' point of view can be heard at the very highest level in a firm. The idea has not been very popular in the UK.

workers' co-operative: a firm that is owned and run by its workers and *managers*. Every member has one *share* which entitles him or her to one vote and gives them a say in the way the business is run. All members get an equal share of the *profits*.

Features of a workers' co-operative:

- Members will be paid a *wage* or *salary* as well as share in the profits. In some co-operatives everyone is paid the same whatever job they do. *Differentials* tend to be smaller than in other forms of business.

- Co-operatives are usually set up as *limited* companies.

- Co-operatives also employ experts such as accountants and marketing staff, who may not be members.

working capital: the funds needed for the day-to-day running of a business.

FORMULA *for calculating working capital:*

Working capital = Current assets – Current liabilities

Working capital:

- is used to pay the everyday debts of a business as they become due. It is used to pay for raw materials, wages, creditors, the heating and lighting and other expenses

- is a measure of a firm's *liquidity*. If it is too low a firm will have a *cashflow* problem and will not be able to pay its bills when they become due. It could therefore become *insolvent* and this might lead to its *winding up*

- can be too large: this means the firm is not using its assets in the most profitable way.

Example:

Extract from Balance Sheet of XYX & Company Limited as at 31 December

	£ 000	£ 000
Current assets:		
Stock	86	
Debtors	67	
Bank	52	
Cash	18	223
less Current liabilities:		
Trade creditors		130
Working capital		93

working capital ratio: a measure of a firm's ability to pay its short-term debts. It is also known as the *current ratio* and the *liquidity ratio*; see these entries for formulae and examples.

working conditions are the physical environment in which a person works. The environment includes how well lit and clean and warm the work place may be. Working conditions will be affected to a very large extent by the *Health and Safety at Work Act*. Other factors include whether the work is inside or out, fellow workers and the kind of equipment that is used, (whether it is modern or old fashioned, for example). Working conditions are not the same as the *conditions of employment* which are set out in the *contract of employment*.

works councils are committees made up of the representatives of workers and managers within a firm. They meet regularly to talk about problems and plans for the future. Works councils provide opportunities for shopfloor workers to air their ideas and make suggestions. They do not negotiate about *wages* and the *terms of employment*. There is a danger that they become little more than 'talking shops'. They are an attempt at *consultation* and industrial democracy. Workers are usually elected, possibly one from each department.

work-to-rule: a form of *industrial action* where workers follow to the letter the rules and regulations for their jobs. Some industries have very complicated and detailed rules that have developed over many years. Such detailed rule books are to be found particularly in industries where safety is very important. Some examples are the railway, mining and building industries. Some of the rules will be out of date. Therefore, if workers stick exactly to the rules, work will be slowed down or even brought to a halt.

written off describes an *asset* which no longer has any value in the books of a company. A piece of equipment may have been depreciated to the point where its value is zero. A debt which becomes a *bad debt* will also be written off.

written warning: this is given to an employee at the second stage of a *disciplinary procedure*. If the conduct that led to a verbal warning carries on, a written warning may be issued. A written warning must clearly state: the nature of the complaint against an employee; what the employee must do to overcome the problem. It must give the employee a time in which to solve the problem.

If the conduct continues, the next stage (a final written warning) will be started. The warning will be entered on the employee's work record and will remain on the record for a stated period, as shown in the company's disciplinary procedures.

yield is another term for the *dividend yield* of shares.

zero rated are products on which the rate of VAT is 0%.

GCSE EXAMINATIONS AND EXAMINERS' TERMS

Introduction

To help candidates, all examination boards structure their questions, that is, questions are broken down into three or four parts. Each part will be a step in the question. Often, but not always, one part will lead on to the next. Usually the more difficult parts will be towards the end of the question. New ideas and topics may be introduced to help show the interrelated nature of business studies.

All GCSE examinations in business studies are set at Foundation and Higher tiers. Questions at the Foundation tier are more structured than those at the Higher tier. Foundation candidates are given more guidance and are steered through questions step by step. At the Higher tier questions are more open-ended and candidates have more control over the way they shape their answer.

The marks given to each part of a question are shown on the examination paper. This gives an idea of:

- how much time should be spent on that part
- how long the answer should be.

A question with one mark need not be answered in a sentence, but with one word or a very short phrase. As a general rule all other questions should be answered in complete sentences. Very often points are worth two marks, with one mark for making the point, plus one mark for developing the point; that is, for saying something extra about it. There may also be a mark for an example. Where possible examples should be drawn from the case study or data supplied.

Questions with more than five or six marks may be marked according to a 'levels of response' system in which marks are not given for specific points. There are bands of marks, into one of which an answer will fall. For example:

1 to 3 marks	– a simple list of the relevant points; points not developed; arguments not supported by examples
4 to 6 marks	– relevant points given; some development; arguments supported by references to case study/data
7 to 10 marks	– a full answer with well developed points and arguments supported by relevant examples from the case study/data.

Many boards combine the questions with the answer booklet. The number of lines they allow for the answer shows the length of answer expected. All the lines do not have to be used as boards provide enough space to meet all styles of writing.

All GCSE examinations have similar Assessment Objectives (AOs) drawn from the National Criteria for Business Studies.

AO 1 Knowledge and critical understanding of the subject content.

AO 2 Application of terms, concepts, theories and methods to address problems and issues.

AO 3 Select, organise, interpret and use information from various sources.

AO 4 Evaluate evidence, make reasoned judgements and present conclusions accurately and appropriately.

All the AOs are tested in every examination paper.

In all questions there are key words, called 'command' or 'trigger' words. They are the words that show what the examiner wants from an answer. These key words are closely linked to the assessment objectives(s) the question is designed to test.

Candidates should look carefully at these key words and the number of marks linked to a question, when planning their answer. The command or trigger words are listed below with the assessment objectives to which they are linked shown in brackets.

advise (AO 3, AO 4): you are being asked to suggest ways of solving a business problem. This should be looked at from several points of view. The benefits and drawbacks of each suggestion should be given, supported by evidence drawn from the case study or the data supplied.

analyse (AO 3, AO4): this is the breaking down of a topic into its parts. A question using 'analyse' is asking you to show how and why something happened. You are being asked to break the event down into various parts to show how certain causes lead to certain effects. You must use the case study or data, and select the parts needed for the answer. Answers should be in sentences that follow each other logically. An 'analyse' question does not necessarily need a conclusion.

apply (AO 2): use your knowledge of business studies and apply it to a business situation. You may have to decide which business studies concepts and theories should be applied to the situation given. Giving examples is also a part of application.

assess (AO 4) means having to weigh up two or more arguments or possible solutions and decide which is the most relevant to a situation. The answer should state the pros and cons of each argument or solution and draw a conclusion. It is another way of asking for *evaluation*.

briefly means write an answer in a sentence or two. It is usually used with another command word such as 'briefly explain'. The length of the answer should be judged by the mark allocation.

calculate (AO 2) refers to numerical questions where you have to work out the answer by arithmetic. You should learn the formulae for answering such questions. Good answers will show the formula and apply the formula to the question. Always show your working. You may score marks for the working even if your answer is wrong. Most GCSE business studies papers will have questions asking for a calculation.

compare (AO 3, AO 4): note the similarities and the differences between two or more ideas or options. Your answer must be in sentences and should give the points for and against each of the items being compared and draw a conclusion. The arguments and the conclusion should draw on your knowledge of business studies and be supported by examples from the data or case study. Marking will probably be on a 'levels of response' basis.

consider (AO 4): another term that requires you to weigh up the arguments for and against alternatives. You should consider things in the light of business studies terms and ideas.

decide (AO 4): make a choice between the options available. You should give reasons for your choice and support your decision with evidence based on the data or case study.

define (AO 1): state the meaning of a term as precisely as possible. You should also give an example. An example on its own is not a definition and may score no marks. For example, SEG has a question asking for definitions. One mark is given for a simple definition, one mark is given for a brief expansion of the point and one mark for a relevant example.

demonstrate (AO 2): show that you understand what is meant by a business studies idea or how the idea can be applied to a problem.

describe (AO 2, AO 3): write a statement that sets out the main features of a topic. It tells the reader what something is like, or how it works.

discuss (AO 4): put forward both sides of a case and draw a conclusion, based on evidence from the data or case study. Such questions are fairly rare at GCSE level in business studies but may sometimes be found in higher tier papers.

do you think (AO 4) is a way of asking you to look at various options and to come to a conclusion. It is not enough just to give the conclusion. You must state the reasons for your conclusion and support it with evidence from your knowledge of business studies and the data or case study.

draw on your knowledge of (AO 2, AO 3): apply your knowledge of business studies ideas to a business situation or problem. You will probably have to decide what business studies ideas are most suitable and show how and why they are appropriate. Support your answer with examples.

evaluate (AO 4) asks you to weigh up the evidence and come to a conclusion. You should give the pros and cons of each option. Points for and against should be supported with evidence, preferably from the case study or data provided. You are expected to come to a conclusion or judgement. It should come at the end, and be based on the arguments. Do not be afraid to give your own opinion but you must say why you hold that opinion.

examine (AO 2, AO 3) asks you to look carefully at a situation or idea. You may have to select the most appropriate information from a case study or data and apply it to a business situation. The question may be asking you to interpret information in a certain situation or to suggest why some factors are more important than others. Answers will usually be in sentences and be supported by information from the data or case study.

explain (AO 1, AO 2, AO 3, AO 4): expand upon a topic to show what it means. It is a very common term that can be used at several different levels. At its simplest level you are being asked to show that you understand a topic. At a more complicated level you may be asked to show how a business studies idea can be applied to a business situation or problem. It can also be used to ask you to interpret data or information (e.g. to look for patterns or trends) or to select data and to show their relevance. Explanations should be written in sentences and be supported by examples from the data or case study. The length of the explanation expected will be shown by the number of marks given to the question.

from the graph/data (AO 2, AO 3): this asks you to select some part of the information provided. In some cases you may just have to extract the information from the data or case study provided. In such a case you need only write it out, not necessarily in your own words. Such questions usually carry few marks. In other cases you may be asked to select and then interpret the information in which case the question will carry more marks and your answer should be in sentences, unless it is a calculation.

give (AO 1) is asking you to give a *list*. Answers can be in a word or in a phrase; a sentence is not necessary. No explanation is needed, but you may need an example.

give an example of (AO 2) may be asking for an example from your knowledge of business studies or are selected from the case study or data provided.

give reasons for or why (AO 4): this is asking for an explanation. You will often be given the number of reasons you are expected to provide. Answers should be in sentences and refer to the specific problem or situation in the question.

how (AO 2, AO 3) is asking for an explanation. This may be to show how a business studies idea can be applied to a situation or problem. Answers should be in sentences. The length of your answer will depend on the number of marks given to the question.

how well (AO 4) is asking for an explanation and a conclusion or judgement. For example, a question may ask 'How well is X company doing?' You are being asked to give reasons why it is, or is not, successful. You have to *evaluate* the points for and against and come to a conclusion. Answers must be supported with examples.

identify (AO 1): name or point out examples relevant to the question. It is very like *give* or *list*.

in your opinion (AO 4): you are being invited to make a judgement or draw a conclusion or make a recommendation. Your opinion must be based upon the pros and cons of the situation. You should state which of the various arguments leads you to your conclusions. Answers should be written in sentences. The length of your answers should be based on the number of marks given to the question.

judge (AO 4): balance the arguments for and against and make a judgement. The arguments for and against must be stated and the conclusion based on those arguments. Arguments should be supported by examples, preferably from the data or case study. Answers must be in sentences.

justify (AO 4): put forward an argument and come to a conclusion. The conclusion should always be based on the arguments, supported by evidence from the data or case study. The conclusion should always be at the end. The length of the justification will depend on the number of marks given to the question.

list (AO 1): the same as *give* or *name*.

name (AO 1) is another way of asking you to *give* or *list*.

outline (AO 1, AO 2): write a brief description of a business studies theory or concept. Answers should be in sentences. The length of the description will depend on the marks allocated.

predict (AO 4): you are being asked to *evaluate* the evidence given to you and to make a judgement about the outcome. You must say why you have made your judgement. The answer should be in sentences. Its length will depend on the mark allocation.

select from (AO 3): choose from a number of options being given to you. It may also be used to ask you to select appropriate information from the data supplied. Sometimes you will only have to make a selection. At other times you may be asked to say *why* you have made your choice, in that case answer in sentences.

show your working (AO 1): in calculation questions it is rare for all the marks to be given to the final answer. There may be marks for showing the formula, and further marks for selecting the right figures and for clearly showing the stages in the arithmetic. If you only put the answer down and have made a mistake you will get nought. If you have shown your working you may score some marks, even if the final answer is wrong.

show (AO 2, AO 3, AO 4) will usually be linked to another word, such as, 'show how' or 'show why' or 'show which'. It is another way of asking you to explain something. Answers should be in sentences. Take examples from the case study or data to support the explanation. The length and depth of the answer expected will be indicated by the mark allocation.

state (AO 1): may be used instead of *give* or *list* or *name*.

state why (AO 1): is asking for a simple explanation. It may be a question about your knowledge of business studies in general. For example, 'state why cashflow is important to a business'. The answer can be written in general terms, although examples may be taken from the case study or data supplied. At other times the question may ask you to answer specifically in terms of the case study or data. The length of your answer will depend on the mark allocation.

suggest (AO 2, AO 4): put forward your ideas about the methods or ways to solve a business problem or to give reasons why a problem exists. If the mark allocation is small a list of points will probably be enough. If there is a larger mark allocation each point should be explained and justified with examples.

use (AO 2): you are being asked to apply business studies theories, concepts or techniques to a business situation or problem. You will usually be told what to use in the situation, e.g. 'use a bar chart to show …'. An explanation is not usually necessary.

what are (AO 1): this may be asking you to *list* or it may be asking you to explain. You will have to decide what is required from the context of the question and the marks available.

what is meant by (AO 1) is another way of asking you to *define* a business term or concept.

which (AO 2, AO 3, AO 4): you are being asked to select or make a choice between options. It can be answered as a *list*, or if it is designed to test AO3 or

AO4 it will require explanations for your choice. It should then be answered in sentences, and include examples or justification based on the data or case study.

why (AO 2, AO 3, AO 4) is another way of asking you to *explain* something.

write a report (AO 4): you are being asked to present your answer in the form of a report. There will be marks given for setting out your answer in the correct report format as well as for the content of your answer. The SEG states how it expects a report to be laid out in business studies. If any other format is used, e.g. a memorandum or business letter, no format marks will be awarded. Reports should have a title, be broken down into subsections and contain a conclusion and recommendations. They should also show whom they are addressed to, who prepared the report and the date.

Common trigger words used in GCSE Business Studies

AO1 Knowledge and understanding	AO2 Application	AO3 Selection, organisation and interpretion of information	AO4 Evaluation
Define	Apply	Advise	Advise
Explain (to show understanding)	Calculate	Analyse	Assess
Give	Demonstrate	Compare	Analyse
Identify	Describe	Describe	Compare
List	Draw on your knowledge of …	Draw on your knowledge of …	Consider
Name	Examine	Examine	Decide
Outline	Explain (in a context)	Explain	Discuss
Show your working	From the graph/data …		
State	Give an example of …	From the graph/data …	Do you think …
State why …	How	How	Evaluate
What are …	Outline	Select from	Explain
What is meant by …	Show how	Show how	Give reasons for …
	Suggest ways …	Which	Give reasons why …
	Suggest reasons …	Why	How well do you …
	Suggest methods …		In your opinion why …
	Use		Judge
	Which		Justify
	Why		Predict
			Show why
			Suggest
			When
			Which
			Why
			Why do you think …
			Why have you chosen …
			Write a report

REVISION LISTS

Lists for GCSE level

Set out below are the key concepts and terms in GCSE Business Studies. The lists include the main topics found in the syllabuses of all the GCSE examining boards. The lists are not definitive but cover the main topics under each heading. They are classified under the following headings taken from the SEG Business Studies syllabus:

1 The business environment

2 Business structures and organisation

3 Marketing

4 Production

5 Finance

6 People in business

7 Communications

1 The business environment

business ethics
capitalism
central government
chamber of commerce
choice
Confederation of British Industry
consumer protection
demand
Equal Opportunities Act
Equal Pay Act
European Community/Union
exchange/exchange rates
externalities
fiscal policy
government intervention
Health and Safety and Work Act
inflation
local government
location of industry
market economy

mixed economy
monetary policy
Office of Fair Trading
opportunity cost
planned economy
primary production/industry
private enterprise/sector
public enterprise/sector
retail prices index
Sale of Goods Act
scarcity
secondary production/industry
social benefits
social costs
supply
tertiary production/industry
trade associations
Trade Descriptions Act
Training and Enterprise Councils
voluntary sector

2 Business structures and organisations

board of directors
business objectives
business plan
centralisation
chain of command
conglomerate
co-operative
decentralisation
delayering
delegation
director
diversification
franchise
growth
integration
limited liability
market share

multinational
organisation chart
organisation
partner
partnership
private limited company
privatisation
profit
public limited company
regulator
shareholder
small firms
sole proprietor
span of control
stakeholder
takeover
unlimited liability

3 Marketing

advertising
Advertising Standards Authority
Boston matrix
branding
chain of distribution
distribution
market penetration
market position
market research
market segmentation
market share
market skimming
market testing
marketing
marketing mix
marketing strategy

merchandising
packaging
point of sale
price discrimination
pricing methods
primary research/sources
product life cycle
product differentiation
promotion
questionnaire
retailing
secondary research/sources
sponsorship
SWOT analysis
wholesaler

4 Production

added value
automation
batch production
capacity
cell production
chain of production
computer aided design (CAD)
computer aided manufacture (CAM)
diseconomies of scale
division of labour

economies of scale
flow production
job production
just-in-time
mass production
production
quality assurance
quality control
specialisation

5 Finance

acid test ration
assets
average costs
balance sheet
bank overdraft
breakeven
budget
budgetary control
capital
capital employed

capital expenditure
cash flow forecast
contribution
cost of goods sold
credit
current ratio
debentures
depreciation
discount
factoring

fixed costs
gearing
hire purchase
indirect costs
interest
interest rates
leasing
liability
liquidity
loans
margin
marginal costs
mark-up
ordinary shares

preference shares
profit and loss account
profit margin
profit, gross, net
rate of turnover
rate of interest
reserves
retained profits
revenue expenditure
sources of finance
stock control
trading account
variable costs
working capital

6 People in business

absenteeism
Advisory, Conciliation and Arbitration
Service (ACAS)
appraisal
basic pay
bonus
collective bargaining
consumer and customers
contract of employment
dismissal
employee
employer
employment agency
equal opportunities
foreman
fringe benefits
human resources
industrial action
industrial tribunal

job satisfaction
labour mobility
manager
motivation
overtime
piece rates
pressure group
recruitment & selection
redundancy
salary
shift work
shop steward
supervisor
trades unions
training
Training and Enterprise Councils
unemployment
wages
working conditions

7 Communications

advertising
bar chart
business letter
communications
formal communication

histogram
informal communication
memorandum
pie chart
reports

Lists for Intermediate GNVQ Business Studies

The key terms in the specifications for the intermediate GNVQ in Business Studies have been identified. In the following pages the main terms necessary to meet the requirements of the end of unit tests have been listed.

Unit 1: Business organisations and employment

Unit 2: People in business organisations

Unit 3: Consumers and customers

Unit 4: Financial and administrative support

Unit 1: Business organisations and employment

advertising
after sales service
business objectives
capital goods
central government
chamber of commerce
choice
competition
co-operative
consumer
consumer goods
consumable
demand
durable goods
employee
employer
European Community
European Union
franchise
government intervention
Health and Safety at Work Act
international trade
labour supply
limited liability
local government
location of industry
market
market share
marketing
marketing mix
owner

partnership
pressure group
primary industry/production
private enterprise/sector
private limited company
product life cycle
production
profit
profit distribution
public enterprise/sector
public limited company
public sector
recruitment
reserves
retained profit
retraining
secondary industry/production
selection
self-employed
service industries
shareholder
small firms
sole proprietor
sponsorship
supply
tertiary industry/production
training
Training and Enterprise Councils
transport
unlimited liability
voluntary sector

Unit 2: People in business organisations

accounting
Advisory Conciliation and Arbitration Service (ACAS)
after sales service
board of directors
centralisation

contract of employment
decentralisation
deductions
delegation
director
disciplinary procedures

distribution
equal opportunities
Equal Pay Act
Employment Acts
Employment Protection Acts
European Court of Justice
flexible working
flexitime
foreman
franchise
grievance procedures
Health and Safety at Work Act
hierarchy
human resources
industrial tribunal
manager
marketing department
negotiations
organisation chart
organisation
partnership
personnel department
production

productivity
quality assurance
quality control
Race Relations Acts
remuneration
research and development
sales department
self-employed
semi-skilled worker
Sex Discrimination Acts
shift work
shop steward
skilled worker
sole proprietor
supervisor
teleworker
trades unions
training
Training and Enterprise Councils (TEC)
voluntary sector
working conditions

Unit 3: Consumers and customers

advertising
Advertising Standards Authority
after sales service
branding
business ethics
business letters
communications
competition
consumer
Consumer Credit Act
consumer protection
customers
demand
earnings
guarantee
Health and Safety at Work Act

market research
marketing mix
memorandum
notices
point of sale
promotion
repeat order
reports
retail prices index
Sale of Goods Act
sample
sponsorship
statement of account
supply
Trade Descriptions Act
trading standards department

Unit 4: Financial and administrative support

accounting
accounting equation
accounts
affinity card
assets
bank loan
bank statement
banking automated clearing services
  (BACS)
budget
business letter
cash
cash discount
charge card
cheque
communications
costs:
  average
  direct
  fixed
  variable
  marginal
credit
credit card
credit note
credit sale
credit terms
current account (bank)
debit card
debit note
delivery note
discount
e-mail
facsimile (fax)
goods
gross profit
hire purchase
invoice
ledger
ledger accounts
liability
loan capital
loss
memorandum
notices
net profit
order
overheads
pay slip
paying-in slip
petty cash
profit
purchases
receipt
reports
sales
spreadsheet
statement of account
trade discount
value added tax

Why not use our range of *Complete A–Z Handbooks* to support your A levels and Advanced GNVQs? All the *A–Z*s are written by experienced authors and Chief Examiners.

0 340 65467 8   *The Complete A–Z Business Studies* Second Edition £9.99
0 340 65489 9   *The Complete A–Z Geography Handbook* £9.99
0 340 64789 2   *The Complete A–Z Leisure, Travel and Tourism Handbook* £9.99
0 340 65832 0   *The Complete A–Z Sociology Handbook* £9.99
0 340 65490 2   *The Complete A–Z Psychology Handbook* £9.99
0 340 66985 3   *The Complete A–Z Economics and Business Studies Handbook* £9.99
0 340 66373 1   *The Complete A–Z Biology Handbook* £9.99
0 340 68804 1   *The Complete A–Z Physics Handbook* £9.99
0 340 68803 3   *The Complete A–Z Mathematics Handbook* £9.99
0 340 67996 4   *The Complete A–Z 20th Century European History Handbook* £9.99
0 340 69131 X   *The Complete A–Z Media and Communication Handbook* £9.99
0 340 68847 5   *The Complete A–Z Business Studies CD-ROM* £55.00 + VAT
0 340 69124 7   *The Complete A–Z Accounting Handbook* £9.99
0 340 67378 8   *The Complete A–Z 19th and 20th Century British History Handbook* £9.99
0 340 72513 3   *The Complete A–Z Chemistry Handbook* £9.99
0 340 70557 4   *The Complete A–Z Health and Social Care Handbook* £9.99
0 340 72120 0   *The Complete A–Z Law Handbook* £9.99
0 340 72051 4   *The A–Z Business Studies Coursework Handbook* £6.99
0 340 74919 9   *The A–Z Sociology Coursework Handbook* £6.99
0 340 73047 1   *The A–Z Geography Coursework Handbook* £6.99

All Hodder & Stoughton *Educational* books are available at your local bookshop, or can be ordered direct from the publisher. Just tick the titles you would like and complete the details below. Prices and availability are subject to change without prior notice.

Buy four books from the selection above and get free postage and packaging. Just send a cheque or postal order made payable to *Bookpoint Limited* to the value of the total cover price of four books. This should be sent to: Hodder & Stoughton *Educational*, 39 Milton Park, Abingdon, Oxon OX14 4TD, UK. EMail address: orders@bookpoint.co.uk. Alternatively, if you wish to buy fewer than four books, the following postage and packaging costs apply:

UK & BFPO: £4.30 for one book; £6.30 for two books; £8.30 for three books.
Overseas and Eire: £4.80 for one book; £7.10 for 2 or 3 books (surface mail).

If you would like to pay by credit card, our centre team would be delighted to take your order by telephone. Our direct line (44) 01235 827720 (lines open 9.00am - 6.00pm, Monday to Saturday, with a 24 hour answering service). Alternatively you can send a fax to (44) 01235 400454.

Title _____ First name _____ Surname _____

Address _____

Postcode _____ Daytime telephone no. _____

If you would prefer to pay by credit card, please complete:

Please debit my Master Card / Access / Diner's Card / American Express (delete as applicable)

Card number _____ Expiry date _____ Signature _____

If you would not like to receive further information on our products, please tick the box